SMALL GROUPS
AN INTRODUCTION

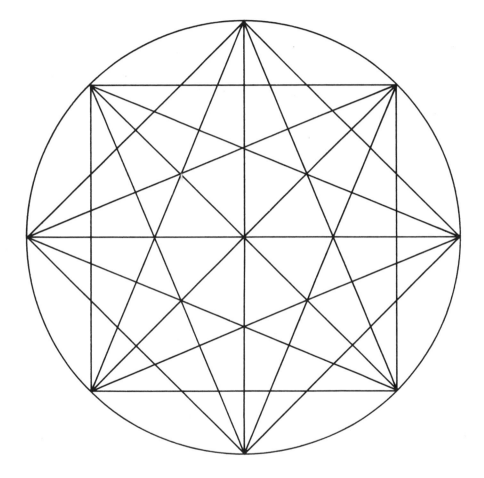

SMALL GROUPS
AN INTRODUCTION

Charles S. Palazzolo
Villanova University

D. Van Nostrand Company
New York   Cincinnati   Toronto   London   Melbourne

The original graphic design used for the cover and part-title pages was done by Stephen J. Reilly. The design symbolizes the complex of two-person interactions possible in a small group composed of eight members.

D. Van Nostrand Company Regional Offices:
New York   Cincinnati

D. Van Nostrand Company International Offices:
London   Toronto   Melbourne

Library of Congress Catalog Card Number: 80-50820
ISBN: 0-442-25868-2

Published by D. Van Nostrand Company
135 West 50th Street, New York, N.Y. 10020

10 9 8 7 6 5 4 3 2 1

Photo Credits

Georg Simmel Courtesy of Bildarchiz Preussischer Kulturbesitz, Berlin, Germany.

George Herbert Mead Courtesy of The University of Chicago Library, Department of Special Collections.

Charles Horton Cooley Courtesy of the Michigan Historical Collections, Bentley Historical Library, University of Michigan at Ann Arbor. Reproduced by permission.

this
book
is
for
Flo

As the science of society, sociology has examined the characteristics and problems of communities, cities, regions, big organizations like factories, and even whole nations, but it has only begun to study the smaller social units that make up these giants. In so doing, it has not followed the order of human experience, for the first and most immediate social experience . . . is small group experience.

From *The Human Group* by George C. Homans

Preface

SMALL GROUPS: An Introduction introduces the student to small-group research and theory. Designed for undergraduate courses in sociology, social psychology, education, and communication, this text is also appropriate for the undergraduate curricula in nursing, social work, and business administration. The study of small-group interaction has become increasingly helpful in gaining a better understanding of business as well as social relationships.

The book coordinates the diverse body of small-group theory and research through the use of the interactionist approach. As applied to the study of small groups, interactionism is based on the premise that the social exchange between and among members of small groups is essential in generating group continuity and cohesion. The usefulness of this approach lies in its adaptability to understanding a wide variety of group types.

The book is divided into three parts. Part One deals with basic small-group concepts and is designed to provide the student with an understanding of the social group, a delineation of the limits of the small group, and a knowledge of the basic elements in small group structures.

Part Two deals with small-group theory. The material on Georg Simmel, George Herbert Mead, and Charles Horton Cooley recognizes their significant contributions to the field of small groups through their early interactionist studies. Biographical sketches, entitled "Life Notes," further illustrate the lives of these three men in personal historical terms. Sections dealing with current contributions to small group theory reveal a continuing development in the field.

Part Three covers selected areas of small-group research. The particular research areas were selected with the goal of representing a wide span of topics in an interesting fashion. In the final chapter, methods of research and modes of data analysis are applied to three different small groups: the family, the friendship group, and the informal work group.

Each chapter includes preview outlines, end-of-chapter summaries, discussion questions, and a list of suggested references. A glossary and bibliography are located at the end of the text.

This book is based upon material that has been class-tested for three years at Villanova University. The cooperation and suggestions of my students contributed to this book in a special way. I welcome this opportunity to thank them for their efforts.

The cooperation of members of the Villanova University community greatly facilitated the writing of this manuscript. Dr. James J. Cleary, Vice-President for Academic Affairs, gave me the time to work without interruption by approving my request for a sabbatical leave, and the Rev. John P. O'Malley, O.S.A., Dean of the College of Arts and Sciences, offered every financial and personal assistance.

I wish to thank my colleagues John E. Hughes, Brian J. Jones, Lynda P. Malik, Lawrence McGarry, Miriam Vosburgh, and Barry S. Young for their willingness to bear the daily burden that my constant inquiries and changing moods placed upon them. Typing the manuscript from the original fell to Mary Ann Griesser, whose ability and perseverance cannot be overestimated. Jill Schwartz was a most helpful library and office worker, and Maureen O'Brien, my student assistant, was of invaluable help in checking and evaluating the manuscript during its preparation. Student assistants Kathy Henneberry and Robert Benincasa were often available to perform a variety of tasks upon request. The final manuscript was typed by my daughter, Beady, whose skill and enthusiasm carried me to the end. Gwen Cassel and Rosanna Hoefling ably assisted me in the final proofreading.

I am pleased to acknowledge the support of my wife, Flo, my daughter, Neesie, and my son, Chuck, who made the hours away from the book more enjoyable than I could have expected.

At D. Van Nostrand, the expert direction and full cooperation I received from my publisher, Judy Joseph, deserves special acknowledgment. My executive editor, Harriet Serenkin, was extremely competent in resolving all problems that surfaced in the preparation of the final manuscript. Donna DeBenedictis, project editor, expertly coordinated all efforts from the submission of the final manuscript to the publication of the text and was the key to making the last months before publication more than bearable.

I finally wish to thank the following persons who made valuable comments and suggestions at various stages of manuscript preparation: Donald Reitzes, Georgia State University; Ronald E. Anderson, University of Minnesota—Twin Cities; Jane H. White, Catholic University;

Timothy J. Curry, The Ohio State University; Barbara Buckwalter, California State University–Long Beach; R. J. Bord, The Pennsylvania State University; R. T. Morris, University of California–Los Angeles.

I know my memory and must assume that these acknowledgments are incomplete. Therefore, to the friend who has contributed to the completion of this book and whose name I have failed to mention, I beg forgiveness and give my thanks. My indebtedness to others in no way absolves me from full responsibility for the final product.

Charles S. Palazzolo

Contents

PART III SMALL GROUP RESEARCH AND ANALYSIS

SMALL GROUPS
AN INTRODUCTION

PART 1
BASIC CONCEPTS

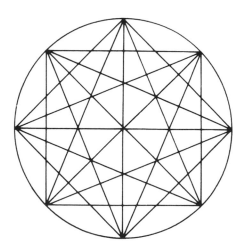

Chapter One

Human Interaction and the Social Group

CHAPTER PREVIEW

ISOLATION AND THE IMPORTANCE OF HUMAN INTERACTION

Early in 1940 there appeared an account of a girl called Anna. She had been deprived of normal contact and had received a minimum of physical care for almost the whole of her first six years of life . . . she remained on the second floor in an attic-like room because her mother hesitated to incur the grand-father's wrath by bringing her downstairs. Anna received only enough care to keep her barely alive. She appears to have been seldom moved from one position to another. Her clothing and bedding were filthy. She apparently had no instruction, no friendly attention (Davis, 1947:432–433).

*   *   *   *

Toward the end of one semester a student complained to a professor about difficulties encountered while studying for final examinations. Studying was difficult because the student could not sit still and kept finding reasons for taking a break: getting a bite to eat, calling a friend, taking a shower, and so on. The student ended the conversation by saying, "I started talking to myself and it was then that I decided to bag it." The student simply was unable to study alone.

The case of Anna and the story of the pre-exam jitters may seem to have nothing in common. Actually, in both instances, the individual was isolated from other human beings. In the second case, the isolation was short-lived with no apparent ill effects; in the case of Anna, the isolation lasted over many years and resulted in her death. Being isolated from the human social environment takes its toll. Isolation highlights the importance of human interaction and the necessity of group identity.

What is human interaction? What is group identity, and why is it so important? Must human beings live in groups? What are social groups? What effects do they have on individuals? The answers to these and other questions are the subject matter of this chapter.

THE INTERACTIONIST APPROACH

HUMAN INTERACTION

Perhaps the most complete definition of interaction both as a concept and as an approach to the study of social groups is the one given by Tomotsu Shibutani (1961:22–23):

What characterizes the interactionist approach is the contention that *human nature and the social order* are products of communication . . . behavior is not regarded merely as a response to environmental stimuli, an expression of inner organic needs, nor a manifestation of cultural patterns. The importance of sensory cues, organic drive, and culture is certainly recognized, but *the direction taken by a person's conduct is seen as something that is constructed in the reciprocal give and take of interdependent men who are adjusting to one another.*

The basis for understanding and analyzing group behavior centers on this theme of interdependent persons and the patterns of communication between and among them. In fact, the most important element of the social group is the rather complex set of relationships which develop within its boundaries. These relationships are the foundation upon which group identities and group strengths are based, and these are the bases for the group's potential for achieving its goals.

These groups, which individuals form and maintain throughout their lives, are natural settings for behavior. They derive from a nature which is, in part, social. But to suggest that human beings have a social nature is not quite sufficient to explain social behavior. One must also understand what the individual does as a group participant and how others in the group respond to such activity. One way of understanding the social element in human behavior is to view the individual as a social person, as one who is part of a network of communication within which behavior is directed toward others and received from them in return. Frederick L. Bates (1957:104–105) suggested this in his view that a group consists of "two individuals who interact with each other as the occupants of two positions, each of which contains at least one role reciprocal to a role in the other position."

By looking at groups from Shibutani's viewpoint, we are using the interactionist approach. Such an approach is by no means a simple one. In fact, it is extraordinarily complex, involving an understanding of the subject matter (content) and structure (form) of each social group and the motivation behind each action performed by an individual while participating in group activity. It is also important that we understand the physical and psychological elements surrounding the behavior performed and, as we are about to discover, the use of the individual's ability to symbolize the external world.

Before looking into the particulars of social groups, we must discuss, at length, one additional element of paramount importance to understanding human social interaction: *human behavior is symbolic.* The manner in which individuals use symbols is special and can be considered the most unique qualifier in the human social interaction process.

Bringing symbols into the picture makes the entire world of human interaction more complex but much more fascinating than one might suppose at first glance. This is so because, with the incorporation of the idea that human interaction is symbolic, we must concern ourselves not only with the fact that individuals behave interdependently in groups but also with the meanings their actions toward each other represent.

THE SYMBOL

A *symbol* is something which represents something else, the meaning of which is given by the user. For example, the letters of our alphabet—b, s, a, t, e, k, and so on—are all symbols which in different combinations represent objects, thoughts, actions, or, in fact, anything else.

Let us take the letters b, s, a, t, e, k. If we recombine them as follows, b-a-s-k-e-t, they represent an object which is so familiar to us that there is no need to depict it on these pages. So, the word, *basket*, represents the object, basket. That object is, of course, real. It also exists in the mind and that is where the symbol is translated into an image of the object which it represents.

A more sophisticated look at human interaction can now be taken. People interact with each other on two levels: (1) The symbol level—here, individuals actually exchange symbols. They speak to each other, gesture to each other, and use facial expressions in a complex of total communication. (2) The meaning level—the symbol level of communication forms the basis for what some might want to call mental communication. In interaction, people exchange meanings with each other and, assuming common agreement as to the meanings their symbols represent, are able to understand the message each is giving to the other. Common meanings for symbols used, then, is the basis for effective group behavior.

This is not to suggest that the actual behavior of individuals is at a lower level of significance. The importance of actual behavior is far too obvious. However, the true reality of human interaction lies not in the behavior of the interacting parties but in the understanding they derive from the meanings communicated. (See Figure 1-1.)

It must be understood that our interests are with the kinds of symbols most frequently used in human interaction—the kinds of symbols used to communicate within the boundaries of group behavior. Anything whatsoever can be designated a symbol if those individuals who refer to a given object agree that it is a symbol which represents something else. Included in this broad category are physical objects such as a flag, a wedding ring, the tassel on a graduation cap, a crucifix, a dove, colors, shapes, and so on (White, 1969). (See Table 1-1.)

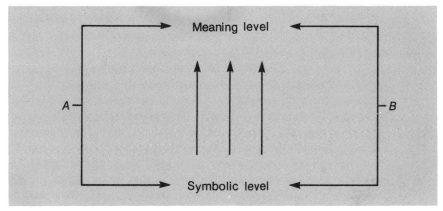

Figure 1-1. Interaction Levels

Table 1-1. Some American Symbols and Related Meanings

SYMBOL	RELATED MEANING
Basket (word)	Basket (physical object)
American flag (physical object)	U.S. government, democracy
Yellow (color)	Cowardice
White (color)	Purity
Thumbs up (gesture)	Yes, all's well
The heart (shape)	Love and affection
A crucifix (physical object)	Christianity
A wedding ring (physical object)	Marriage
A dove (animal)	Peace
Head shaking side to side (gesture)	No, disapproval
$A \leftrightarrow B$	Two-person group (dyad)

SYMBOLIC INTERACTION

Symbolic interaction is a framework for understanding human social behavior which combines the concepts of human interaction and the symbolic nature of the individual's relationship to the external world. Our particular concerns are with the use of symbols as a means for developing and maintaining relationships between and among individuals in groups. According to Herbert Blumer (1969) there are three propositions which represent the symbolic interactionist view:

1. The meanings that objects have for individuals form the bases upon which the individual acts toward these objects.
2. The meanings of these objects come from the social interaction between and among individuals.
3. The mechanism used by individuals in dealing with the meanings of objects themselves and with all the circumstances of human interaction is essentially the individual's interpretative ability.

When group interaction is viewed in these terms, our understanding of interaction is dependent upon the definition and use of three words — symbol, meaning, and interpretation. We are already familiar with the symbol but need to define meaning and interpretation. The word, *meaning*, includes all those things to which symbols refer. If we use language as a symbol structure, meaning refers to that which we intend to convey to others through the use of language. In interaction terms, meaning refers to the things individuals intend to communicate to others in the performance of an act. *Interpretation* is a process going on inside an individual by which that individual attempts to understand the meanings intended by others as they interact with each other.

One special characteristic of the symbolic interaction approach is that it does not deal with interaction as a straight-line phenomenon — that is, one in which two or more individuals are viewed as interacting with each other in, for example, a communication network. For the symbolic interactionist, the interpretation aspect of interaction suggests an interruption in the interaction between and among individuals so that the simple $A \leftrightarrow B$ becomes $A \leftrightarrow B$. The vertical line indicates that there is an interruption in the direct relationship A and B have with each other. That interruption is, in fact, the interpretation required of each group member before that member can respond to the symbolic behavior of others. (See Figure 1-2.)

If, as indicated in Figure 1-2, meanings are to be reciprocated by the interacting parties, the question of agreement of meanings arises. If social groups are to maintain themselves well over extended periods of time,

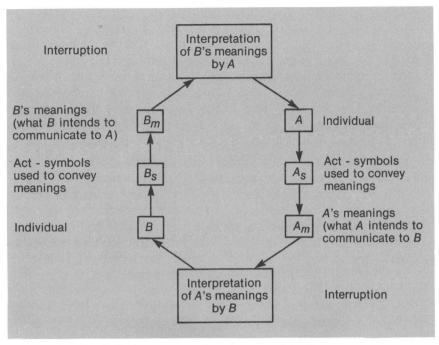

Figure 1-2.   Symbolic Interaction —Interruption of the Act

agreement as to the meanings of the symbols used is an absolute necessity. Ordinarily, developing a body of symbols having common meanings
is a rather normal circumstance of group behavior. In those instances
where shared meanings do not result from interaction between or among
group members, difficulties in maintaining the group will arise. Many of
the problems which develop within social groups—difficulties in communication, in expectations, and in understanding the common rules laid
down for all members—grow out of a failure on the part of group members to come to an agreement about the meanings intended as members
communicate with each other. Figure 1-2 is best explained by considering the following statements:

1. Individuals are symbol users and symbol makers.
2. Individuals respond to the meanings they give to external objects.
3. Interaction is possible because the meanings given to behavior are
   shared.

Individuals are symbol users and symbol makers. If we stop to think about it, we are surrounded by a vast number of symbols. Although we are not always aware of it, we are seldom without some relationship to one or another symbol. This book is a collection of symbols. The words you are reading are symbols; they represent the thinking of the writer. When you attend your classes you are, for as long as you listen, bombarded with symbols by your professor who lectures to you, uses the blackboard, passes out book lists, and so on. Speech and the written word are complexes of symbols. As a category, the kinds of symbols just mentioned are called language symbols. There are, of course, many other kinds of symbols. Gestures, such as the "O.K." gesture or the shoulder shrug, are symbols. Facial expressions—the smile, the frown, the down-turned mouth—are symbols. However, as we mentioned earlier, there are many kinds of symbols available, and all of us use these symbols every day.

We not only use these symbols, we make them. The language which we all use—and take for granted—is constructed by man, as are all other symbols. We use symbols, we make symbols, and we change the meanings of symbols. When we all agree that the symbols we are using have a certain meaning, that is, when we develop symbols which have common meanings, we are able to communicate with each other in a most effective way.

Leslie White's (1969:22) statement on the symbol leaves little doubt that it is a force in the development of man's social character:

> All human behavior originates in the use of symbols. It was the symbol which transformed our anthropoid ancestors into men and made them human. All civilizations have been generated, and are perpetuated, only by the use of symbols. It is the symbol which transforms an infant of Homo sapiens into a human being. . . . The symbol is the universe of humanity.

It is important that we emphasize one point. It is not only man's ability to symbolize that is important in understanding human interaction. Simply to know that a certain object or sound or gesture is a symbol is not enough to explain human social behavior. The importance of the symbol in defining human interaction lies in the meanings individuals give to them.

Individuals respond to the meanings they give to external objects. Individuals respond to the meanings they give to the behavior of others. Individuals also respond to the meanings they give to *all* elements in the situation in which an interaction takes place. Herbert Blumer (1962:187) remarks that "action takes place in and regard to a situation . . . any particular action is formed in the light of the situation in which it takes place."

When we approach symbolic interaction from the broad perspective of the situation rather than the specific perspective of interaction, we find that individuals respond not only to a single object but to the many objects which combine to form the situation in which interaction takes place, including the behavior of other individuals. Of course, the most important elements in any social situation are the elements of the interaction itself. Individuals take symbols from other individuals, interpret the symbols, and respond to them by communicating to the others in a symbolic way. In taking the view that individuals respond to situations, we are presenting a view of symbolic interaction which is more inclusive of all the elements to which individuals respond. The process which describes the individual's response to situations is exactly the same as the process by which individuals respond to other individuals.

We will look at the situational environment in terms of the meanings people give to it. The *situational environment* is the sum of all the social elements at a given point in time which individuals perceive as determiners of how they will perform their social or group roles. The key phrase in the definition, for our purposes, is "the sum of," indicating that an individual must take into account any number of elements in deciding upon an appropriate response to a given situation. When confronted with a situation, the individual must take into account each element separately and all the elements taken as a whole. In assessing these, the individual must formulate and carry out a plan of action which is deemed appropriate.

Most situations present no serious problem or concern for the individual. The reason is that, having been socialized to the ways of the society, the individual develops expectations about situations as well as about other individuals. In this way, the individual can anticipate not only self behavior and the behavior of others, but also the situation which develops from the interaction.

There are, however, situations which individuals cannot anticipate, situations about which expectations cannot easily be formed. Unexpected situations are uncommon but they can occur at any time, causing a good deal of anxiety and embarrassment. We are all only too familiar with situations such as the following ones, offered here as examples.

A young woman is on a date with a young man and is enjoying an evening capped off by a late-night snack at the local eatery. Another young man, who considers himself the young woman's boyfriend, enters the eatery alone. He and the young woman see each other, and he approaches the table where she is sitting with her date. The situation is complicated by the fact that neither of the young men is aware that the young woman is dating both of them. This is the kind of situation in which the young woman feels like crawling under the table. She may consider a hasty retreat to the ladies' room or introducing her date as her brother. However, the young woman will be forced to face up to the situation eventually.

Judy Smith, a student, is told by her professor that, unless she begins to perform better on tests and the final examination, she stands a good chance of failing the course. The professor recommends that the student make an appointment to see "what can be done." The student is faced with the unfamiliar situation of meeting with the professor outside the classroom. She must decide how she is going to "handle" the situation, which is another way of saying that she must decide how she is going to behave when meeting the professor in an office situation.

Professor Stephen Jones has always assumed that in the classroom he is the expert. He is accustomed to fielding questions, even difficult ones, with competence and flair. From the beginning of the fall semester, one student exhibits a knowledge of the subject matter which severely tests Professor Jones' expertise. Professor Jones may well ask himself: "Now, how am I going to handle *this* situation?"

In these, as well as in other more predictable situations, the individual must gather a good deal of information about the elements in the situation in order to develop an appropriate response. We have concentrated on the sum of all the social elements which confront individuals and which produce "situations." There are other elements which individuals must consider as well. For example, social situations occur in a physical setting and are governed, in one way or another, by culturally based expectations. There are, then, three sets of environmental elements (all taken together as a collection of stimuli) which individuals must consider and interpret when defining a situation. They are:

1. *Social Environmental Elements.* These refer to all the actions individuals perform in response to each other and include the definitions which individuals give to the interaction. Individual activity results in a complex of relationships which form the "center" of the situation.
2. *Physical Environmental Elements.* These elements include a host of objects such as the place in which the interaction takes place and all other physical elements including space, distance, and any physical object in the situation.
3. *Cultural Environmental Elements.* Most situations carry with them pre-situational expectations or guidelines. Included here are the standards of conduct of participating individuals. These standards function to limit the possible responses to situations but also have the funnelling effect of "forcing" appropriate responses. This

is so because such standards limit the number of plans of action from which an individual may select his behavior.

The individual, in accounting for all the elements in a situation, is giving meaning to the situation. It is important to note that each individual's perceptions occur on a highly selective basis. In fact, we observe that the meanings an individual gives to a situation are the ones perceived as correct. It is not surprising to hear someone say, "I wouldn't have handled the situation in that way." The phrase suggests that the speaker would have defined the situation differently and would have decided upon a different course of action. Individuals perceive the situations in which they find themselves in different ways, and it is this subjective variability which adds to the uncertainty of how any given individual will respond to any given situation.

Interaction is possible because the meanings given to behavior are shared. From the point of view of the interactionist, this proposition is most important since it is the principle upon which individuals are able to initiate and maintain a relationship. We mentioned earlier that the ability to make and to use symbols is not the most important issue for us. We may now suggest that this ability to give meaning to a symbol is not as important as the ability to share meanings with other individuals. Individuals can interact and can form social groups because of their ability to share with others the meanings given to things in the external environment. The meanings individuals give to things (included here, most especially, are the meanings we give to those objects which are of immediate value as communication tools, such as our language, gestures, and so on) are the result of a subjective process by which the individual internalizes the meaning to which a symbol refers. If these meanings, subjectively given, become part of a common referent, then cooperating individuals can form social bonds through meaningful communication. If this were not possible groups could not exist.

There are difficulties which stem from our attempts to share meanings and to make them common points of reference for individuals interacting as group members. These difficulties may arise from conflict in meanings at the normative, temporal, linguistic, and intergenerational levels.

Individuals must be alert to normative change in the meanings attached to patterns of behavior. For example, the traditional view that females should not move about the society freely or without an escort has undergone some serious revision in recent years. Established patterns of marriage and sexuality have changed, as has the view that the support of a family is the sole responsibility of the adult male family member. We are suggesting that as changes occur in the behavior individuals exhibit, changes also occur in the meanings given that behavior. And when the behavioral changes become increasingly commonplace, we are prone to suggest that normative changes have occurred. As a result of such changes and the failure of some to accept the new norms, individuals experience difficulties in their relationships with others who have accepted the norm changes. These difficulties may be attributed to their inability or simple reticence to adopt the new meanings given to any specific pattern of behavior.

We must also consider the temporal nature of shared meanings. There is no assurance that once the meanings for objects are established and agreed upon as a common basis for communication and group interaction that those meanings will always remain the same. The meanings we share with others are in a constant state of flux. We all agree, for example, that our language is constantly changing. These changes include not only the addition and deletion of words but changes in the meanings we give to words as well. Therefore, individuals must agree not only about the meanings words have for them, but also to change their common agreement when the meanings change. Since the use of language as a symbol structure is at the center of our ability to communicate and to interact with each other, we will consider changes in language a major concern in this regard.

We are suggesting that individuals do not always share the same meanings. The structure of language is very complex, and we are all subject to linguistic error. In interaction, the requirements for behaving appropriately, in terms of language, must include not only attributing the correct meanings to the words we use but making certain that others who receive our communication attribute to the words used the same meanings as intended. In some cases, difficulties arise. Glenn Vernon (1965:40) suggests that some of our phrases carry meanings other than the literal ones. For example, "He has a heart of gold," "My heart is broken," and "Don't beat around the bush," are all phrases which cannot be taken literally. In these instances, meaning can be determined only when one understands the idiom and the situation in which it is used.

We might consider what would happen if, for example, parents did not share their meanings with their young. Children cannot be socialized adequately without the willingness of parents to share commonly accepted meanings intergenerationally. Also, the difficulties encountered in relationships between adults and adolescents result from the adolescents' establishment of meanings for symbols, especially word symbols, which do not fit the traditional meanings adults have for them. We all experience some difficulties in communication when we cross over certain lines. Behavioral differences occur subculturally, socioeconomically, and educationally as well as intergenerationally. Difficulties result from shifts in meanings given by individuals from different regions or with different economic and educational backgrounds as well as by shifts in meanings intergenerationally.

The patterns of behavior which adolescent generations adopt mystify many adults. There is no mystery to the behavior of adolescents. Much of the difficulty lies in the older generation's refusing or being unable to understand and accept the new meanings which adolescents give to their actions. One of the most interesting examples of intergenerational changes in meanings involves the use of words which for the older generation are profane, dirty, and unfit for polite company. There is, of course, no need to provide a list of these words. It should suffice to note that words which are taboo for one generation may be perfectly acceptable to another. There is, in such instances, no sharing of meanings intergenerationally. However, *within* peer relations in each generation the meanings given behavior, including our use of words, are shared. This is not to suggest that adult generations do not use words which are unfit for polite company. Many do, and often. An understanding of the commonality of meanings also suggests that in adult generations there is complete agreement that these special words are profane. The only difference between the use of such words by adults today as opposed to adolescent usage is that adults believe and accept that the words are unfit but choose to use them anyway.

In these discussions of interaction and the individual's use of the symbol we have, in effect, described the mechanism by which individuals develop and maintain group relationships. Figure 1-2, used to describe the symbolic nature of interaction, may now be considered a diagrammatic representation of the mechanism of human group behavior. We turn now to the concept of the social group and begin our discussion by distinguishing group relations from other kinds of social relationships.

TEMPORARY SOCIAL RELATIONS

All social relationships are not group relationships. Especially in the urban, industrial society of today, we find ourselves moving daily into and out of relationships which do not fit the category of established group relations but which are very much like them (Goffman, 1959). These relationships are usually small in number of participants and are usually short-lived.

We shop for food, clothing, and other such needs and so we must deal with shop clerks and checkers. We dine out and must deal with waiters and cashiers. When on the job, we must deal with individuals whom we have never met or individuals whom we know only slightly. On a given day, we may meet friends of our relatives, friends of our friends, and unfortunately, in some cases, friends of our enemies. We have continuing, but hardly established, relationships with letter carriers, service station attendants, doctors, dentists, and lawyers. At least once a year, on a given day, we may meet with an accountant whom we hope will give the necessary aid, if not comfort, at federal income-tax time! Seldom does any one of these qualify as an established long-term group relationship. But they are *like* established group relations. Although these relationships are not of long duration or frequent, they include many of the basic elements found in small group systems of interaction. They are characterized by a rudimentary social structure, as in the dominant-submissive association between doctor and patient. Temporary social relations have explicit or implied goals, and they satisfy individual needs.

Because these social relations have many of the elements which form social groups, when we enter into them we tend to behave in a manner similar to the way we behave in our more established group relationships. A temporary social relation, then, has the spirit of the social group, but little of its reality.

We are all caught up in the business of interacting with others in one way or another every day of our lives. However, the degree to which these groups and group-like social relations affect our lives is by no means the same. Many of the temporary social relations which we encounter have little or no serious effect upon us. We might even suggest that they are the least important parts of our daily interaction routine. Group relations, as we shall see, are quite another matter.

THE SOCIAL GROUP: DEFINITIONS

Although sociologists who are concerned with the study of the social group have some agreement on certain common elements in their definitions, their interpretations of the group phenomenon have differed greatly. Here are a few of the many definitions which abound in the literature:

1. We mean by a group a number of persons who communicate with one another often over a span of time, and who are few enough so that each person is able to communicate with all the others, not at

secondhand, through other people, but face to face (Homans, 1950:1).

2. A group is an identifiable, structured, continuing collectivity of social persons who enact reciprocal roles according to social norms, interests, and values in the pursuit of common goals (Fichter, 1957:110).

3. The following excerpts consider groups as systems of interaction and approach the group in terms of the *range* it encompasses:

   From the standpoint of the extensity of the interaction process, they range from the all-embracing unlimited totalitarian (maximally cumulative) to the slightest, where the interacting relationship is limited to one unimportant 'interest.'

   From the standpoint of duration, from the most durable and continuous to the groups existing only a short moment, sometimes a few seconds.

   From the standpoint of the direction of the interaction, from the maximally and relatively solidary through the mixed groups, to the limited and all-embracingly antagonistic.

   From the standpoint of organization, from the highly organized to the barely organized and unorganized groups (Sorokin, 1970:444).

4. A group, in the social psychological sense, is a plurality of persons who interact with one another in a given context more than they interact with anyone else (Sprott, 1969:9).

There is certainly variety in the above definitions, but among these and most other definitions there is one common factor—the highlight of all social groups—interaction. Marvin Shaw (1976:11) remarks that " . . . interaction is the essential feature that distinguishes a group. . . . " With this understanding of the importance of interaction as a qualifier of group behavior, Shaw (1976:11) defines a group as " . . . two or more persons who are interacting with one another in such a manner that each person influences and is influenced by each other person."

Shaw's definition, at first reading, is simple enough. Once the importance of interaction within the group is established, it must be considered that the process of interaction involves a system of relations in which individuals become meaningful participants in a kind of association which is lasting and which is committed to the achievement of a goal or set of goals.

COMMON BASES FOR GROUP ASSOCIATION

Once there is a basic understanding of what a social group is, a logical question might be: "How do these groups come about?" Groups form in a great variety of circumstances, and for a great variety of reasons. The following is a simple classification scheme suggesting the most common bases for the origin and development of social groups:

1. Physical proximity
2. Familial bonds
3. Common interests
4. Common physical characteristics
5. Positional expectations

(1) *Physical Proximity*. Social groups are real, observable social facts, and the interactions which prevail within them are necessarily limited by the real environment. That is to say, social groups are limited by space and place. This basis for group association is obvious when one realizes that human interaction is a face-to-face phenomenon. It would be extremely difficult, if not impossible, for two friends to meet and maintain a relationship if they were separated by great distances. Members of families live together, collections of families form neighborhoods, and neighborhoods form communities. At each level, physical proximity is an absolute necessity. In fact, when the spatial element is lost or is in the process of being lost, sociologists begin to talk about the disorganization or breakdown of social bonds.

(2) *Familial Bonds*. The basic form of group organization in any society is the human family. The ties which bind family members are those of blood. Group associations based on familial bonds include associations by marriage, by birth, and by adoption. The social groups which are based upon these bonds are the marital dyad, the nuclear family, and extended families which include a number of nuclear families and other individuals connected by common ancestry.

(3) *Common Interests*. This classification is very likely the most all-inclusive one since it suggests common motivation among group members and an expressed need to cooperate in the pursuit of personal interests. Included here are all those groups within the economic, political, educational, recreational, and religious spheres in which individuals associate because they agree on the most basic values and goals each group specifies. Educationally, for example, individuals associate in order to

learn and to prepare themselves for their futures. Within the higher educational institution, faculty groups, student organizations, and clubs are examples of groups based upon common interests.

There is another view of common interests which sociologists have recognized for a long time. The interest is that of companionship. In group terms, Robert MacIver and Charles Page (1949:445) observe that "... the interest of companionship is so pervasive that it is in some degree satisfied by every association. ... "

(4) *Common Physical Characteristics.* Until recently, groups based upon common physical characteristics were more clearly distinguishable than they are today. Changes resulting from both an elimination of patterns of racial segregation and the advent of the Women's Liberation Movement have militated against the easy classification of groups by race and sex. Youth groups, of course, suggest the division of some group associations by age, and, in the sports world, physical ability and talents are characteristics distinguishing sports clubs and organizations.

(5) *Positional Expectations.* There are other groupings which form, usually ones peripheral to specific institutional positions which some individuals occupy. These expectations are often associated with one's job situation. Businessmen, for example, may feel the need to join such groups. To improve business contacts and thereby increase potential profits, businessmen will frequently join local community and political groups, social clubs for purposes of entertaining clients, and even establish friendships for business purposes. The most interesting aspect of these types of group relationships is that there is a certain pressure to join. Failure to do so is often considered a disadvantage to the individual and an indicator of reduced success in the specific position occupied.

THE SOCIAL GROUP: CHARACTERISTICS

Whichever definition one adopts or constructs for social group, it should include interaction. And although interaction is clearly the most important characteristic of groups and group behavior, there are others which help our understanding of the human social group. The remainder of this chapter will deal with four important group characteristics. They are:

1. Interaction
2. Duration
3. Needs and goals
4. Group structure: norms and roles

(1) *Interaction*. Every social group needs participants who will contribute to the development and success of the social group as a whole. Practically speaking, each member should function in an active manner, seeking rewards not only for oneself, but for the entire group. Although it is hoped that each member will behave in a cooperative and useful manner, such is not always the case. Activity among members in the group, be that activity cooperative, competitive, conflict-oriented, or otherwise, is all part of the circumstances surrounding group interaction.

Interaction may be defined as the exchange of meaningful activity between two or more individuals. In simplest diagram form, the interaction between group members can be identified by $A \leftrightarrow B$, where A and B are interdependent group members and where $\leftrightarrow$ is the symbol for the reciprocity (interaction, exchange) between the two. Increasing the size of the group will, of course, increase the number of possible single units of reciprocity. A simple numerical increase in size will result in a proportionately greater increase in the total number of interactions possible between any two members within any group setting. This is a very important function of the size of the group and the complexity of the reciprocity within. Table 1-2 will help make the point clear. The three-person group produces an equal number (three) of two-person interactions but the four-person group (an increase of one person) produces six two-person interactions (an increase of three) and the five-person group (an increase of another person) produces ten two-person interactions (an increase of four).

(2) *Duration*. Many groups endure over long periods of time. One can expect that the long duration of group bonds produces group cohesion and, ultimately, success in achieving group goals. For groups that require long periods of time, this is so. However, the characteristic of group duration is not so much dependent upon long periods of time as it is on the quality of the interaction during the time the group is active. It is reasonable to suggest that depending upon the needs of the group members as individuals and the needs of the group as a whole, *duration* is best interpreted as the amount of time sufficient to allow for the attainment of the desired group goal or goals.

Some groups do not require years to achieve their goals. Ad hoc committees, for example, may require only short periods of time to achieve the ends for which they were organized. Other types of groups, such as American nuclear families, require the lifetimes of its members to achieve the ends for which they were formed.

There are three effects which result when groups maintain themselves over any given period of time: (1) the group's desired goal may be

Table 1-2.   Symbolic Representations and Number of Two-Person Interactions for Groups of *n* Size

NUMBER OF MEMBERS IN GROUP	SYMBOLIC REPRESENTATION	NUMBER OF TWO-PERSON INTERACTIONS
2	$A \longleftrightarrow B$	1
3		3
4		6
5		10

achieved, (2) the group direction may change and goals other than the expressed or desired ones may be achieved, and (3) the group may actually fail to achieve any goal at all. What is being suggested here is that group activity should be distinguished from actual goal attainment with the qualification that without the expectation of achieving some goal, maintaining a group for any length of time would be extremely difficult, if not impossible.

(3) *Needs and Goals.* A major reason why people form groups is that they have needs which are best realized in concert with others. We all know that certain needs cannot be met alone and that when we cooperate

with others in certain ways our needs, particularly our social needs, will be met. It is important to recognize, however, that there is a difference between individual needs and the needs of the group. The distinction, however, is not an easy one.

Individual needs may be defined as forces within the individual, the existence of which is inferred through behavior directed toward the achievement of a goal. Individual needs are presocial or socially derived. Presocial needs refer to the basic survival forces present in the human being. Social needs derive from the experiences individuals have within the social environment from birth. For example, if an individual internalizes the social value placed upon wealth, power, and prestige, it is reasonable to assume that the individual will develop need-dispositions which will orient behavior in the direction of achieving those goals which reflect the values which were internalized.

Group needs, on the other hand, are forces which develop out of group affiliation, and which promote concerted activity directed toward the achievement of a goal acceptable to the group as a whole. All groups, for example, need structure. Groups need some system of norms, statuses, roles, and relationships which is based upon a sense of order and differentiation. Group behavior under any other condition would be chaotic and without goal direction. It might also be argued that all groups need leadership. What is meant here is not only a leader who is elected or appointed but also any individual who emerges from the membership and attains a status above other members. This is the case even between two friends who, under the specific conditions of a given situation, require direction which ordinarily comes from one or the other.

Although the distinction between individual and group needs is an important one, individual and group needs often blend or appear to blend so that it is difficult to distinguish one from the other. Such blends of individual and group needs combine to produce an environment of motivation which is ideal as a basis for achieving individual and group goals.

Since it is often extremely difficult to separate individual and group needs, our discussion is centered around the relationship between the two and the importance of their compatibility. The presence of individual and group needs in any given situation will result in any one of four possibilities: (1) Individual and group needs may be so diverse that they interfere with each other with no positive effects accruing either to individuals within the group or to the group as a whole. (2) Group interaction may result in the realization of goals desired by the group as a whole, while individual needs are not met. (3) Individual needs may be realized by one or more group members to the detriment or destruction of the group. (4) Individual and group needs may blend so completely that the needs realized by the group as a whole are the same needs individuals wish to realize.

It is this last possibility which group analysts consider as the ultimate in group organization and integration. Group integration is facilitated by need compatibility. Such integration will come about if the group as a cooperatively functioning unit can provide: (1) an environment for the mutual satisfaction of needs, (2) an environment in which individual needs, though different from those of the group, become interdependent need components of the group, or (3) an environment in which individual needs develop because of membership within the group, thus suggesting compatibility between individual and group needs. In each of the above instances, the success of the group in finally attaining its goals and the realization of goals which satisfy the needs of the individual will result.

Individual needs are often generalized and lack clarity and substance. A good example of this is the individual's need for companionship. A need such as this becomes more specific and much more clearly defined when the individual becomes an active member of a friendship group or social club. Through participation in the system of interaction within the group, the individual's vague need for companionship is translated into the clear and continuing goal of developing and maintaining a friendship. Table 1-3 suggests some individual needs which, through group association, are translated into goals.

We are suggesting that human behavior needs direction. Individuals seem to perform best when there is some sense of achievement anticipated for their behavior. This being the case, understanding goals and the direction of people's actions is a necessary part of the analysis of groups. *Goals* can be defined as the ends for which social groups are organized and maintained. These ends form the basis for the satisfaction of individual and group needs.

Goals and goal achievement can be viewed at two levels: the personal level and the group level. Individuals may join social groups in order to achieve goals which are highly personal. Ordinarily, such goal orientation suggests the use of group activity and the interaction within it in a purely utilitarian and self-enhancing way. Using group situations in order to achieve personal goals is not a problem as long as the goals of the individual are consistent with those of the group as a whole. R. B. Cattell's (1951:167) definition of the social group highlights personal goals: "The definition which seems most essential is that a group is a collection of organisms in which the existence of all (in their given relationships) is necessary to the satisfaction of certain individuals' needs in each."

The emphasis here should be placed not on the appropriateness of achieving individual or personal goals, but upon the consistency of these

Table 1-3.   Relationship between Needs and Goals and Appropriate Group Choice

NEED	GROUP CHOICE	GOAL
Companionship	Friendship group	Friendship
Love and affection	Marital dyads Family groups	Sexual and emotional support
Achievement	Occupational groups	Recognition and promotion
Knowledge	Educational groups	Diploma, degree, honors
Public recognition	Political groups	Elected or appointed office
Competition	Athletic teams	Winning
Aggression	The military	Defeating the enemy, domination
Altruism	Social service groups Volunteer groups	Well-being of others, helping the under-privileged

with the goals of the group as a whole. This issue is important enough for one author, Clovis Shepherd (1964:122), to remark, "Generally a successful group has clear objectives, not vague ones, and the members of the group have personal objectives which are identical or compatible with the group's objectives." Without such compatibility, the setting of common goals for the development and maintenance of group cohesion would be meaningless. It should be noted that the degree to which these goals blend and complement each other can be an efficient measure of the success a social group may expect.

Although goals and goal achievement is not the major focus of the interactionist approach, the significance of social group analysis would be diminished without the perspective which an understanding of goals and goal achievement provides.

(4) *Group Structure: Norms and Roles.* All social groups have some kind and some degree of structure. This generalization and its implications are absolutely necessary in order to fully understand the group process.

From the interactionist's viewpoint, the *A* and the *B* of group interaction mentioned earlier are symbols which stand for individuals who behave toward one another and who expect responses in return. Each individual in the group interaction system must have a set of expectations about each other in the social group. For the group process to be a viable one, the position which each individual occupies in relation to each other individual in the group must be fixed. In other words, every social group must have a structure. *Group structure* is defined as a set of fixed positions which individuals occupy in relation to each other and which carry with them well-defined levels of expectations for behavior which each group member can more or less rely upon as a basis for ordering present as well as future behavior.

Alvin Bertrand (1967:142), in discussing the concept of structure, indicates that it ". . . denotes a fixed relationship between the elements or parts which make up a whole." For the social group as well as for other structures, the idea that the parts are fixed and work well only in relation to each other is basic to an understanding of the importance which many sociologists place on the concept of structure.

For the interactionist studying the social group, the structural element is crucial. If interaction is to be studied at all successfully, it must be within the framework of a controlled and organized group setting in which the analyst can observe and interpret the interpersonal components of the interactions within the group setting. This would be impossible without understanding and insight into the structural components of the group itself. Simply put by Robin M. Williams, Jr. (1970:25): ". . . human interactions show structure. . . ." Human beings exhibit, in groups, behavior which is repeated, patterned, and organized around a system of expectations about individual activities within the boundaries of a given group. This is precisely what structure is about—the consistencies in group behavior. Appropriate to the subject is the view offered by Vernon (1965:5): "Sociologists talk about the *structure* of human interaction. In doing so they are emphasizing the uniformities found therein. A study of human interaction is essentially a study of the arrangement or relationship of various units."

Without the fixed and patterned elements in group analysis, it would be extremely difficult to understand anything about the relationships taking place over long periods of time. It would be next to impossible to identify all the forces and group components which identify a particular relationship or set of relationships within a particular social group.

Groups may have either formal or informal structure. The distinction is simple enough and will serve as a worthwhile reference in future discussions about relationships found within various types of groups. *Formal structure* involves clearly defined positions in fixed relationships to other positions. These positions are governed by explicit rules and regulations for individual and interpersonal behavior. *Informal structure* involves less clearly defined positions within groups, and these are usually governed by an informal code of behavior which develops out of previous experiences of the group members with each other. Although the distinction between the two types of structures is not a difficult one, it may be more easily understood through the following example: Family groupings are usually associations bound by ties which stem from the personal needs and interdependencies of their members and which have little need for formal, rigid, written rules and regulations. This type of grouping should be thought of as having an informal structure.

A business office, however, does not require such an informal basis for defining relationships among its workers. Relationships within a business office would dictate, for purposes of efficiency and high productivity, at both the personal and interpersonal levels, a clear and explicit set of rules and regulations. Sometimes, such specific and limiting regulations are found written out in a Book of Rules or Job Description. Such rigid regulation of behavior simply would not do for the day-to-day relationships in a family. The American nuclear family, friendship groups, and informal work groups are all examples of informal group structures; and bureaucracies such as the American military, the federal government, colleges and universities, and prison systems are examples of formal group structures.

One note of caution: There is no reason to assume that members of informal group structures are less aware of the privileges and responsibilities of their positions and that members of formal group structures are ever alert to the requirements of theirs. In each, the controls over both individual and interpersonal behavior are strong, but deviation from those expectations is an individual rather than group decision. On the whole, most people follow most of the rules of their group most of the time.

Joseph Monane's (1967:16–17) insight into the regulation of individual behavior by group structures comes from his understanding of systems analysis: "A component's identity appears strongly dependent upon the social systems to which he belongs. A person's attitudes, for instance, tend to be those of the groups in which he holds membership: his family, his friendships, and his co-workers. This pressure of system upon its components may be called system determinism." What Monane is suggesting is that the individual who identifies strongly with the group in which membership is held accepts the regulations of that group, and, in large measure, behavior is determined by those controls.

In describing formal organizational structures which are systems of low organization, Monane (1967:22) finds a ". . . diversity and a tolerance of diversity, in action and opinion. . . . " and suggests that "Autonomy goes with heterogeneity, and both are especially likely in large rather than small social systems. Meaningful communication and reciprocal impact of components become less as the size of a social system mounts."

Monane (1967:23–24) distinguishes between low and high organizations and his distinction parallels our formal and informal one. He states, "Families throughout the world are usually highly organized social systems." He goes on to say, "Psychological disturbance in one member of a family, for instance, carries a profound impact on other family members and upon the family as a system."

NORMS. College students during the late sixties were fond of using the phrase "doing my own thing" with disturbing regularity. The implication was that the individual would or should not be limited by the rules and regulations of the university in which he was matriculating. The following situation involving a student "doing his own thing" will serve to explain student deviation from college norms. One requirement for a small groups course was a term paper due three days before the scheduled final examination date. The assignment was given early in the semester, and there was more than enough time to complete the requirement especially since administrative approval had been given for eliminating the final examination. The day before the term paper was due, a student entered the professor's office and explained that the term paper had not been written and one would not be submitted as required. When asked why, the student replied: "I wouldn't get any pleasure out of doing a paper, and you should respect my right to do my own thing." The professor explained that the student's rights were respected as long as they did not infringe upon the rights of others and hinder the fulfillment of course requirements. The student was told that the "F" grade would result from failure to complete the course requirements. Refusing to accept this decision, the student requested at least the "B" grade, but would not complete the requirement. The student had internalized the individualism of the times thoroughly enough to resist the pressures to conform to the rules established for receiving a passing grade.

In our culture, individuality has been elevated to the status of a highly valued item, as has conformity. There are times, however, when one object of value (individuality) is in direct conflict with the expected behavior (conformity) demanded in certain group situations. The traditional view of group norms and member conformity states that individuals are controlled by the norms and normative expectations to which they have been socialized as a member of the larger society and as a participant in a specific group interaction system. The implication is that individuals conform to norms because they have internalized them and actually believe that conformity to group norms is best for them and for the group as a whole.

Robin M. Williams, Jr. (1970:29–30) presents an interpretation of norms and conformity to norms which suggests that social or group control and the standardization of member behavior "is not achieved by socialization into specific norms . . . but rather is derived from *lack of perceived alternatives.*" Williams explains that individuals often accept the norms imposed upon them simply because they are unaware of other possibilities. This interpretation is interesting but is not substantially different from that of the traditionalist. The lack of perceived alternatives to which Williams refers is, in fact, one effect produced by socialization into a group or social system. Socialization is the process whereby individuals learn how to behave appropriately and how, either explicitly or implicitly, not to behave. Being socialized to accept the normative structure of a given social group includes the rejection of alternatives. Norms are elements which set the limits of acceptable behavior. In this sense, adherence to a normative system requires individuals to eliminate perceived alternatives. It is not the lack of perceived alternatives which necessitates conformity to a set of normative expectations. Socialization to norms places limitations upon the individual's right or wish to select certain courses of action over those which have been approved by the group.

Group norms define the limits within which behavior is deemed acceptable or appropriate. They establish the group basis for controlling behavior, and set the standards by which individual behavior is judged. When individuals enter groups they subject themselves to all the influences which groups exert upon members, and they are expected to conform to the established norms. Group influences also include the means whereby members are pressured to conform to the norms established by the group as a whole. These means by which conforming behavior is exacted from group members are called group or social controls. The basis upon which norms are established and controls are developed exists in the belief that the interests of individual group members and the group as a whole are best served when behavior remains within prescribed limits.

ROLES. Within the group system, the structural element which connects group norms to the behavior of the individual group member is the social role. *Roles* are sets of expectations which members in groups share concerning the behavior of each individual who occupies a position within the group structure. When individuals interact with each other over significant periods of time within the same group, a pattern of expectations develops and forms the constellation of expectations which we call roles.

There are a number of reasons why roles are important to groups and group structure. Roles are the bases of interaction. Effective interaction within group settings is based upon the assumption that individuals internalize their roles and perform accordingly. Assuming that all roles are reciprocal and complementary, interaction proceeds without hindrance toward the achievement of group goals. The reciprocal nature of roles is reflected in the degree to which group interaction based upon role expectations coordinates the activities of all members of the group. The reciprocal and complementary qualities of social roles are observable in the most common role relationships found within the complex of group activity. For example, it is impossible to conceive of the role of parent without the role of child or that of husband without the role of wife. Friendship is based upon the assumption that there is another individual who shares the identities and interests common to all friendships. More formal associations also reflect the reciprocal and complementary nature of social roles. The professional roles of doctors and dentists are complemented only by those who perform the roles of their patients; lawyers and clients are complements of each other. The superordination-subordination character common to many role relationships suggests the logical reciprocity and complementarity of the leader-follower relationship. The theme of dominance and submission in role relationships reached a point of clear distinction in the traditional relationship between master and slave.

ROLES AS TOOLS OF SOCIALIZATION. Children learn how to behave in a variety of situations and internalize those roles which they will be expected to perform as adults by taking others' roles. Children, by taking the roles of parents, are also internalizing the behavior of those others and, in the process, are able to understand better how they, as children, fit into the relationships which have developed between them and their parents. Roles control and limit the extent to which individuals will deviate from group norms. Roles function as translators of group norms for each individual member of the group and determine the limits within which behavior is approved and rewarded and outside of which behavior is rejected and punished. Since individuals occupy different positions within the group, it is necessary for the group as a whole to make explicit what is expected of each group member.

ROLES AND POSITIONS. Group structures have been identified as complexes of positions which group members occupy. For each position there should be a clear, precise, and appropriate statement of the expectations which determine the behavior of those individuals who occupy the group positions. In this sense, roles form an overlay which fits the complex of group positions perfectly, at least on paper. In reality, actual performance usually varies from the stated expectations and is influenced by such individual factors as personality, motivation, ability, and skill. Group structure is an important concept in understanding groups and group organization; roles and the complex of activity and interaction which they promote are the essentials of group behavior. The static quality usually associated with the analysis of structure and position is converted into the dynamics of group interaction by the incorporation of an overstructure of roles which is designed to control the behavior of group members and to order the relationships of those who occupy group positions.

*   *   *   *

The material covered in this chapter should be considered as an introduction to the study of the small group. For some readers, the chapter will provide a useful review of the concept of the social group; for others, the chapter will provide new insights into group behavior which are necessary for a full understanding of the small group and the interaction which occurs within its limited boundaries. The larger hope is that students of the discipline will be better equipped to handle the concepts, theoretical orientations, and research which have developed around those social groups whose size limitations have provided ideal boundaries for serious investigations into understanding human behavior.

summary

This chapter was designed as an introduction to (1) the interactionist approach to the study of small groups, (2) the symbolic nature of interaction, and (3) the social group, by way of definitions and characteristics. The interactionist approach was defined and discussed in terms of the interdependency of individuals and the patterns of communication which characterize interdependency. The interactionist approach was viewed as complex because it includes not only an understanding of the structure of group interaction and the motivation of individual actors, but of situational elements which surround human interaction as well.

Interaction was identified as symbolic. Explanations of the symbolic nature of interaction centered around a need to understand the ability of human beings to use and change symbols, interpret behavior, and define the meanings associated with the symbols used in group interaction. It was observed that human interaction takes place on two levels: *the symbol level* and *the meaning level*.

The concept of the social group was introduced and explained in terms of the common element—interaction—found in all definitions of the social group. The common bases for group association were listed as follows: (1) physical proximity, (2) familial bonds, (3) common interests, (4) common physical characteristics, and (5) positional expectations. The four most important characteristics of group association were identified as (1) interaction, (2) duration, (3) needs and goals, and (4) group structure: norms and roles. These characteristics distinguish the social group from other collectivities such as categories and aggregates.

discussion questions

1. What do cases of isolation, such as the case of Anna, tell us about our social nature?
2. Recall some social situations which may have resulted in embarrassment to you or to a friend.
3. Under what conditions are the needs of the individual and the group compatible?
4. Is the concept of a formal structure alien to the organization of all friendship groups, of a football team, of a small business office?
5. Consider the possible effects on discipline in a family organized as a formal rather than informal group.

references

Bates, Frederick L. "A Conceptual Analysis of Group Structure," *Social Forces*, 36 (1957): 103–111.

Bertrand, Alvin L. *Basic Sociology: An Introduction to Theory and Method.* New York: Appleton-Century-Crofts, 1967.

Blumer, Herbert. "Society as Symbolic Interaction," in Arnold M. Rose (ed.), *Human Behavior and Social Process.* Boston: Houghton-Mifflin, 1962.

Blumer, Herbert. *Symbolic Interactionism: Perspective and Method.* Englewood

Cliffs, New Jersey: Prentice-Hall, 1969.

Cattell, Raymond. "New Concepts for Measuring Leadership in Terms of Group Syntality," *Human Relations*, 4 (1951): 161–184.

Davis, Kingsley. "Final Note on a Case of Extreme Isolation," *American Journal of Sociology*, 50 (1947): 432–437.

Fichter, Joseph H. *Sociology*. Chicago: The University of Chicago Press, 1957.

Goffman, Erving. *The Presentation of Self in Everyday Life*. Garden City, New York: Doubleday, 1959.

Homans, George C. *The Human Group*. New York: Harcourt, Brace and World, 1950.

MacIver, Robert M.; and Page, Charles H. *Society: An Introductory Analysis*. New York: Holt, Rinehart and Winston, 1949.

Monane, Joseph H. *A Sociology of Human Systems*. New York: Appleton-Century-Crofts, 1967.

Shaw, Marvin. *Group Dynamics: The Psychology of Small Group Behavior*, 2nd ed.; New York: McGraw-Hill, 1976.

Shepherd, Clovis R. *Small Groups: Some Sociological Perspectives*. San Francisco: Chandler, 1964.

Shibutani, Tomotsu. *Society and Personality: An Interactionist Approach To Social Psychology*. Englewood Cliffs, New Jersey: Prentice-Hall, 1961.

Sorokin, Pitirim. *Social and Cultural Dynamics*. Boston: Porter Sargent, 1970.

Sprott, W. J. H. *Human Groups*. Baltimore, Maryland: Penguin Books, 1969.

Vernon, Glenn. *Human Interaction: An Introduction to Sociology*. New York: Ronald, 1965.

White, Leslie A. *The Science of Culture*. New York: Farrar, Strauss and Giroux, 1969.

Williams, Robin M., Jr. *American Society: A Sociological Interpretation*, 3rd ed.; New York: Alfred A. Knopf, 1970.

Chapter Two
The Small Group

CHAPTER PREVIEW

WHY STUDY SMALL GROUPS?

The small group may be seen as a microcosm of the larger society. From the point of view of the individual, the small group *is* the society because so much of one's life is spent within its confines. Many of the individual's values and rules of social behavior are determined by that individual's membership in a variety of small groups. For example, in tracing the social activity of an individual from birth to death, one finds that in every stage of development, the most significant environments for socialization are those which occur within small groups. Day-to-day social activities of all sorts occur within the boundaries of the small group. These groups include the family, friendship groups, and children's play groups in neighborhoods, small groups of influence and association in the political, economic, religious, and other sectors of social life, and the less numerous and less frequent family and friendship associations (institutional or other) of the aged. Most individuals may be expected to participate in many or all of these at one time or another in their lives. We study small groups because they are the environments in which we conduct the great majority of social life activities.

As students of society, sociologists spend a great deal of time attempting to explain the relationship between the individual and the society. Small groups become connecting links which help explain not only the interdependence between and among individuals but, also, the interdependence between the individual and the society.

There is, of course, the more general explanation that there is a continuing need to better understand our human surroundings so that we might improve the social environment. In this sense, we can consider the study of small groups as social ecology.

DEFINITIONS: SMALL GROUP SIZE

To continue this investigation of small groups without first considering the limits of size would be folly. It is logical to assume that if we want to concentrate on small groups, we must decide which groups are small and which groups are too large to fall within the small group category.

It is considerably easier to ask the question about small group size than to answer it. If you were asked whether or not groups having four or five members fall into the small groups category, you would reasonably agree that they do. But, if you were asked the same question about groups with twenty members, would you agree that such groups are small? Consider the same question for groups with thirty, forty, and fifty members. Where would you draw the line?

An early contributor to our general understanding of the size of small groups was Georg Simmel (Wolff, 1950:87):

> It will immediately be conceded on the basis of everyday experiences, that a group upon reaching a certain size must develop forms and organs which serve its maintenance and promotion, but which a smaller group does not need. On the other hand, it will also be admitted that smaller groups have qualities, including types of interaction among their members, which inevitably disappear when the groups grow larger.

In this passage, Simmel highlights the need to distinguish small and large groups and, by implication, points out the difficulty encountered in attempting to determine the size at which groups should be considered large. But Simmel does not help us in deciding on the numerical lower and upper limits of the small group. As we shall see in Chapter Three, Simmel concentrates on groups of very small size, emphasizing the three-party relationship which small groups analysts call the triad.

There is no agreement among sociologists as to the minimum and maximum size of small groups. This is understandable since common sense tells us that any rigid set of limits would be arbitrary at best. If, for example, we agreed that groups of fifteen should be included within the range of small groups, does that mean that groups of sixteen should not? At the lower end of the size question, are we to include groups of two or should we go no lower than three?

THE LOWER LIMIT

Joseph H. Fichter (1957:109) suggests that ". . . the briefest definition of the group is 'human beings in reciprocal relations.'" If we accept the obvious simplicity of this definition, we could interpret the lower limit of all small groups as two individuals in reciprocal relations. Two-person relations are referred to as dyads.

Students of small groups might be willing to agree on groups of two individuals as the acceptable lower limit were it not for Simmel, who insisted that three interacting individuals was the smallest number acceptable as a social group. He believed in a superpersonal group life, a sense of group identity beyond the individual, which is possible only when the loss of one individual does not hinder the ability of a group to function as a whole. This is possible only in groups of three or more members. The following example will describe Simmel's view that groups persist beyond the presence of one member, and that the superpersonal life of the group is a quality which allows for member replacement without hindering group organization or group activity. In a five-person group composed of members a, b, c, d, and e, one member, a, departs at a certain point in time and is replaced by individual, m. The new member is socialized by the four members remaining from the original group. Assuming that this process continued through the remaining four original members, the result is a group composed of five individuals, none of whom is an original member. If we follow Simmel's logic, the final group is the same group as the original one since the superpersonal or cultural life of the group continued beyond the membership of any one individual. The following series of changes in group membership at different points in time expresses the procedure by which a group persists beyond any one member's existence in it:

		TIME ELEMENT
Original group:	a, b, c, d, e	
Departure:	$a\!\!\!/, b, c, d, e$	h
Replacement:	m, b, c, d, e	
Departure:	$m, b\!\!\!/, c, d, e$	i
Replacement:	m, n, c, d, e	
Departure:	$m, n, c\!\!\!/, d, e$	j
Replacement:	m, n, o, d, e	
Departure:	$m, n, o, d\!\!\!/, e$	k
Replacement:	m, n, o, p, e	
Departure:	$m, n, o, p, e\!\!\!/$	l
Final group:	m, n, o, p, q	

According to Simmel's thinking, group m, n, o, p, q is the same group as a, b, c, d, e since, over time, each new member is socialized to the group by original members and by those who were socialized into group membership at an earlier time.

Simmel (Wolff, 1950:126) argued, "In the dyad, the sociological process remains, in principle, within personal interdependence and does not result in a structure that grows beyond its elements." For him, then, the dyad is not a social group because it does not have the superindividual quality of group life. He adds that with the loss of one of the two interacting members, there is nothing left of the relationship.

Some believe that Simmel's argument is not a compelling one. The opposing view suggests that as long as the two-person relationship exists as an ongoing, viable interaction it has a level of intimacy, an intensity, and a face-to-face identity which is very close to the ideal form for an integrated small group relationship. There is another argument against the view that all groups persist beyond any one member. Certain types of social groups develop a level of identity and integration based upon feelings and personalities. Individuals within these kinds of associations base their relationships on a subjective evaluation of others in the group. These are groups, such as friendship groups, which are concerned with continuing a relationship with given individuals and not any other persons who might fulfill some objective criteria for membership. There is little chance of Simmel's view applying under these conditions. Group relationships such as those found in business, political, and military systems are another matter. Simmel's idea is more acceptable under conditions in which criteria such as educational level, skill, and other objective qualities determine group membership.

THE UPPER LIMIT

Every small groups analyst has an opinion on the maximum size of small groups. Again, there is little agreement. But the upper limit which seems to occur most frequently in the literature is twenty. Michael S. Olmstead and A. Paul Hare (1978:12) offer the supposition that ". . . approximately twenty persons represents the upper limit of small group size. . . ," and Marvin E. Shaw (1976:11) suggests ". . . a group having twenty or fewer members. . . ." Clovis Shepherd (1964:4) explains that a large proportion of small groups studied by sociologists "have had no more than twenty members and usually fewer than fifteen."

The entire question of small group size is not only arbitrary but problematic as well. The size distinctions made here are important ones. Sociologists believe, and small group research supports the position, that: (1) the type of behavior performed by individuals in small groups is different from that observed in groups of larger size, (2) the form of organization required for small group interaction differs from that observed in larger groups, (3) the kinds of emotions and sentiments individuals exhibit in their behavior toward each other differ according to group size, and (4) the kinds of rules and regulations that relationships within groups require are dependent upon the size of the group. The position taken here regarding group size is as follows: *Small groups are those whose size extends from a minimum of two to a maximum of twenty.* John James (1951) researched the size factor in small groups and reached some interesting conclusions. In reporting his findings, which are based upon empirical observations, James indicates that 91.82% of his cases (N = 9,129) of group membership were groups of two or three individuals (71.11% two-person groups and 20.71% three-person groups) and less than 1% of his cases included groups of six or more individuals. Such reporting suggests that the most frequent interaction characteristic of small group behavior occurs within a size range of five or fewer individuals.

CHARACTERISTICS OF SMALL GROUPS

INTERACTION: QUANTITATIVE ASPECTS

Even with the most meticulous empirical investigations into group size, one must doubt that there will ever be a totally clear and specific statement concerning lower and upper limits. However, the size of the group is an important consideration because the number of individuals interacting within the group has a significant influence upon the patterns of interaction which occur in the group as a whole.

The discussion of interaction as a group characteristic in Chapter One suggested the relationship between interaction and the size of the group. Here, the earlier theme is developed fully and will include the most complex possibilities in the relationship between size and interaction. There are two levels on which the analysis centers: Level I deals with the number of possible dyadic relationships in groups of different size (Type 1), and Level II deals with the number of possible dyadic relationships (Type 1) *plus* the number of possible individual to subgroup relationships (Type 2) *plus* the number of possible subgroup to subgroup interactions (Type 3) possible in groups of different size.

Let us assume the existence of a five-person friendship group composed of individuals *a*, *b*, *c*, *d*, and *e*. At any one point in time the system of group interactions may take on one of the following configurations:

Type 1

Dyadic
relationships

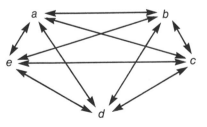

Note: Type 1 occurs at both levels of analysis.

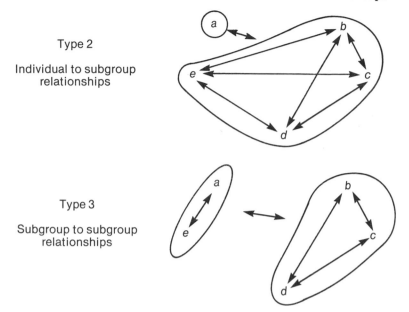

Type 2

Individual to subgroup
relationships

Type 3

Subgroup to subgroup
relationships

The longer the group continues to function, the greater the chance that
the combinations and a great variety of others will occur with some combinations recurring. It is important to remember that any combination is
possible at any time. In fact the combinations of relationships within any
given group will shift from time to time suggesting that changing combinations of relationships within a group are more likely than one stable
combination.

Level I — *The Number of Possible Dyadic Relationships in Groups of
Different Size.* An understanding of the relationship of group size to the
interactions within was provided by James H. S. Bossard's (1945:293)
Law of Family Interaction:

> With the addition of each person to a family or primary group, the number of
> persons increases in the simplest arithmetical progression in whole numbers,
> while the number of personal interrelationships within the group increases in
> the order of triangular numbers.

Bossard used the formula below to determine the number of possible
two-person relationships (dyads) within groups of any given size:

$$X = \frac{N^2 - N}{2},$$

N is the group size and X is the number of two-person relationships.

Table 2-1 presents the results of applying the formula to groups consisting of up to eight members.

Table 2-1. Results of Application of Bossard's Formula to Groups of Size N

GROUP SIZE (N)	NUMBER OF POSSIBLE TWO-PERSON (DYAD) RELATIONSHIPS (X)
2	1
3	3
4	6
5	10
6	15
7	21
8	28

Level II — *The Number of Possible Dyadic Relationships, Possible Individual to Subgroup Relationships, and Possible Subgroup to Subgroup Relationships in Groups of Different Size.* Basing his analysis upon Bossard's Law, William Kephart (1950:548) derived the formula below for measuring the total number of possible complex relations in groups of different size:

$$P.R. = \frac{3^N - 2^{N+1} + 1}{2} \, ,$$

where N is the group size and $P.R.$ is the number of possible relationships.

Table 2-2 presents the results of applying this formula to groups of specific size.

The quantification of the interaction elements as they relate to the size of small groups is a useful aid to understanding the character of interaction and its many complexities. The results depicted in Table 2-2 indicate the difficulties inherent in small group analysis and suggest one way of looking at the problems encountered when trying to keep track of rela-

Table 2-2.   Results of Application of Kephart's Formula to Groups of Size N

GROUP SIZE (N)	NUMBER OF POSSIBLE RELATIONSHIPS (P. R.)
2	1
3	6
4	25
5	90
6	301
7	966
8	3,025

Note: P.R. includes the number of possible dyadic relationships, the number of possible individual to subgroup relationships, and the number of possible subgroup to subgroup relationships.

tionships within small groups. Eight individuals interacting may appear small enough in size until we try to cope with all the possible relationships.

SOCIAL STRUCTURE

The term *structure* is used to explain the patterned regularity of people's relationships with each other in clearly defined settings. Social groups are such settings and all social groups have structure. Interaction in the small group is organized; it is patterned. Individuals in small groups occupy positions which are usually clearly defined, and they interact with each other in terms of dominance and submission, superiority and inferiority. Members of small groups establish communication networks and hierarchies based upon dominance and submission. In short, small group interaction is controlled by elements other than personality although less serious discussions—for example, of friendship groups—do not commonly refer to such elements.

As is true for all social groups, small group members develop expectations which arise from the structure for behaving in ways acceptable to the group as a whole. Simply put, structure takes the guesswork out of interaction within the group. This is so because group members, understanding the structure of the group, can interact with each other in expected ways.

Figure 2-1 identifies the elements of structure in parent-child interaction within the American nuclear family. The diagram is designed to give one example of social structure in a small group and does not include all the psychological, emotional, and support elements inherent in family relationships (see Chapter 9).

Formal and Informal Structures: Qualitative Aspects. Here we will discuss not only the traditional elements of small group structure as outlined above, but also the nature of the relationships which develop out of the structural organization of the small group. The following story has been told in many different ways, and most of us have heard one version or another. The best known of these comes from the movie *Boy's Town* and centers around the line: "He ain't heavy, Father, he's my.brother."

The story is told of two brothers who, as brothers will, fought on occasion. One of these occasions was observed by a friend of the older brother who was busy letting his younger brother "have it." The friend, for whatever reason, joined in the fight. At that point, the older brother turned and directed his fighting prowess towards the friend. When it was all over, the friend, stunned by the sudden turn of events, asked the older brother why he had started fighting him. The older brother replied: "Because you were hitting my brother." When the friend reminded the older brother that he, too, was guilty of the crime, the older brother replied: "Yeah, but he's my brother."

One might question the license by which the older brother felt free to "beat up" on his younger brother, but license for such action is not our concern. What is interesting to note is that the older brother saw his relationship with his younger brother as privileged. In some way or another, the relationship was special; it possessed an integration and identity which, clearly, did not include the friend.

This informal quality of group structure suggests qualitative aspects of group interaction which emphasize the individual and how other individuals in the group think of him as a whole person. The following list identifies the characteristics of informally structured groups:

1. Cooperation is the dominant social process
2. Strong sense of group identity and involvement
3. Interaction is face-to-face
4. Emotional involvement based upon sympathy and empathy

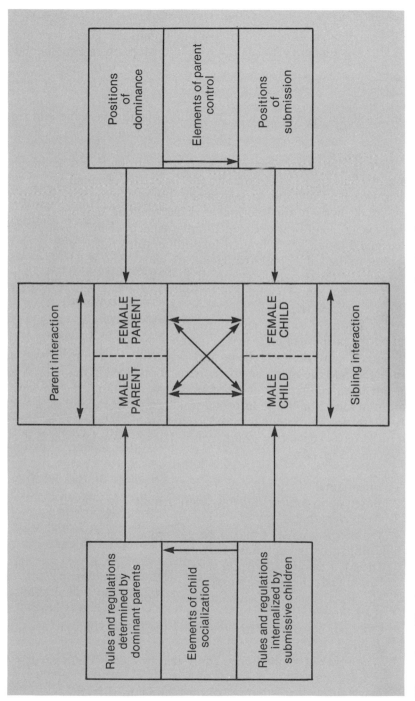

Figure 2-1. The Structure of Parent-Child Interaction in the American Nuclear Family

5. Socialization effects are intense and dominant
6. Strong tendency to maintain relationships over long periods of time
7. Members interact on the basis of personal knowledge of each other
8. Symbolic representations are unique to the membership of the group

If there is a stereotype for small groups, it can be found in the above listing of characteristics. Certainly, the basic list of small group types suggests such a view: the nuclear family, friendship groups, play groups of preschool children, and informal work associations, to name a few.

There is a second view of the qualitative aspects of small groups which has received much less attention in the literature but which is no less important to the subject matter. These are small groups which originate and maintain themselves, not out of feelings of personal affection or familial ties, but out of a strong desire to achieve material goals such as wealth, power, and social position.

We are referring to such small groups as business conferences organized for the purpose of increasing efficiency or sales, boards of directors, U.S. Senate committees, college and university committees and subcommittees, and the many business associations based, not upon friendship, but upon contractual obligations. These and other like groups are different in kind from those informal small groupings mentioned earlier. In the literature, contractually based groupings are referred to as formally structured or as secondary group types. These secondary small groups can be characterized as:

1. Impersonal
2. Based upon contractual obligations (implicit or explicit)
3. Nonsympathetic
4. Promoting a sense of high achievement and success
5. Competitive (sometimes conflicting)
6. Oriented toward self-interest or the interests of the larger structures of which they are a part
7. Having a system of behavior expectations limited to the terms of the contract
8. Oriented towards clearly defined ends through highly organized means
9. A complex of relationships controlled by clearly defined rules and regulations
10. A system of clearly defined rewards and punishments

These two views suggest the great variety of small group types which are included within the small groups field. They also support the observation that a very large portion of our social lives is spent within the confines of small group boundaries.

The distinction between informal and formal small groups is paralleled, in the literature, by a distinction between primary and secondary groups. In approaching the qualitative differences between small group types from the point of view offered by primary/secondary distinctions, we are afforded the opportunity to discuss the concept of the primary group. Additionally, recent interpretations of this concept and of the secondary group type will enhance our understanding of the qualitative differences found in groups of small size.

The Primary Group. The most enduring discourse on the qualitative aspects of informal small groups is that of the primary group by Charles Horton Cooley. Cooley believed that primary relationships are basic to an understanding of man's social nature and to an understanding of the development of the concept of the self. Cooley (1962:23) defined primary groups as:

> . . . those characterized by intimate face-to-face association and cooperation . . . it is a "we"; it involves the sort of sympathy and mutual identification for which "we" is the natural expression. One lives in the feeling of the whole and finds the chief aims of his will in that feeling. . . . It is not to be supposed that the unity of the primary group is one of mere harmony and love. It is always a differentiated and usually competitive unity, admitting of self-assertion and various appropriate passions . . . .

Since Cooley's identification of the concept, interest in primary relationships has been continuous despite suspicions that the high complexity and impersonality characteristic of an expanding industrial urban complex reduces the importance of such strong, personalized relations. The best example of continued interest in the primary group is the work of Dexter Dunphy (1972) in which the author reinforces Cooley's belief in the significance of primary relationships in human society and updates the areas in which primary groups are to be found. Dunphy (1972:5) adds to the list free association groups of all ages including delinquent gangs, informal groups which develop in formal organization settings, and re-socialization groups such as therapy and rehabilitation groups.

Somewhat earlier, Tomotsu Shibutani (1961:404) redefined the primary group as one which ". . . consists of people whose relationships with one another approach the primary pole on the continuum of social distance. It is an association of people who know one another on an individual basis." This recent surge of interest is perhaps a reflection of growing concern with the rise of large, formal, industrial, political, and business organizations and their increasing influence and control over the lives of individuals.

Cooley's definition of the primary group did not, as is often suggested, identify these groups as utopian associations of high integration and affectivity. Ordinarily, the primary group concept is presented as characterized by intimacy, face-to-face interaction, cooperation, "we-ness," sympathy, mutual identification, harmony, and love. These elements, said Cooley, are necessary for the development of man's social nature.

But Cooley was aware of the true realities of all group life. He argued that primary groups are also characterized by differentiation, competition, and "various appropriate passions." These are the characteristics often forgotten in presentations of the concept of primacy. Nevertheless, they are as important to a full understanding of the primary group as those characteristics listed in the previous paragraph.

With the incorporation of characteristics such as differentiation and competition, Cooley was identifying primary elements which indicate that members are sometimes forced to cope with status differences and unique, sometimes colliding, personalities within the group. Cooley was acutely aware that all social groups are structured, that all groups are composed of individuals who are unique entities as well as cooperating members, and that the competitive spirit is as much a part of human behavior as is cooperation. The following list includes all the characteristics of Cooley's primary group:

Intimacy	Love
Face-to-face interaction	Social differentiation
Cooperation	Competition
"We-ness"	Self-assertion
Sympathy	Ambition
Mutual identification	"Various appropriate
Harmony	passions"

Some might want to consider the last five items in the above list as nonprimary characteristics. However, this is not the case. Cooley intended to present a view of integrated group relationships as a complex of behavior, the characteristics of which include all normal human responses to situations. Recognizing that individuals in social groups, especially long-lasting social groups, become involved in tension-producing relationships as well as the more integration-enhancing, affective relationships, Cooley presented a view of primacy in keeping with the realities of group life as he observed it.

Contemporary interpretations of primary groups seldom refer to the two characteristics which, for Cooley (1962:26), must be present in such associations: "a certain *intimacy* and *fusion of personalities.*" The true meaning of primary group relationships, then, includes social bonds based on intimacy, a high level of affectivity and closeness, and the development of a sense of identification of each individual member with the whole. This latter element might be termed group or social unity or "we-ness."

In consideration of the seemingly dichotomous elements which Cooley said belonged to primary group relations, we will discuss two other issues relevant to modern interpretations of the primary group: (1) the primary group as an ideal type, and (2) the concept of the secondary group which developed out of Cooley's primary group analysis.

The Primary Group as an Ideal Type. The presentation of the primary group as an ideal type suggests that the primary group, as so defined, is not one which exists in reality. Highly integrated nuclear families and friendship groups, for example, are not pure primary groups. The concept of the ideal type is used as a construct from which groups may be analyzed in terms of the degree to which they are more or less primary. One group is said to be more like the ideal type than another group. Using the ideal construct allows us to understand social groups in relation to each other; groups can be ranked according to the degree to which they are primary.

For example, if we make a list of groups in American society, chosen at random, we should be able to rank them from most primary-like to least primary-like. The following is such a list, presented here without consideration of rank order:

A board of directors
A nuclear family
A friendship group
A neighborhood bridge club
An informal work group
A university curriculum committee

In ranking these groupings, all the characteristics which identify primacy would have to be used, and, depending upon the subjective interpretations of the person doing the ranking, a ranking of the groups based upon Cooley's concept of primacy would result. The procedure for ranking in this manner is difficult and tedious. Let us work through the procedure using only the two characteristics of intimacy and fusion of personalities (social unity or "we-ness").

If we take each item on the list at face value, that is, without imposing problem-oriented interpretations on them, we conclude that the family would be placed in the first rank since family intimacy and "we-ness" is deeply rooted in the long-standing societal traditions. For the children within the family, it is an intimacy and unity of which they have been a part from birth. The second-place ranking would be occupied by the friendship group which is, characteristically, an intensely intimate association although it does not have the tradition or the duration of the nuclear family. These observations are especially true of friendship associations which develop during adolescence. The third position in the rank order would be given to the neighborhood bridge club. We might assume, for example, that such an association grew out of the development of a complex of neighborhood friendships among individuals who discovered they have bridge playing as a common interest. The informal work group would be placed in the fourth position since the relationships, although not as intensely intimate as those of the groups already ranked, are nonetheless strong enough to influence the work performances of its members. The informal work group does not receive a more primary ranking because such associations do not automatically spill over into the friendship associations away from the proximity of the work situation. In such cases, the friendship is limited by a factor from outside the group. The fifth-ranked group would be the university curriculum committee. Ordinarily, a curriculum committee is a standing committee of members of an academic community, including administrators, faculty, and students whose function is to oversee and regulate the curriculum established by the university. Members have a strong chance of knowing each other outside the committee meetings since they are all part of the community within which the committee functions. When meeting, however, the relationships are determined by the impersonal organizational responsibilities of the committee. The last-ranked group would be the board of directors whose concern is decision making at the large corporate level. The relationships among board members might be thought of as reflecting the highly impersonal characteristics of the large corporation rather than those of groups more like the primary group type.

It should be noted that although we have bothered to rank a curriculum committee and a board of directors, neither of these is very close to the primary group type. The distance between each of these last two and the ideal type would be disproportionately greater than the distances between any one of the other groups ranked and the primary group type. The rank order for these groups is readily observable when placed on a continuum of primary group types. (See Figure 2-2.)

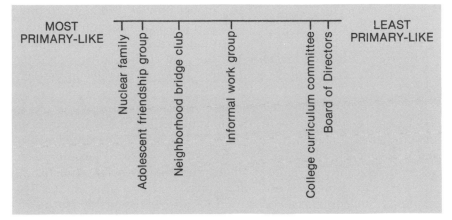

MOST PRIMARY-LIKE

Nuclear family
Adolescent friendship group
Neighborhood bridge club
Informal work group
College curriculum committee
Board of Directors

LEAST PRIMARY-LIKE

Figure 2-2. The Primary Group Type Continuum

At this point, the reader may be thinking that the last two items on the list should not have been included because they bear little or no resemblance to the kinds of associations Cooley intended to include in his primary group framework. The reader is quite correct. If we look at Cooley's concept of primary groups as a conceptual scheme which aids our understanding of a special, highly integrated, intimate, socially unified set of differentiated and sometimes competitive relationships, we recognize that groups such as boards of directors do not qualify. These last two items, the curriculum committee and the board of directors, were included to suggest to the reader the need for developing a view of certain small groups which is opposite from the view offered by Cooley. The development of the secondary group concept fulfills this expressed need and affords us the opportunity to consider a basis, other than the primary group concept, by which groups can be compared.

The Secondary Group. In contrast to the primary group, the secondary group can be characterized as impersonal, formal, contractual, rational, nonemotional, and concerned with ability, not personality. The secondary group is thought of as everything the primary group is not. There is no clear source for the origin of the secondary group concept. The concept entered the literature out of a need to explain the idea of primacy more completely. There are only vague references in Cooley's writings which point to a group type other than the primary group. Cooley did recognize that individuals associate with each other within group settings other than those limited by his definition of primacy. For example, Cooley

(1962:26) observed: "Besides these almost universal kinds of primary association, there are many others whose form depends upon the particular state of civilization . . . ." And: "In our own life the intimacy of the neighborhood has been broken up by the growth of an intricate mesh of wider contacts which leaves us strangers to people who live in the same house."

The field of small groups has not concerned itself with small secondary associations because, for many, the most immediate reference for secondary group interpretation is the element of large size. This size identification of secondary associations is understandable since large bureaucracies such as the federal government, the military establishment, and large corporate structures are commonplace on lists of secondary type groupings. Such organizational structures are clearly outside any reasonable identification of small group types.

Nevertheless, within these large, formally organized systems of human interaction there are numerous types of groupings which are well within the limits of small group size. Behavior within these small units often reflect the expectations which the larger systems impose upon them. They are usually highly differentiated in terms of the positions the members occupy, and they are the subsystems within which the terms of the organizational contract of each member are carried out. Although cooperation is necessary for these small formal groups to achieve their goals, relationships within are often characterized by high levels of competition and, in some cases, conflict.

The difference between these subsystems and their larger counterparts is size. Their small size, however, does not automatically place them in categories of informal groups or groups more like the primary group. They are special types of small groups which we will call secondary.

Although researchers in the small groups field have not concentrated on the small secondary group, some studies have considered, for example, the impact of leadership in large organizational systems (Bass & Norton, 1951), and the use of group interaction (lecture and discussion groups) to change supervisory norms in an industrial plant (Levine & Butler, 1952).

The Small Conference by Margaret Mead and Paul Byers (1968) discusses the conference as a form of group process and uses photographic materials to interpret three types of conferences. The authors (Mead & Byers, 1968:vi) state that their work is ". . . devoted to a discussion of those aspects of the conference process that are relevant to the small substantive conference . . . ."

The Secondary Group as an Ideal Type. The development of a secondary group concept has an interesting function in relation to that of the primary group. Since the secondary group as an ideal type is in direct opposition to the primary group concept, it functions to legitimize Cooley's suggestion that all groups are not primary. Because of the concept of secondary association, we are no longer required to think of group associations of widely varying types as more or less primary. We may now consider the differences between and among social groups on a primary-secondary group type continuum on which the least primary-like endpoint is replaced by the secondary group ideal type.

The reader will recall the earlier view that certain types of small secondary groups are so different from Cooley's thinking about primary-type relations that to place them on a scale which considers only the primary group as an ideal type is essentially nonproductive. Let us use the list of small groups we used earlier: a board of directors, a nuclear family, a friendship group, a neighborhood bridge club, an informal work group, and a university curriculum committee. Using a primary-secondary scale we are able to consider not only the degree to which each small group is primary, but also the degree to which each of the groups is secondary. For example, a board of directors is understood more reasonably as a system of interaction of members based upon the contractual arrangements each has with the larger system organization and as a system in which there are clear limits as to the content of their relationships, relationships which are by no means intimate. Placing such a small group a great distance from the primary group ideal type and, therefore, very close to the secondary group end of the continuum allows us to understand the truer nature of the kinds of relationships which prevail within. Rather than having to say such a group is not a very good example of Cooley's primary group, we are able to say that such a group is an excellent example of the small secondary group type. Figure 2-3 presents our list of small groups on a scale, the endpoints of which are primary and secondary group types. The rankings are exactly the same as in Figure 2-2.

DURATION

We stated earlier that the life span of the social group is determined by the amount of time required to achieve the goals of the group. This is true for all groups, regardless of size. For small groups, however, the time factor can be distinguished according to the degree to which the structure of the small group is formal or informal.

In groups having informal structure there is a strong tendency for members to maintain their relationships over longer periods of time than in small groups whose structures are of a formal type. This is so because in informal small groups, individual and group goals are often generalized, that is, they are not limited to the terms of a contract. The

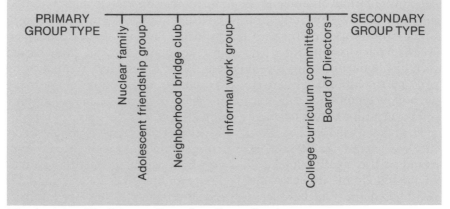

Figure 2-3.   The Primary-Secondary Group Continuum

informal work group (Homans, 1950) will serve as an example. Informal work groups develop for three reasons: (1) to control the work environment of its members along lines other than those defined by the formal work organization, (2) as an unpremeditated outgrowth of the relationships workers have with each other on the job, and (3) to break the tedium and boredom produced by some work environments. The relationships which develop within the informal work group may extend beyond the limits of a workday or workweek. The friendships formed would then become the basis for maintaining associations built around nonwork situations such as after-work relaxation, extrawork activities including company sports, and work breaks. When such group identities are formed, they tend to maintain themselves for longer periods of time.

GOALS AND GOAL ACHIEVEMENT

The specifics of needs and goals at the small group level are, of course, subject to the generalizations which we have made about all social groups. The unique aspects of goals and goal achievement in small groups refer mainly to the fact that, realistically, certain goals are best achieved in group associations of small size. It is impossible to overstate the case for small groups in this regard.

For example, the tendency in every sector of society is for its members to function, often by personal preference, within small social groups rather than in large, impersonal superstructures such as corporations, bureaucratic systems, and the like. Robin M. Williams, Jr. (1970:516–517), in referring to the development of informal organizations, observed:

" . . . every formal organization that continues for any considerable period develops an informal organization alongside the formal one." This is exactly the basis for the development of the informal work group. It is within such small personal identity groups that the motivation for and identification with one's job is found. We might say that the large system of corporate enterprise is not sufficient to achieve its goals or the personal goals of its members.

The need for companionship and the achievement of the friendship goal may be realized in any social relationship, but the chances of greatest success in developing and maintaining a friendship are to be found in the small, personal, emotionally supportive groupings. Small friendship groups are best suited because in such groups one finds: (1) a heightened sense of belonging, (2) high levels of emotional reinforcement, (3) understanding of each individual friend in terms of the whole person, (4) the intimacy and privacy of relationships not available in groups of more complex organization and large size.

The list of examples is a long one. It includes the marital dyad, the subgroup relations of parents and children within families, and groupings of children at play. These groups have their counterparts in formal, small group types. Boards of directors, university and college committees, sales meetings, and other formal or secondary small groups, although based upon contract and impersonal in nature, give to their larger parent organizations an environment more conducive to efficient production, increased sales, and decision making than the larger systems of which they are a part.

THE ORIGIN AND DEVELOPMENT OF SMALL GROUPS

We cannot assume that because individuals happen to meet by chance or by design that their associations will result in the development of a small group. Certain elements are necessary for the early association to result in the kind of relationships which promote group interaction. First impressions of each other which produce positive results set the stage for further meetings. During this early stage of interaction, preliminary patterns of reciprocity and consensus about symbols and meanings are formed and may well result in continued and more complex associations among the members. When individuals begin to form a system of values and goals combined with very clear expectations about each other's roles and positions in the group, we may refer to the relationships among the individuals as those characteristic of a social group. At this point, the members have a common past and may anticipate a common future with

a high degree of certainty. The hope and expectations which the anticipated future suggests indicates a high level of common identity and

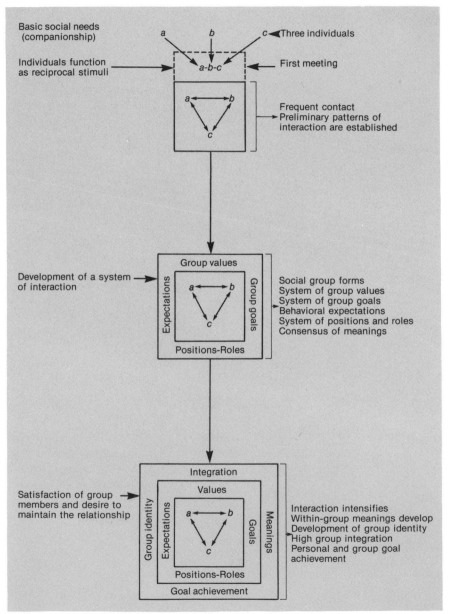

Figure 2-4.   The Origin and Development of a Small Friendship Group

integration which results in a degree of satisfaction necessary for the maintenance of the system of interaction and for the achievement of personal and group goals. Figure 2-4 presents a tracing of three individuals whose first meeting results in the development of a small social group.

---

summary

In this chapter the social group was given size limitations usually associated with small group analysis. Small groups were identified as groups whose size limits range from two to twenty individuals. Observations about the size of small groups included the difficulties associated with determining the lower and upper limits of small group size. The lower limit was determined to be two even though interpretations by Georg Simmel suggest the lowest possible number to be three. The upper limit of twenty appears rather large but was accepted with the understanding that the majority of small groups function with a membership well below that number.

There was an attempt to understand small group interaction as a function of size. It was noted that there are two levels on which the analysis centers: (1) the number of possible dyadic relationships, and (2) the sum of the number of possible dyadic, individual to subgroup, and subgroup to subgroup relationships possible in groups of different size. First level results were determined by applying the James Bossard formula: $X = (N^2 - N)/2$; and second level results were determined by applying the William Kephart formula: $P.R. = (3^N - 2^{N+1} + 1)/2$.

The discussion on the qualitative aspects of formal and informal structures identified small group types which are characteristic of each. Small groups such as families and friendship groups were classified as informal in type, and groups such as boards of directors and U.S. Senate subcommittees were classified as formal. Explanations of these two basic types of small group structures included a list of characteristics which indicate that relations in the informal small group are cooperative, face-to-face and sympathetic. These were found to be in contrast to the impersonal, contractually based relationships characteristic of formally structured groups. Discussions of the duration of small groups of differing structure suggested that, as a rule, informally structured small groups maintain relationships over longer periods of time than do small groups whose structures are of a formal type. Certain goals were found to be achieved best in group associations of small size. It was suggested that the tendency in every sector of society is for individuals to function within small social groups rather than in large, impersonal ones.

Qualitative differences were also discussed in terms of the distinction made between primary and secondary small group types. Charles Horton Cooley's early identification of the primary group was discussed, and it formed the basis for a comparative analysis of small groups based upon the concepts of primary and secondary ideal types.

The last section of this chapter discussed the origins and development of small groups and indicated that the following occurrences were necessary: (1) first meeting, (2) frequent contact, (3) the development of group values, goals, and common expectations, and (4) intensification of patterns of interaction, meaning consensus, emergence of group identity, and sense of integration.

discussion questions

1. Why is it difficult to reach agreement on the lower and upper limits of small group size?
2. Do groups of different size require different behavior for group members? Why?
3. Why do groups have a tendency to divide into subgroups?
4. How does group structure take the "guesswork" out of group interaction?
5. Discuss the statement: All primary groups are small; all small groups are not primary.
6. Why is it impossible for any individual to belong to a large number of primary groups?
7. Are individual goals different in groups of different size and structure?

references

Bass, Bernard M.; and Norton, Fay-Tyler M. "Group Size and Leaderless Discussions," *Journal of Applied Psychology*, 35 (1951): 397–400.

Bossard, James H. S. "The Law of Family Interaction," *American Journal of Sociology*, 50 (1945): 292–294.

Cooley, Charles Horton. *Social Organization: a Study of the Larger Mind*. New York: Shocken, 1962.

Dunphy, Dexter. *The Primary Group: A Handbook for Analysis and Field Research*. New York: Appleton-Century-Crofts, 1972.

Fichter, Joseph H. *Sociology*. Chicago: The University of Chicago Press, 1957.

Homans, George C. *The Human Group*. New York: Harcourt, Brace and World, 1950.

James, John. "A Preliminary Study of the Size Determinant in Small Group Interaction," *American Sociological Review*, 16 (1951): 474–477.

Kephart, William M. "A Quantitative Analysis of Intragroup Relationships," *American Journal of Sociology*, 55 (1950): 544–549.

Levine, Jacob; and Butler, John. "Lecture vs. Group Discussion in Changing Behavior," *Journal of Applied Psychology*, 36 (1952): 29–33.

Mead, Margaret; and Byers, Paul. *The Small Conference*. Paris: Mouton, 1968.

Mitchell, J. Clyde (ed.). *Social Networks in Urban Situations*. Manchester, England: Manchester University Press, 1969.

Olmstead, Michael S.; and Hare, A. Paul. *The Small Group*, 2nd ed.; New York: Random House, 1978.

Shaw, Marvin E. *Group Dynamics: The Psychology of Small Group Behavior*, 2nd ed.; New York: McGraw-Hill, 1976.

Shepherd, Clovis R. *Small Groups: Some Sociological Perspectives*. San Francisco: Chandler, 1964.

Shibutani, Tomotsu. *Society and Personality: An Interactionist Approach to Social Psychology*. Englewood Cliffs, New Jersey: Prentice-Hall, 1961.

Williams, Robin M., Jr. *American Society: A Sociological Interpretation*, 3rd ed.; New York: Alfred A. Knopf, 1970.

Wolff, Kurt H. (Trans. and ed.). *The Sociology of Georg Simmel*. New York: The Free Press, 1950.

Chapter Three

The Basic Components of Small Groups

Small groups are very complex systems of human behavior. In Chapter Two we explored the surprising complexity of interaction possibilities in groups of twenty or fewer members. We discovered some reasons, relating to the size of the group, why so many of us experience difficulties in, for example, keeping a family of five organized, coping with a friendship group of four members, and maintaining a semblance of organization in an eight-member board of directors or a committee of eleven. But small groups are complex systems of human interaction for reasons other than size.

Small groups are composed of *individuals* who are *interacting* with each other in a meaningful way and who are influenced by the *environments* in which these interactions occur. The three italicized words in the sentence above are three reasons, beyond the size of the group, for considering the small group as a complex social system. In this chapter, we will consider each of these group components—the individual, group interaction, and group environments—as parts of the complex system of human group behavior.

THE INDIVIDUAL

For our purposes, an *individual* is a symbol-using animal who is capable, by nature and through social care, of participating in patterned interaction within human social groups. This definition is necessary but difficult. To simplify matters, let us take each part of the definition and discuss it separately. By referring to the individual as a symbol-using animal, we mean that the individual is someone who is capable of internalizing, in a symbolic way, the environment—including other individuals. A person uses symbols (language) to communicate with others and to give meaning to surroundings. We may say that individuals live in a world of symbolic representations and that their connection with the real (objective) world is not direct, but through those representations. For example, in human interaction one individual perceives the behavior of another individual and interprets what the other intends to communicate. The individual, then, assigns meanings to the other's behavior and behaves in terms of those meanings rather than the behavior of the other. In other words, the individual is responding to the meanings, and not to the other's behavior directly.

When we say that the individual is social by nature we mean that, at birth, the individual has the potential to function as a member of society and its social groups. We mean that the individual has the materials necessary to behave according to the specifications which human society lays down for all its members. But the newborn infant cannot actually behave as a full-fledged participant in the social world of interaction. In order to do so, the infant must have social care. *Social care* refers to the relationships an individual has with others—such as parents, friends, and teachers—as the individual adapts to the expectations of society. Adaptation and, finally, social maturation is the result of a process which sociologists call *socialization*. It is a process through which the individual through interaction with others learns how to behave according to the rules and regulations of the society into which he is born.

Socialization is not a one-way street, however. It is true that the direction of the relationships between the learner and the others who are doing the caring (social agents) is toward the one doing the learning, but the social agents are also being influenced by those to whom their efforts are being directed. And this is, in part, what we meant when, in the definition, we referred to interaction. Patterned interaction results from certain forms of group interaction being repeated with some frequency over a significant period of time. When we, as children or as adults, develop a set of expectations about each other's behavior, as in social groups, and when those expectations are internalized by all individuals in the group, the interactions which result are patterned. We refer to *patterned interaction* as behavior, in group settings, which has become a habit. The phrase, "human social groups," will not be commented upon here since groups are the subject of this entire text, except to point out that it is within the social group that the individual finds the opportunity to function in a completely social way.

Joseph H. Fichter (1957:19–20) characterizes the individual, whom he calls the social person, as a "composite and complex being." By this he means that every individual can be viewed as a physiological unit, a moral unit, a psychological unit, and a sociological unit. It is this last identification, wherein Fichter defines the social person as ". . . the irreducible physical unit of social categories, aggregates, groups, and society . . . ," which is the subject of our present interest.

It is simply impossible to study the small group without discussing those who occupy positions within the group. A family, for example, can be looked at sociologically in a variety of ways. It can be viewed as a small group with clearly defined goals. It can be studied as a major force in the early socialization of the child. The family can be diagrammed in terms of its structure (authority)—as a hierarchy of superordinate-subordinate positions. Whichever way one chooses to approach the family grouping, that way must include a view of the family as a group composed of individuals who interact in a specific setting, are influenced by specific internal and external forces, and, in turn, influence those very same forces. In this sense, the family is a collection of individuals who have internalized the patterns of family interaction and who behave toward other family members in a highly personal way. The youngest child in a family may have the least amount of pull or authority in terms of the position of youngest sibling. It would appear, on the surface, that the child is powerless to control the behavior of other family members. Yet, that child may very well change the conventional arrangement of positions and come to exercise some degree of control over one parent or sibling by forming a coalition with another member. In such a situation, it is the individual with the ability to recognize possible changes in the structural arrangements within the family through changes in self behavior, who determines—in that situation and at that time—where the power really lies. Another child, under the same conditions, might not be so inventive behaviorally. It would appear that the position of a given individual in the group is important to understanding the group process and cannot be excluded from our thinking about it.

It is important that we accept the premise that the individual is one key to understanding group behavior. As in the above example, the child who manipulates a parent to the point of restructuring the authority and control system in a family is behaving in a manner which suggests that self decisions are part of the phenomenon of group interaction. Children can change their behavior to fit their definition of a situation as well as their personal needs. In a more general sense, individuals are capable of looking at situations in which they are involved and, after deciding what kind of behavior is appropriate and what kind is not, selecting from a variety of possible actions the one felt to be most appropriate to the situation.

What is it about an individual which allows that individual to select behavior from a storehouse of possibilities and to do so, in most circumstances, appropriately? The explanation lies in the ability of an individual to see the self from the point of view of other group members and then to judge anticipated self performance before actually participating in the group interaction. Tomotsu Shibutani (1961:91–93) referred to this process within the individual as the self-control mechanism. *Self-control* refers to the individual's ability to make appropriate decisions about, to organize, and to execute a plan of action within the group which will satisfy not only personal needs and the needs of other individuals, but also those of the group as a whole. When all members of a group are able to do this in a concerted way, we refer to the process as group or social control.

THE ISOLATED INDIVIDUAL

Georg Simmel believed that the individual belongs among sociological categories. In a unique interpretation of the individual as a social fact, Simmel discusses the sociological significance of the individual in isolation. Although the idea that an isolated individual is a sociological fact appears to be a contradiction, Simmel argues that isolation is a state in which the individual continues to interact with others in a relationship existing within the individual's mind.

The question here is: How can isolation (meaning the isolated individual) have sociological significance? In Chapter One our short statement on isolation helped to highlight the importance of social interaction. Here, we will look at the isolated individual as a sociological fact—that is, as an individual who has a social existence beyond actual participation in the group.

The central theme of the isolated individual is that the socializing influences received by a person while a member of the social group can never be eliminated from the individual's experiences. When an individual leaves the group, it is only in the sense that that individual no longer experiences the concrete, physical reality of group participation and interaction. The individual leaves but remains unquestionably social. Group experiences are remembered and relived because they have been internalized. Also, the individual continues to live within the group since group members, in the past, had internalized that individual and, in the future, remember him.

The isolated individual, then, is someone who has internalized the entire group experience and is capable of maintaining a sense of that experience well beyond the life of the group. The phenomenon of isolation according to Simmel's interpretation can be considered from two different time perspectives: (1) past experiences and identities, and (2) future group experiences.

Past Experiences and Identities. Each individual has a social history, the particulars of which form a *social frame of reference*, which is the accumulation of all past experiences from birth to the present. New experiences are incorporated continually into this reference system so that it is always up-to-date. These experiences are instrumental in developing a structure of attitudes about past experiences and in facilitating expectations and interpretations about future ones.

It is, of course, difficult to think of individuals who are involved in the dynamic activity of group interaction as isolated or frozen in time so that there is a definite past and definite future. With apologies for the static quality suggested in this explanation, we note that the individual uses his past experiences as a reference for participation in groups in the future. (See Figure 3-1.)

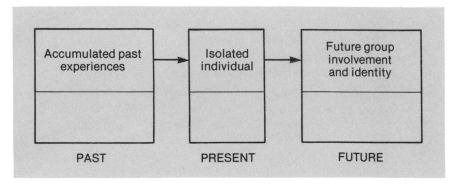

Figure 3-1. The Individual as a Sociological Fact

Simmel's (Wolff, 1950:118–119) explanation of isolation as a remembrance is noted in the following passage:

> . . . isolation . . . refers by no means only to the absence of society. On the contrary, the idea involves the somehow imagined, but then rejected, existence of society. Isolation attains its unequivocal, positive significance only as society's effect at a distance—whether as lingering on of past relations, as anticipation of future contacts, as nostalgia, or as an intentional turning away from society.

The sociological significance of isolation is apparent in the above quotation but is clearer still in Simmel's (Wolff, 1950:119) observation: "Isolation is interaction between two parties, one of which leaves, after exerting certain influences."

Isolation and Future Group Experiences. Simmel's explanation of isolation as "anticipation of future contacts" suggests that individuals have a sense of the future based on the past. The combination of past experiences and the structure of attitudes which develop from past experiences function as a basis for determining, before the experience occurs, the meanings associated with future group activity.

There is another interpretation of isolation connecting the individual with future behavior. The individual who is isolated from a particular group through exclusion, free choice, or death is not completely lost to the group. Individuals contribute to the character of social groups, and their contributions remain after contact is lost. Remarking on the residual qualities of group participation, Simmel (Wolff, 1950:119) observed: "The isolated individual is isolated only in reality, however; for ideally, in the mind of the other party, he continues to live and to act."

Recognition of the individual as a group component is important to understanding the group concept, not as the primary subject of investigation, but as an acting part of the whole whose behavior contributes to the larger reality of group process and interaction. Consideration of the individual as part of this larger reality does not direct interest away from the group as a functioning unit with identities beyond those of its individual members. Rather, a view of group life which considers the role of the individual as a functioning group member enhances attempts to understand the nature of group life.

Individuals combine in a great variety of ways to form groups. The forces which develop within the social group are forces which derive from the members and which direct, to a significant degree, their patterns of association within its boundaries.

Simmel's consideration of the individual as isolated from society provides a unique means whereby we are able to understand the impact which group life has upon the individual social person. Once the individual is socialized to group life there is no escape from its influence either in terms of experiences remembered or experiences anticipated.

INTERACTION

It is important to note that every change in the behavior of one individual presumes changes in the behavior of every other group member. This fact not only suggests the importance of interaction as a component of the small group but highlights the importance of viewing the individual as a major factor in the process of group interaction as well.

The group is composed not only of individuals but of interactions (relations between and among group members) as well. For the interactionist, of course, relationships between and among group members are the central focus of interest. They are the best indicators of the true position individuals occupy in the sociological analysis of small groups: individuals occupy positions in groups in relation to the positions occupied by other individuals. Individuals are, then, parts of a larger system of group interaction.

These relationships between and among individuals are the most basic facts of human group behavior. Although looking at the facts of such ongoing relationships within larger complex groups is cumbersome, such a view applies extremely well to groups of small size.

In discussing group interaction, a number of elements begin to come together. Group interaction is communication, and communication, as we have discovered already, is symbolic. Since we are dealing here with human beings, the symbolic character of group interaction takes the external form of verbal communication. Understanding that the total external communication system which links individuals to each other in group relations includes gestures, facial expressions, and, in the interest of completeness, body language, we will concentrate on the verbal element and consider it dominant in group interaction. On this issue, Schellenberg (1970:245) observes that:

> Animals, other than humans, communicate quite effectively with their own kind, but without language. The signals with which they communicate to each other are not primarily symbolic. This is not to say that such communication may not be highly sensitive and show significant learning. But the sensitivity and learning are directed to dealing with natural reactions rather than the artificial and conventional system of representations that we call languages. So humans are apparently the only animals who have clearly developed language systems.

The unique factor in human communication is the incorporation of a language—a system of verbal and written symbols—which forms the actual substance of interaction between and among individuals. Put quite simply, if an individual does not acquire language as part of the socialization process, that individual would not be able to perform even the minimum requirements of human social interaction demanded by group membership. Humanity presumes sociality, and the means for realizing this is the incorporation of a language into the system for learning appropriate behavior.

Unquestionably, this ability to develop and use a set of symbols representing the objective environment is crucial to our understanding of human behavior in all social contexts. Language, however, must be seen in a somewhat larger context: as part of communication within the interaction framework. We refer then, not only to language (verbal behavior requisite for interaction), but also to forms of communication (Mills, 1958) and to communication networks (Bavelas, 1950; Leavitt, 1951). All are significant in the study of group interaction. It should be understood that although the central element in communication is verbal behavior and its attendant intentions and meanings, elements such as those mentioned above are nonetheless crucial.

Language is at the core of the socializing process and is an absolute requirement for normal social development. Acquiring a language has usually been thought of as commonplace, so commonplace that we seldom take the time to reflect upon and applaud the achievement of each individual who has learned an acceptable pattern of language behavior. The process of acquiring language is extraordinarily complex, involving the intricate coordination of mental, sensory, and social factors. This being the case, the social scientist has for some time time been interested in language behavior and the circumstances surrounding it. For sociologists, it is necessary to understand the field in which language is used, that is, to understand interaction as the situation in which verbal communication takes place. Glenn Vernon (1965:38) states:

> One of the most important capacities of the human being with normal symbolic equipment is the capacity to respond to symbols, to manipulate symbols, and to engage in symbolic interaction. Using language is a universal human characteristic, with each group having at least some distinctive language patterns of its own. Man lives in a symbolic world.

In accepting the symbolic nature of the individual, we should qualify the use of symbols in systems of interaction. Symbols, as we have seen, have no utility save for the meaning each individual gives to the symbols he uses. It is precisely the individual's ability to internalize the meanings which symbols represent which makes one's symbolic nature significant. Using symbols and giving symbols appropriate meanings are facts of man's social nature. It is only in the human social community that symbols and meanings take on significance. The use of symbols to establish an orderly and controlled environment of meaningful communication is the truly distinguishing factor of the human social animal and is at the center of our understanding of group interaction.

For the sociologist interested in group interaction and the forms which interaction takes, verbal behavior has been a particularly interesting area of investigation. In this the sociologist is not alone. Others, including psychologists, social psychologists, and linguistics analysts, have all looked at this phenomenon from their special analytical perspectives. Additionally, social workers, family counselors, educators, and students of child development have all pursued a course of interest in the communication aspect of interaction for obvious reasons.

The sociologist, however, in attempting to understand the organization of society and its parts, has recently started interpreting the interaction construct in human behavior from a microsociological point of view. While investigating the unit of interaction with extreme care and thoroughness, the student of human interaction has also concentrated upon the mechanical aspects of the social relationship. One area of investigation centers around the proposition that the core of all interaction involves an understanding of the form which the communication takes. In this regard, particular emphasis has been placed upon verbal and attendant behavior as crucial to the relationships between and among individuals, particularly in the group setting. Let us now attempt to construct a basic diagram which suggests the most general form taken by group interaction. We will call the scheme the base unit of group interaction.

The unit of analysis best suited to understanding interactive behavior has already been described in the diagram, $A \leftrightarrow B$. You will recall that A is the Actor (Communicator) who initiates a relationship and who, by communicating appropriate meanings and intentions through the use of verbal and other kinds of symbols, suggests the preliminary direction of the relationship. B is the Reactor (Recipient) who responds to the Actor's symbols and who, through adequate interpretation of the meanings and intentions of the Actor, maintains the relationship. The interaction factor connecting the Actor and the Reactor, therefore, involves the constant interchange of meanings and intentions through the use of verbal and other symbols.

The major concern of the interactionist is with the reciprocity of the relationship, with the interaction itself. The Actor (A) and Reactor (B) are crucial, of course, but the major thrust of the analysis is the interaction between and among the participants in the relationship. Given this perspective, an understanding of the form of the relationship, the mechanism involved, and the symbols used for communication is essential. We are suggesting that when one enters into the study of human verbal behavior as a major communicative device, the implications are interaction-oriented. By its very definition, *verbal behavior* is a means whereby two or more individuals communicate their intentions and meanings to each other.

Enlarging upon the simple interaction model $(A \leftrightarrow B)$, the meanings and intentions on the part of the Actor (A) and the interpretations of the other (B) suggest a complex system in which interaction is maintained or within which serious error in transmission of a communication can also occur. (See Figure 3-2.) It should be noted, at this point, that interaction in the group actually functions as a kind of interface between the individual and the group as a whole. And further, interaction is not only the link between the individual and the group, it is also the key to understanding the nature of the group itself.

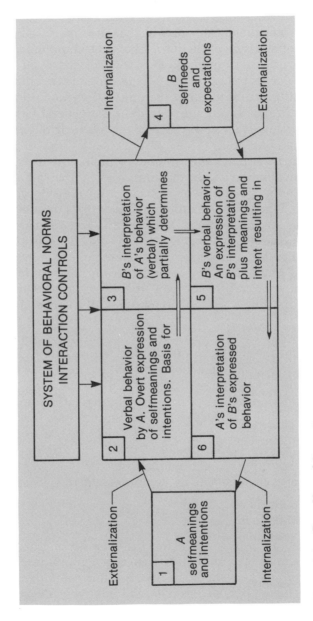

Figure 3-2. Base Unit of Group Interaction

THE DYAD

A great deal of our understanding of interaction in small groups is derived from Simmel's interpretations of two- and three-party relations. The characteristics of dyads and triads suggest features of interaction which are applicable to all social systems. Part of Simmel's analysis of the nature of society as an object of scientific inquiry centers around these two microsystems of human interaction. In this regard, Simmel directed his interest to the size of the group and the forms of relationships found within. The ongoing dyad, defined as a two-party group relationship, is the most crucial of all group relationships. It is the one in which each member stands to lose the most if the other is lost. Robert Nisbet (1970:85–86) has observed that because:

> . . . the dyad is in a sense the most "natural" of unions, the most elemental in terms of size, does not mean that it is the least complex or the easiest to sustain . . . . By very virtue of the affinity between the dyad, the feelings and sentiments of deepest unity, intimacy, and separateness from the rest of the world, the dyad can become, where surrounding contexts fail to give reinforcement and nourishment, the most precarious and fragile of all relationships.

In earlier chapters, we discussed interaction and used $A \leftrightarrow B$ as its symbolic representation. The same symbol can be used for the dyadic relationship. In this case, the symbol represents two individuals who are involved in a direct relationship, one in which each individual is totally dependent upon the other. If the dyad is to endure, the two interacting parties must accept each other and develop a special set of symbols and meanings appropriate only to their relationship. If the relationship does endure, it can be considered the ideal or pure group type because the interaction maintained between the two is not exposed to the intrusion of even a third individual who could shift the group balance away from the two and become the focus for a disruption of the unity developed between the two.

The dyad is the only relationship in which individuals can give themselves to each other totally. In the dyad, an individual's thoughts, actions, intentions, and meanings are forwarded only to the other individual, who then responds in a manner unrestricted by the presence of additional group members.

In American society, the marital dyad is a good example of the total absorption of two people in a group setting. The sentiments which flow from marital relationships are clearly exclusive of any third party. Friends of one or the other married partner have a different relationship with each of them, but the marital dyad remains the same. Even the birth of a child, extending the dyad by a simple increase of one, does not break the unity of the married partners. The husband and wife will interact with the child but in the role of parent; the unity of the marital dyad will remain intact. The dyad maintains an identity different from the identity which includes the child. The best indicator of this seemingly impregnable unity is the development of a set of symbols which carry meanings to which the child has no access.

The problems of sharing the special sentiments and meanings attached to the marital dyad are apparent in the triadic relationship commonly referred to as the "love triangle." The traditional sharing of feelings, physical love, and the meanings associated with the intense marital relationship are, in the love triangle, shared by one member of the marital dyad and the third person. It is the presence of the third person as a participant in the circumstances of the marital dyad which threatens and often destroys it.

Talcott Parsons and Edward Shils present a different view of the dyad. Their analysis of the structure of interaction in the dyad attempts to integrate all the basic elements present when two individuals interact with each other over an extended period of time. In identifying these elements, Parsons and Shils (1951:105–107) argue that the dyad is ". . . the most elementary form of a social system. The features of this interaction are present in more complex form in all social systems."

According to them, the dyadic relationship exhibits the following structural elements:

1. *The two interacting parties are objects of orientation for each other. These orientations are reciprocal and complementary.* The actions of ego are contingent upon the actions of alter. Also, ego becomes oriented to alter's probable overt behavior and ego becomes oriented to his own interpretations of what alter expects of ego. When the system of interaction becomes integrated, these orientations to the expectations of each other become reciprocal or complementary.

2. *Reciprocity of expectations requires the development of a system of communication involving the use of common symbols.* Integration of this two-person system of interaction requires the development of a common culture in which the orientations and expectations of both parties are to be found. One determiner of the presence of culture in such a relationship is the development of a system of communication, the symbols of which have common meanings for ego and alter. The function of a common culture is to mediate the interaction.

3. *The symbol system (common culture) has normative significance for the interacting parties who must observe its conventions in order to "understand" each other.* The culture of the interactive relationship of ego and alter functions as a definer of the range of appropriate reactions by alter to ego's behavior and by ego to alter's behavior. The pattern of communication which develops between ego and alter becomes a pattern of appropriate reactions by the interacting parties. This pattern of appropriate behavior results from the development of a common culturally based set of meanings which ego and alter now share. The culture of the interactive relationship, then, is composed of a set of common symbols for communication and a set of norms for action.

4. *The motivation of the interacting parties becomes integrated with the normative patterns through interaction.* Ego and alter are motivated to behave within the limits of appropriate behavior as defined by the culture. This results from the realization that behavior defined by the culture as inappropriate is negatively sanctioned, and behavior defined as within appropriate limits is positively sanctioned. Behavior consistent with the role expectations placed upon ego and alter results from the structure of sanctions which develop in the interactive relationship.

5. *The interactive system involves the process of generalization.* Generalization occurs at the normative, behavioral, and attitudinal levels. Ego and alter maintain an integrated relationship by supporting the normative system, behaving appropriately, and developing sensitivity to the attitudes about the relationship and about each other. The relationship between ego and alter, at the integrated level, implies mutuality of gratification but not necessarily equal distribution of gratification. These characteristics indicate that the structure of human interaction for all social systems includes: (a) individuals as objects of orientation for each other, (b) reciprocity of expectations, (c) the presence of a system of common symbols, (d) a normative basis for interaction, (e) a system of positive and negative sanctions, and (f) normative, behavioral, and attitudinal generalizations.

Parsons and Shils refer to the applicability of this structure to all social systems. It should be understood, however, that the simple structure of the dyad is by no means an indication of the complex structures which develop in group associations of increasing size. One index of the complexities associated with defining the structural elements of groups of increasing size is the eventual need to externalize normative and other structural elements—for example, the need to develop a written statement of the rules and regulations which define appropriate behavior.

THE TRIAD

The triad is considered the most classic of all small group types. Three-person relationships are distinguishable from dyads in that they tend to divide the membership into a subgroup of two and isolate the third person. It is this tendency which hints at the complexities associated with groups of increasing size. We will define the *triad* as a system of interaction among three members who maintain their identity as a group over a significant period of time.

Georg Simmel's Triadic Formations: Mediator, Tertius Gaudens, Divide et Impera. In Georg Simmel's explanation of the triadic relationship, three formations are used to explain the view that three-person relationships are prone to coalition formation, a circumstance in which the three $(a+b+c)$ become two persons and a third $(a+b)$ *and* c. The three formations are: (1) The Mediator, (2) the *Tertius Gaudens* (Enjoying Third), and (3) *Divide et Impera* (Divide and Conquer).

THE MEDIATOR. This triadic form describes a dyadic relationship which requires outside assistance (mediation) in order to maintain itself. Although we are not concerned presently with relationships between large groups or collectivities, they provide excellent examples of triadic mediation. Two nations, unable to cope with the circumstances of their relationship at a particular time (possibilities of war, trade relationships, etc.), may require an outside party (third nation in the form of its representatives) to function as an intermediary in order to reach agreement. Similarly, marriage partners who are incapable of maintaining their relationship may require a third party (marriage counselor or some third member of the family) to aid in maintaining the marriage. The key to functioning as the mediator lies in that individual's ability to remain neutral. Lack of involvement in the content of the two-person relationship is essential. The failure to remain neutral may result in extreme disorganization and possibly separation, as in the case of the married couple, or war in the case of international diplomacy.

THE *TERTIUS GAUDENS*. The "enjoying third" either finds or places himself in the position of receiving some benefits from the three-person relationship. Simply put, the third, and usually weakest member, uses the relationship as a means to his own ends.

Caplow has constructed an interesting example of the *tertius gaudens*: Ahab, Brutus, and Charlie are smugglers who, in order to escape the controls of civil authority, decide to divide their ill-gotten gains on an isolated island. Brutus and Charlie are equal in strength and power; Ahab is slightly more powerful. His position of power in relation to the combined power of Brutus and Charlie disallows any rewards proportionate to his power since he could be easily overwhelmed by a coalition of the other two. If Ahab's power would, for one reason or another, be reduced to slightly less than that of the other two, he would be in the position of the *tertius*:

> The greatly diminished and enfeebled Ahab is now sought out as a coalition partner by both Brutus and Charlie and, within reason, he can make his own terms with one of them. The causes of this new popularity are self-evident, nearly reversing the reasons he was avoided in his more powerful days. Both Brutus and Charlie, now giants to his pygmy eyes, are enthusiastic about a coalition partner whom they can readily dominate and with whose help they can subdue an otherwise equal adversary. The offers Ahab would receive from them might reach an equal share or more (Caplow, 1968:3).

DIVIDE ET IMPERA. The unique quality of a triadic relationship characterized by "divide and conquer" is simply that the third person intentionally functions as a disruptive force moving in the direction of an organized two-person relationship. The purpose, in most cases, is to gain a position of power or superiority over each of the other two, which position can be achieved only by separating their combined power. The split, if such occurs, may be temporary or permanent; the effect of the split may or may not result in the ascendency of the third party; the force of the disruption may be so great that whatever power the third party enjoys will be useless in the face of thoroughly disorganized or dissolved relationships.

Coalition Formation. There are three major interaction configurations in triads. They are:

1. SEPARATION. The breakdown of the three-party relationship resulting in loss of group identity.

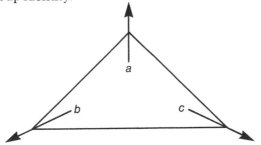

2. UNIFICATION. The integration of all three members into a balanced relationship.

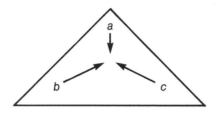

3. COALITION FORMATION. The breakdown of the three-party relationship into a relationship of two against the third.

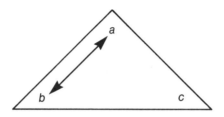

Separation and unification are opposites of each other. In separation, the interaction among the three members results in the breakdown of the triad. Systems of common identity—including symbols, meanings, and a sense of belonging—are lost, as are the original group goals. In unification, all the elements necessary for group formation and group maintenance are present. Beyond these, there develops a high level of integration in which the individual members feel their sense of involvement in the group in terms of primary group qualities.

In coalition formation the triad exhibits the possibilities for variation between and among group members. Theodore Caplow (1959:488–493) has developed a theory of coalition formation in which he identifies eight types of triads which are actually models for predicting coalitions in terms of the relative power of each member in the triad. The eight types of triads are presented in Figure 3-3.

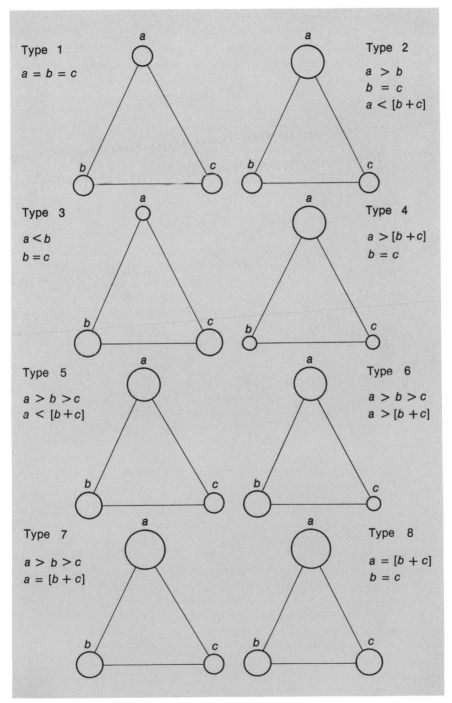

Figure 3-3. Caplow's Eight Types of Triads

Coalition formation in triads refers to the three possibilities surrounding the organization of groups into individual to subgroup relationships. (See *Type* 2 in Chapter Two.) For the triad, these possibilities are: $(a+b)$ against c, $(a+c)$ against b, $(b+c)$ against a. The important point to remember is that, in the triad, coalition formation of one kind or another is the most likely form taken for interaction. Although separation and unification are realistic possibilities, they are not the most likely. If, for example, interaction does result in unification, the chance of a triad maintaining itself in this form is very slight. The strongest tendency, then, is for triads to form into coalitions of two against the third.

For example, coalitions occur with some frequency within the boundaries of the American nuclear family: Two parents form a powerful coalition $(a+b)$ in relation to their child (c). The effective maintenance of the powerful parent coalition is an important element in the socialization of the child. When the coalition remains intact, the child's association is characteristically consistent and secure. There is a sense of stability in the position the child (c) occupies within the family.

At any point in time, however, the child may attempt to restructure the relationships which have been set and pit one parent against the other in order to attain some end not acceptable to the parent coalition. If the child succeeds in weakening the parent coalition, the structure of the family interaction system changes. There occurs a new coalition of the child (c) with one parent (a) against the other parent (b). The result: $(a+c)$ against b. These observations on coalition formation are derived from Simmel's (Wolff, 1950:135–136) discussions of the disturbing character of the third party:

> No matter how close a triad may be, there is always the occasion on which two of the three members regard the third as an intruder. The reason may be in the mere fact that he shares in certain moods which can unfold in all their intensity and tenderness only when two can meet without distraction: the sensitive union of two is always irritated by the spectator.

SHIFTING COALITIONS IN TRIADS

As a three-person relationship, the triad is a stable group. However, the coalitions which form within the boundaries of the triad are seldom stable; they are usually in a state of flux, shifting from time to time. (See Figure 3-4.)

We are aware that there are numerous external forces which influence behavior within groups. When the forces surrounding the group change,

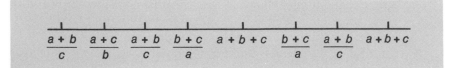

Figure 3-4.   Shifting Coalitions in Triads (Time Continuum)

changes can be expected to occur within the group. For example, in the American family the needs of a child, at a certain point in time, will force a coalition with one parent against the other, or with a sibling against a third, or with a sibling against one or another parent. We are suggesting that the circumstances at any point in time will determine the state of coalition formation within the triadic relationship.

If we can understand that one of the basic characteristics of triads is the formation of coalitions, then we should understand that the stability of the triad is dependent upon the shifting of relationships which occur within. If any one of the three coalitions possible forms and stabilizes, the third party in the group is isolated from the relationship formed. The result of such a stable coalition would be the loss of the triad as a small group, having been replaced by a permanent coalition and an isolate.

We have argued that the numerical bases for small group behavior are those sociologically significant elements found in the isolated individual, the dyad, and the triad. The dyadic and the triadic constructions are fully legitimate small group systems in themselves; they are also the numerical bases for small group systems of larger size and more complex organization. In discussing this point, Simmel (Wolff, 1950:162) says that ". . . we must preface the treatment of this constellation by pointing out that the number, three, is merely the minimum number of elements necessary for this formation, and that it may thus serve as the simplest schema."

GROUP ENVIRONMENTS

Very little has been said or implied about group environments to this point; so, we will spend some time on the subject. Individual group members and within-group interaction do not exist in a vacuum. Although individuals and the interaction aspects of social groups are of the greatest importance, the present analysis would be incomplete without an understanding of the environments within which group interaction takes place. Group environments may be viewed as:

1. Situational—sum of all social and personal elements surrounding group interaction (defined by each individual in the group)
2. Physical—settings in which the group performance occurs
3. Cultural—value, belief, and norm elements influencing behavior within the group

THE SITUATIONAL ENVIRONMENT

The situational environment is the sum of all the social elements at a given point in time which individuals perceive as determiners of how they will perform their group roles. The social elements include other members within the group, the entire complex of relationships with others in the group, and individual perception of the group as a whole.

Blake and Mouton (1970:413–426), in their discussion of situations in which a conflict arises about a basic issue or an issue important to the group members, present a Conflict Resolution Grid which is an excellent example of a situational environment. (See Figure 3-5.) The grid is ideal for helping us understand small group situations in which individuals openly discuss issues which might possibly produce a change in the cohesive bonds present in the group.

The authors identify five ways in which a conflict situation may be handled. We may identify these on the grid as:

1. Smoothing (upper left corner)
2. Confronting (upper right corner)
3. Balancing (center)
4. Withdrawing (lower left corner)
5. Suppressing (lower right corner)

We are safe in assuming that each of us has been in group situations which require that we and others in the group use one of these five ways for handling the conflict at issue. If we used a conflict model for interpreting behavior within group boundaries (see Chapter Five) we would argue that behavior within groups is in a constant state of conflict resolution—a situation natural to all social groups.

In studying the grid, the reader will notice that the vertical axis is scaled from 1 to 9 as is the horizontal axis. The vertical axis identifies individual concern for people; the horizontal axis individual concern for getting results. The five ways for handling conflict situations are placed in grid positions which suggest more or less concern for people and for getting results.

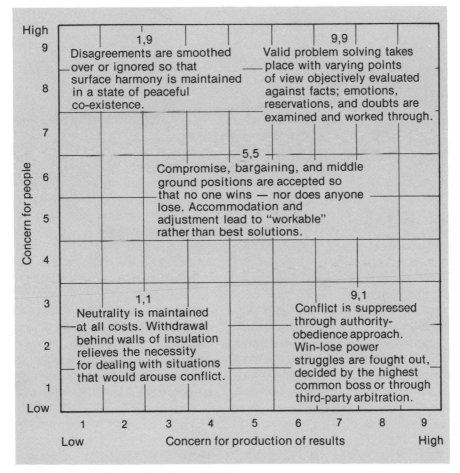

Figure 3-5. Collective Resolution Grid

Reproduced by special permission from *The Journal of Applied Behavioral Science*, "The Fifth Achievement," by Robert R. Blake and J. S. Mouton, Volume 6, Number 4, p. 4, NTL Institute for Applied Behavioral Science.

In applying the grid to an actual situation of group conflict, the author notes that no one way of handling conflict is consistently characteristic of any one individual. Individuals may have a strong tendency to behave in a consistent manner when conflict situations arise, but different issues and different others in various groups may work against any individual using a preferred mode for conflict resolution.

We have all used phrases suggesting the situation in which we find ourselves. "The situation is this," and "How did I ever get into this situation," are examples. When relations within the group become strained we might feel like saying, "What a hell of a situation I'm in now!" Sometimes, others admonish us for getting too involved and offer the following advice: "You got yourself into that situation, now get yourself out!"

The word *situation* refers to the circumstances surrounding behavior in a given set of relationships. These circumstances include the behavior of others with whom we must cope, the direction in which the relationship is moving for good or ill, and the general state of group affairs at any point in time. The situation of a given group at a given time might be described as tense or relaxed. Situations may be found "wanting" or described as a "snafu" (situation normal, all fouled up).

Hare, Borgatta, and Bales (1966:196) offer the following definition of a social situation:

> The social situation for a given individual may be another individual, or a relationship with a series of other individuals, or it may be, as he conceives it in his own mind, a relationship between himself and the group as a whole.

This view highlights two important features of the situational environment:

1. The environment is a functional reality only in terms of how the individual group member interprets the elements of a situation.
2. Definitions of the situational environment of a group are given by individuals, and in any given group, perceptions will differ from group member to group member.

Bossard and Boll (1966:19) define a situation as consisting ". . . of a number of stimuli, external to the organism but acting upon it, organized as a unit and with a special relatedness to one another as stimuli of the specific organism involved." This view is, again, suggestive of selective perception on the part of individual group members and indicates that the situational environment is made up of many stimuli which combine as an influence upon each group member. Actually, these authors were attempting to understand child development within group contexts such as the American nuclear family. But, for our purposes as well as theirs, the idea of a situational environment is a useful tool for understanding the elements in all small groups.

THE PHYSICAL ENVIRONMENT

The physical environment presents an interesting contrast to the seemingly less concrete situational environment. Marvin Shaw (1976:117), in discussing small group environments, suggests that such groups are ". . . embedded in a complex environmental setting that exerts a strong influence on almost every aspect of the group process." Part of that "complex environmental setting" is the physical environment in which group members interact.

The physical environment is composed of the concrete objects and spatial elements which surround activity within a group. It includes concrete objects such as rooms, buildings, color, lighting, temperature, and noise, and spatial elements such as distances between and among group members while interacting, personal space, and group space.

If you are wondering what the physical world has to do with small group behavior, consider the following example. Whether or not a college professor lectures at a consistently high or low level of excellence must be for the students to judge. But, in one particular instance, it was the professsor who felt that the lecture was going badly and was unable to determine why.

A number of years ago upon entering an opening semester class which, incidentally, was a class in the Sociology of Small Groups, the professor began to introduce the subject matter but was unable to "get things going." The professor had taught the course many times before and, being in the profession for more years than anyone would care to remember, could not plead poor preparation or nervousness. Nothing was going as had been expected. Errors in specch, hesitations, and loss of control over the lecture situation all proved embarrassing. There was no alternative but to stop the formal lecture, apologize to the students, and ask them if they knew what was wrong. One of the students offered an explanation which the professor accepts to this day. The student, clearly in control of herself, and not suffering as was the professor, suggested that the problem might have to do with something the students were discussing before class began. The classroom was small for the number of students registered and in attendance and the walls were painted a "very sick" salmon color! The student suggested that unless one likes salmon-colored walls and small, congested areas, one might have difficulty lecturing in such a classroom. This reasoning not only got the professor off the hook, but served as the basis for a lively lecture on the importance of the physical environment in which human interaction takes place.

Is color really so important as an influencing agent on human interaction? Consider entering someone's home and finding that all the walls are painted black! We give meaning to colors just as we give meaning to all other elements surrounding us. These meanings, internalized by each individual, are culturally based and find a high degree of consensus within the population.. For a great majority of people, going about the business of daily family interaction in a house filled with black walls is out of the question. Brides wear white, cowards are yellow, the sinner's soul is black; such language usage is common and suggests that we all give meanings to colors beyond the objective significance which color carries in itself.

At the risk of overkill on this point, consider the cultural meanings of the colors yellow, black, and white in the context of intergroup relations. Students of that discipline will surely note their significance in the nature of the system of segregation, discrimination, and prejudice in America's past.

Some groups of individuals who have established strong, intimate, personal relationships are going to behave in a given way depending upon numerous factors outside of those in the physical environment. The presence of an immediate or long-range goal to be attained, the changing interests of group members, and the presence of nongroup members will serve as factors in changing the behavior of the members of the group. However, one factor in the physical environment which must be considered is the place in which the interaction is occurring. It should be obvious to all that family members, as a group, do not behave in the same way when dining at home and when dining at a restaurant. We are certainly not suggesting a Jekyll and Hyde transformation in member behavior—that is, that they behave as totally different personalities. It would appear, however, that the restaurant, as a specific physical environment with a specific set of behavior expectations, forces a pattern of interaction quite different from that which occurs in the home. The people are the same, their relationships to each other are structurally the same, and their goals may be the same in both environments, but their behavior changes.

Concrete objects such as color, buildings, and rooms are some of the most visible elements in our physical environment. Less obvious, perhaps, but no less significant as influencers of group behavior are the elements of space. Interaction distances and personal space function as modifiers of human behavior. As in the case of concrete objects, spatial elements are culturally determined, and the variations observable cross-culturally are many.

Interaction distance is defined as the measurable distance between and among group members while they are interacting with each other. Intimacy in highly integrated small groups, for example, refers not only to the psychological condition of a relationship but to the physical closeness, including physical contact, of the interacting parties as well. In discussions of more formally organized small groups, such as boards of directors, the characteristic of impersonality has as much significance for physical distance as it has as a definer of the interaction itself. Intimate relationships are close, tactile relationships and impersonal relationships are those which require breathing room, that is, distances measurable in feet, not inches.

Personal space is "owned" space surrounding an individual while he is interacting with others. In using the phrase, "owned space," we are referring to a kind of personal territory surrounding an individual's body into which others may enter only with the approval of the individual whose space it is. The American handshake is one means of preserving personal space for both parties. The handshake, then, has a twofold function: to symbolize a meeting with the appropriate greeting form and to set limits of personal space between the individuals who are meeting.

Space and distance as factors in human behavior have been the subject of interest for more than a decade. Much of our continued interest stems from Edward T. Hall's work, *The Hidden Dimension*. Hall traces the origins of space and distance investigations to the experimentalists whose research on animals predates present-day interest in space and distance in human groups. Bridging the gap between these animal experiments and human group behavior, Hall (1966:107–122) identifies four distances in man and gives definite linear measurements for each distance. (See Table 3-1.) These observations suggest that behavior changes as the distance from the point of contact increases between or among interacting individuals. The characteristic intimacy of bodily contact between a mother and her child in the Intimate Distance Close Phase is contrasted, at the other end of the distance scale (Public Distant Far Phase), with relationships in public settings with, for example, political figures such as the President of the United States or a Justice of the United States Supreme Court.

Attempts to apply Hall's Distances in Man to small group behavior must necessarily exclude the Public Distance Phases. Even those small groups which are more formally structured, such as corporate committees, function at distances no greater than those described for the Social Distance Phase.

As a final note, W. H. Auden's poem best expresses the significance of personal distance in our lives:

> Some thirty inches from my nose
> The frontier of my Person goes,
> And all the untilled air between
> Is private *pagus* or demesne,
> Stranger unless with bedroom eyes

I beckon you to fraternize,
Beware of rudely crossing it:
I have no gun, but I can spit.

Table 3-1.   Edward T. Hall's Distances in Man

INTIMATE DISTANCE

Close Phase—contact to 6 inches
Far Phase—6 inches to 18 inches

At intimate distance, the presence of the other person is unmistakable and may at times be overwhelming because of the greatly increased sensory inputs. Sight (often distorted), olfaction, heat from the other person's body, sound, smell, and feel of the breath all combine to signal unmistakable involvement with another body.

PERSONAL DISTANCE

Close Phase—1½ to 2½ feet
Far Phase—2½ to 4 feet

"Personal distance" is the term originally used by Hediger to designate the distance consistently separating the members of noncontact species. It might be thought of as a small protective sphere or bubble that an organism maintains between itself and others.

SOCIAL DISTANCE

Close Phase—4 to 7 feet
Far Phase—7 to 12 feet

Impersonal business occurs at this distance, and in the close phase there is more involvement than in the distant phase. People who work together tend to use close social distance. It is also a common distance for people who are attending a casual social gathering. To stand and look down at a person at this distance has a domineering effect, as when a person talks to a secretary or receptionist.

PUBLIC DISTANCE

Close Phase—12 to 25 feet
Far Phase—25 feet or more

Several important sensory shifts occur in the transition from the personal and social distances to public distance, which is well outside the circle of involvement.

CULTURAL ENVIRONMENT

The cultural environment is by no means a concrete, measurable set of facts. When we speak of the cultural environment, we are not referring to individuals, or interaction, or communication within group situations. Nor can we continue to think in terms of colors, places, or personal distance.

Let us begin by defining culture. *Culture* is a system of standards of conduct which orients individuals in their organized, meaningful relationships with one another. The elements which compose culture are values, beliefs, and norms. These are transmitted through a system of language which links individuals to each other and to their culture in a meaningful way. We cannot see or feel culture but without it we would have no orderly basis for human conduct. Without values, beliefs, and norms, human beings would be lost and would live truly chaotic lives.

It is usual for sociologists to discuss culture in terms of the larger society and to view cultural facts in these terms. But the true reality of social behavior lies in the circumstances of group interaction, and it is here that culture has its greatest impact. It is in the organization of group behavior that values, beliefs, and norms are translated into meaningful, appropriate behavior.

We have stressed values, beliefs, and norms. What are these cultural facts? *Values* are ideas which are shared and which define behavior as appropriate or inappropriate, good or bad. They form a system of social morality which places constraints upon the behavior of individuals. For example, success is highly valued in the American society and, for many individuals, achieving some measure of success becomes a control over the choice of career, the purchase of items which are symbolic of success, and, for some, the selection of a marriage partner. For those whose lives fall short of being successful, the criteria for which are wealth, power, and prestige, the vocalization of high expectations for success in the future is mandatory.

Perhaps the most complete and telling identification of values is by Robin M. Williams, Jr. (1970:452–500) who, in his book, *American Society*, identifies the following as major value orientations in America:

1. Achievement and success
2. Activity and work
3. Moral orientation
4. Humanitarian mores
5. Efficiency and practicality
6. Progress
7. Material comfort

8. Equality
9. Freedom
10. External conformity
11. Science and secular rationality
12. Nationalism-Patriotism
13. Democracy
14. Individuality
15. Racism and related group-superiority themes

Although Williams is concerned with values as constructed within the American society, the impact of these values is no less when discussing the small group. Human behavior of the day-to-day variety occurs with greatest frequency within small groups of influence, and it is in these microsystems that social values reinforce and direct the lives of individuals who are society's members. What we are suggesting is that the significance of values as an environmental factor lies in the influence these cultural facts have on the lives of those who hold them. In this sense, the worth of a value system is best discerned in those small group situations in which they are used.

The importance of values at the level of small group behavior can be identified through the following distinction. Values which have no applicability to the lives of society's members are dormant or mythical values. Active or real values are those which influence the lives of society's members every day. Active values are those which people internalize as the basis for interaction with others. This distinction places the small group at the center of the value system. It is within the small group that we conduct our lives and give meaning to our societal identity.

Beliefs are mental concepts by which we judge elements of culture to be true or false and which exert control over individuals in certain situations. Beliefs are conceptions of what should be in a given situation. A religious belief system tells those who accept its limitations that if they wish to participate in a given community of worship and if they wish to accept the identity of a particular religious affiliation, they must follow a particular set of beliefs.

Norms are systems of expectations or standards of conduct which define appropriate behavior in specific situations. These expectations may be written or unwritten, and they define what is expected of the individual when interacting with others under specific conditions of time and place. Norms answer the question, "What am I supposed to do?" In business firms and corporations, Job Description Manuals answer this question. Norms also answer the question, "How am I expected to act?" For most social situations there are rules of etiquette learned through socialization or written à la Emily Post. Table 3-2 identifies some of the more prevalent values, beliefs, and norms present in American society.

The cultural environments of small groups are exactly the same as those of the larger society. In small groups which, at this point, we may view as microsystems of interaction within the larger society, actual behavior is based upon how individuals perceive the culture surrounding the particular groups of which they are members. We might look to the following examples to see how culture is reflected in the behavior of individuals in small group systems of interaction.

Table 3-2. American Values, Beliefs, and Norms

	VALUES	
Humanitarianism		Success
High achievement		Conformity
Individuality		Freedom

	BELIEFS	
Religious systems		Economic systems
Political systems		Systems of racial beliefs

	NORMS	
The Criminal Legal Code		Corporate regulations
The Civil Legal Code		Rules of etiquette

Values. It is not uncommon in the informal work groups which develop among young corporate executives to think of one or more of their number as nice guys who are all too anxious to move up (*high achievement*). True friendships, in times of stress or need, often require sacrifice on the part of one friend for the good of the other in terms of money, time, or energy (*humanitarianism*). Parents will often admonish their peer-conforming adolescents with the words, "When are you going to start thinking for yourself?" (*individuality*). Many children proceed through their preadult years with the constant echo of their parents' and teachers' hopes for them: "You can become anything you want to be as long as you put your mind to it" (*success*).

Beliefs. Religious beliefs, whether learned as part of early child socialization in the family or as part of a later adult commitment, are strong and difficult to throw off. In general, Christians hold tenaciously to their belief that Jesus Christ is God. In particular, Catholics espouse belief in the virgin birth and the forgiveness of sins through the sacrament of confession. The tenets of capitalism as the basis for a system of economic organization have pervaded the American social structure for many years, and democracy is believed to be a solid basis for the organization of the American political system. All these beliefs seriously influence behavior on a day-to-day basis and are reflected in the ways in which individuals organize their families, select their friends, and choose their work environments. In group situations, the individual is known by what he tells others his beliefs are, and, in part, it is upon the acceptance or rejection of the belief systems of others that we accept or reject them as group members. Once the group members agree on a basic system of beliefs, the chances of the group maintaining itself at a high integrative level are good even in the face of conflict between and among its members.

Norms. We have only to look at the common, daily reactions of individuals to the crimes of murder, robbery, and rape, to the unbelievable consistency with which people adhere to traffic regulations, to common eating habits, and to the ritualistic behavior of individuals at weddings and funerals to understand the impact of norms on the daily routines of people as they interact with each other. In fact, all our relationships with others, in groups or outside the boundaries of group interaction, are, in

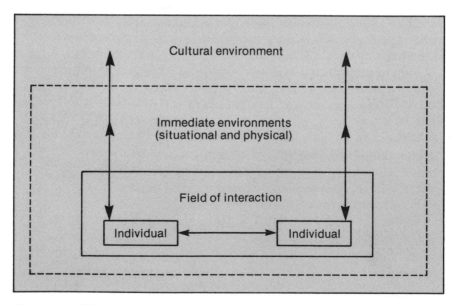

Figure 3-6.   Major Components of the Group

large measure, controlled by a system of normative expectations which is internalized from very early childhood within the confines of family, friendship, and educational groupings.

*   *   *   *

We have stated that the three major components of groups are the individual, within-group interaction, and group environments. Although these may appear to be three distinct elements, they are not. They are only analytically distinct, separated for purposes of analysis and interpretation, and should be viewed as three facets of the very same social phenomenon—the group. Figure 3-6 presents the relationships among these three group components.

---

summary

The individual, interaction, and group environments were identified as the basic components of small groups.

THE INDIVIDUAL

As a symbol user the individual is capable, by nature and through social care, of participating in meaningful, patterned interaction within social groups. The individual was observed to behave appropriately in group settings when able to control behavior in order to satisfy self needs and the needs of other group members.

As a social fact, the individual was viewed in terms originally described by Georg Simmel as a sociological fact even when isolated from group environments. It was noted that isolation is a state in which the individual continues to interact with others in a relationship existing in the individual's mind. The sociological implications of isolation were described in terms of the individual's past experiences and future contacts.

INTERACTION

Two perspectives on interaction were discussed: (1) the symbolic nature of interaction with emphasis on language symbols, and (2) interaction as a function of the size of the group. This latter perspective included interpretations of dyads and triads based upon Simmel's early discussions.

Groups are composed of systems of interaction as well as individuals. Group interaction was identified as communication and language as the most important communication tool. Language was considered to be at the core of early socialization and found to be much more difficult as a learning process than some might suspect. Further discussion of interaction included the ability to verbalize and use language as a symbolic tool of communication. The basic unit of interaction was identified (Figure 3-1); it included the elements of verbal behavior, self and other meanings, and the use of these in order to communicate. The transmission of a verbal communication of meanings was identified as an act of externalization, and receipt of a communication as an act of internalization. Discussions of interaction viewed from the perspective of group size included observations about the interaction aspects of Simmel's dyadic constructions and a more modern view of the interactive relations as presented by Talcott Parsons and Edward Shils.

Dyadic interaction was considered a relationship in which the two individuals are dependent only upon each other. According to Simmel, the two-party relationship, if it does endure, must be considered ideal or pure because the interaction maintained by the two members is not exposed to the intrusion of even a third individual. The addition of a third member increases the complexities of interaction within the system and often results in a disruption of the unity developed between the two.

Parsons and Shils identify the dyad as "the most elementary form of a social system." The basic structural elements of the dyadic relationship were identified as: (1) individuals are objects of orientation for each other; (2) a system of communication involving the use of common symbols is a requisite of expectation reciprocity; (3) the symbol system has normative significance; (4) interaction is the connecting link between individual motivation and normative group patterns; and (5) the interactive system includes the process of generalization. The authors indicate that the basic structure found in two-party relationships is applicable to all social systems.

Interaction in the triad is distinguished by the tendency to divide into a subgroup and an isolated third member. Three interaction configurations were observed in three-member relationships: separation (group breakdown resulting in loss of group identity), unification (integration resulting in a balanced relationship), and coalition formation (restructuring in terms of "two against one").

Discussions of interaction in the triad centered around coalition formation since the strong tendency in triads is for such coalitions to develop. Caplow's eight types of triads were considered models for predicting coalitions in terms of the relative power of each member.

The three most classic triadic formations by Simmel were identified as the mediator, the *tertius gaudens*, and *divide et impera*. A triad characterized by mediation was described as a dyadic relationship which requires outside assistance in order to maintain itself. The classic formation of *tertius gaudens* was described as a noncoalition formation, involving threat, in which the "enjoying third" (weakest member) either finds or places himself in the position of receiving some benefits from a less advantageous position.

The special character of *divide et impera* was determined to be simply that the third person intentionally functions as a disruptive force moving in the direction of an organized two-person relationship in order to gain a position of power or superiority. This process requires the separation of the combined power of the organized dyad.

The tendency of triads to form coalitions suggests a three-party relationship which is tenuous at best. However, the stability or duration of triadic relations are dependent upon the shifting character of these internal formations. It was noted that if any one coalition forms and stabilizes, the continued isolation of the third member foreshadows the breakdown of the three-party relation, which is replaced by a permanent dyad and an isolated individual.

GROUP ENVIRONMENTS

Systems of group interaction and the individuals who behave within them do not exist in a vacuum. Group environments form the situational and physical and cultural circumstances in which group activity occurs.

The situational environment is the sum of all the social elements at a given point in time which individuals perceive as determiners of how they will perform their group roles. These social elements include other group members, the group interaction complex, and the individual's perception of the group as a whole. The discussion of conflict situations by R. Blake and J. Mouton included the construction of a Conflict Resolution Grid which identified five ways in which conflict situations may be handled: smoothing, confronting, balancing, withdrawing, and suppressing. When viewing situational environments from the perspective of the individual group member, two features of situational environments were noted: (1) individual response to environmental features depends upon individual interpretation, and (2) perceptions of situational elements—the significance given to each will differ from group member to group member.

The physical environment was defined as one composed of the concrete objects and spatial elements which surround group activity. Included in the list of physical and spatial elements were such objects as rooms, buildings, color, lighting, temperature, noise, and spatial elements such as distances between and among group members, personal space, and group space.

Interaction distance was given special consideration and was defined as the measurable distance between and among group members while they are interacting with each other. Individuals were determined to occupy *personal space*, defined as "owned" space surrounding an individual while he is interacting with others.

In *The Hidden Dimension*, Edward T. Hall elaborates on the concept of space by identifying four distances in man. They are:

1. Intimate distance—contact to 18 inches
2. Personal distance—18 inches to 4 feet
3. Social distance—4 feet to 12 feet
4. Public distance—12 feet to 25 feet or more

Culture was defined as a system of standards of conduct which orients individuals in their organized, meaningful relationships with one another. Culture includes systems of values, beliefs, and norms. These are transmitted through a system of linguistic communication linking individuals to each other in a meaningful way.

Values were defined as ideas which are shared and which define behavior as appropriate or inappropriate, good or bad. Values form a social moral system which constrains individuals. According to Robin M. Williams, Jr., major value orientations in America include, for example, achievement and work, efficiency and practicality, equality, democracy, and individuality.

Beliefs are similar to values and are defined as mental constructs which we use to judge cultural elements as true or false and which exert control over individuals in certain situations. *Norms* are systems of expectations or standards of conduct which define appropriate behavior in a specific situation.

---

discussion questions

1. What kinds of symbols are used in group interaction?
2. Comment on the statement: Group interaction is communication.
3. Are Caplow's Eight Types of Triads all-inclusive?
4. Behavior in groups changes as group situations change. Apply this observation to your own group experiences.

5. Explain the reasons why Hall's Public Distance Phase must be excluded from small group analysis.

references

Auden, W. H. *Collected Poems* (Edward Mendelson, ed.). New York: Random House, 1965.

Bavelas, Alex. "Communication Patterns in Task-Oriented Groups," *Journal of the Acoustical Society of America*, 22 (1950): 725–730.

Blake, R. R.; and Mouton, J. S. "The Fifth Achievement," *The Journal of Applied Behavioral Science*, 6 (1970): 413–426.

Bossard, James H. S.; and Boll, Eleanor Stoker. *The Sociology of Child Development*, 4th ed.; New York: Harper & Row, 1966.

Caplow, Theodore. "Further Development of a Theory of Coalitions in the Triad," *The American Journal of Sociology*, 64 (1959): 488–493.

_____. *Two Against One: Coalitions in Triads*. Englewood Cliffs, New Jersey: Prentice-Hall, 1968.

Fichter, Joseph H. *Sociology*. Chicago: The University of Chicago Press, 1957.

Hall, Edward T. *The Hidden Dimension*. Garden City, New York: Doubleday, 1966.

Hare, A. Paul; Borgatta, Edgar F.; and Bales, Robert F. *Small Groups: Studies in Social Interaction*. New York: Alfred A. Knopf, 1966.

Leavitt, Harold J. "Some Effects of Certain Communication Patterns on Group Performance," *Journal of Abnormal and Social Psychology*, 46 (1951): 38–50.

Mills, Theodore M. "Some Hypotheses on Small Groups from Simmel," *The American Journal of Sociology*, 63 (1958): 642–650.

Nisbet, Robert. *The Social Bond*. New York: Alfred A. Knopf, 1970.

Parsons, Talcott; and Shils, Edward A. (eds.). *Toward a General Theory of Action*, Torchbook edition; New York: Harper & Row, 1951.

Schellenberg, James A. *An Introduction to Social Psychology*. New York: Random House, 1970.

Shaw, Marvin E. *Group Dynamics: The Psychology of Small Group Behavior*, 2nd ed.; New York: McGraw-Hill, 1976.

Shibutani, Tamotsu. *Society and Personality: An Interactionist Approach to Social Psychology*. Englewood Cliffs, New Jersey: Prentice-Hall, 1961.

Vernon, Glenn. *Human Interaction: An Introduction to Sociology*. New York: Ronald, 1965.

Williams, Robin M., Jr. *American Society: A Sociological Interpretation*, 3rd ed.; New York: Alfred A. Knopf, 1970.

Wolff, Kurt H. (Trans. and ed.). *The Sociology of Georg Simmel*. New York: The Free Press, 1950.

PART 2

SMALL GROUP
THEORY

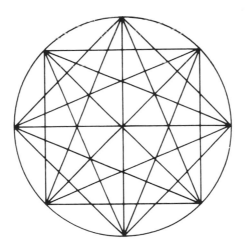

Chapter Four

Major Theoretical Orientations in Small Groups

CHAPTER PREVIEW

THE IMPORTANCE OF SMALL GROUP THEORY

In 1950, George Homans (1950:1) wrote:

> As the science of society, sociology has examined the characteristics and problems of communities, cities, regions, big organizations like factories, and even whole nations, but it has only begun to study the smaller social units that make up these giants. In so doing, it has not followed the order of human experience, for the first and most immediate social experience of mankind is small group experience.

Since the publication of Homans' *The Human Group*, research in the field of small groups has not been neglected. Journals have been reporting the results of investigations into the field with great regularity over the last thirty years (Hare, 1976).[1] Included in the literature are the works of Kurt Lewin, Jacob Moreno, Robert F. Bales, and, of course, the more recent publications of George Homans (see Chapter Six). These combine with a host of others whose works have produced the large and ever-increasing volume of information on the small group.

The amount of research has been so great and the directions taken by researchers so varied that it has become almost impossible to get a clear and orderly view of the content of the small groups field and, especially, of the theoretical lines which it has followed. In 1965, A. Paul Hare, Edward F. Borgatta and Robert F. Bales (1965:vii) recognized the importance of identifying the theoretical origins of small group analysis when they observed:

> There is a saying that "it is a wise child that knows its own father." The field of small group research is so new that it has not yet recognized sufficiently even the more important of its ancestors.

We are able to trace the origins of the small groups field directly to three sources: the sociology of Georg Simmel, the symbolic interactionism of George Herbert Mead, and the social psychology of Charles Horton Cooley. These three theoretical systems have had a lasting impact on the study of the small group. In studying these systems we hope: (1) to place the small groups field in theoretical perspective, (2) to use the

---

1. The most complete list of publications can be found in A. Paul Hare, *Handbook of Small Group Research*. The *Handbook* lists 6,037 publications of which only 319 (5.0%) were published before 1950.

theoretical perspective as a basis for understanding and interpreting research findings, and (3) to present the field of small groups as a complete discipline—an impossible task without an understanding of its theoretical origins.

Theory is part of the history of sociology; it is the foundation upon which a system for understanding and interpreting human social behavior is constructed. The wise student is the one whose knowledge is built upon the same foundations as the subject he hopes to master. A *Life Notes* section has been included for each of the three theorists so that the reader will know the theorist as a human being and not just as a thinker having functioned somewhere in an ivory tower. Georg Simmel's life, personal and academic, was part of the fabric of his thinking about society and human interaction. The theorist and his theories were not separate entities—they flowed one from the other. These sections, therefore, might be studied in terms of the influences which all three theorists' small group associations had on their lives and works.

THE MICROSOCIOLOGY OF GEORG SIMMEL

The general and specific interpretations of Simmel's sociology will afford the reader a deeper understanding of the theorist as well as of his theories. Our major concern, of course, is with the impact of Simmel's theory on the small groups field, and the direction of our interpretations will reflect that concern.

FORMAL SOCIOLOGY: SOCIETY AS INTERACTION

Although Simmel was known for his interest in a variety of disciplines by his European contemporaries, his acceptance by American scholars is due mainly to his sociology, which includes the famous interpretation of sociological forms as the bases for a science of society. Because of Simmel's insistence that the study of society must concentrate upon the forms relationships take, he is considered the father of Formal Sociology. Simmel had no desire to develop a complete and systematic theory of man's social behavior or of society. He wanted only to discover the limits of society as a system of interaction and wanted the method of discovery to be bound by principles of scientific investigation.

Simmel saw society and all its components in terms of the relationships which exist between and among individuals behaving within its boundaries. To this end Simmel (Coser, 1965:5) defined society as "an intricate web of multiple relations established among individuals in constant

Life Notes

Georg Simmel

Georg Simmel (1858–1918) was born in Berlin, Germany. His father, co-owner of a chocolate factory, died when Simmel was very young. Having only a distant relationship with his mother, Simmel, under the guardianship of a close family friend, had little opportunity to develop a sense of personal security which stems from an integrated family life. His religious identities were equally strained. His Jewish father had converted to Catholicism, and his Protestant mother insisted on raising young Simmel in her faith. Having graduated from the *gymnasium*, Simmel studied at the University of Berlin and began teaching there in 1885.

Simmel's academic life was a contradiction in itself: he was a brilliant scholar and lecturer but, having been rejected for promotion, was not given official recognition for his abilities until shortly before his death. Simmel did not achieve an academic position higher than extraordinary professor until 1914 when he was accepted, finally, as a full professor at the University of Strasbourg. He died four years later of cancer. Earlier in his career, Simmel taught as a lecturer (*privatdozent*). Until he was promoted to full professor, Simmel received no financial remuneration for his labors and supported himself with inheritances from his father and guardian.

There were numerous factors which contributed to Simmel's failure to gain official acceptance. Some have been obscured by time, others are suggested in a letter of recommendation to the University of Heidelberg by the Minister of Culture, Dietrich Schaefer, in 1908. Simmel had applied for a post at Heidelberg and needed the official approval of Schaefer. The following passages from the letter are relevant:

> As you no doubt expect, I will express my opinion about Professor Simmel quite frankly . . . . He is a dyed-in-the-wool Israelite, in his outward appearance, in his bearing, and in his manner of thinking . . . his academic and literary merits and successes are very circumscribed and limited . . . he spices his words with clever sayings. And the audience he recruits is composed accordingly. The ladies constitute a very large portion—even for Berlin. For the rest, there [appears at his lectures] an extraordinarily numer-

ous contingent of the oriental world . . . I regret that I must render an unfavorable judgment. (Coser, 1965:37–39)

Simmel, then, received no official recognition from the academic establishment. The recognition he received from his students is another matter. He was known to them as a brilliant thinker and lecturer on a great variety of subjects. Alfred E. Laurence (1975:34), in speaking of Simmel as a lecturer, states:

When he lectured at Berlin for the last time, his desk had been totally covered with rose petals by his grateful listeners . . . . No figures are reported, but his listeners certainly went into the huadreds [sic], and he was so famous that he attracted "everybody who was anybody."

Simmel's lectures were innovative, thought-provoking, and enjoyable. He lectured in the areas of sociology, philosophy, and aesthetics, on subjects including *The Metropolis and Mental_Life*, *The Adventure*, *The Stranger*, *On the Significance of Social Life*, and *The Isolated Individual*. Simmel had no systematic approach to his subject matter and was often found to have contradicted himself. His writings are characterized by the same difficulties. However, the lack of a systematic approach and the presence of contradictions did nothing to reduce the strong impact of his thought in the field of sociology, most particularly, in the small groups area.

Simmel was never part of the integrated life of the German academic community. He was, in Coser's (1965:29–37) view, *The Stranger in the Academy*. We must assume that Simmel's brilliant essay, entitled *The Stranger*, is as much an autobiographical sketch as it is a recognized treatise on marginality and alienation. In the essay Simmel (Wolff, 1950:402) observes that:

The stranger is thus being discussed here, not in the sense often touched upon in the past, as the wanderer who comes today and goes tomorrow, but rather as the person who comes today and stays tomorrow.

interaction with one another." Society is to be viewed as a configuration of individuals who are interacting with each other and who develop associations of some duration by maintaining a system of formal relationships.

In arguing that interaction is the life blood of society, Simmel rejects the notion of interaction as a psychological phenomenon. He argues that individual social behavior is dependent upon the element of sociation. *Sociation* is a sense of unity between and among interacting parties—an awareness which derives from the form which the interaction takes. Of course, each individual must experience the sense of sociation if the interaction is to be significant. Individual awareness is the one psychological element which Simmel incorporates into his interpretation of interactive behavior.

The psychological interpretation of interaction (Tenbruck, 1965: 66–74)[2] which Simmel rejects suggests that two individuals who are interacting with each other are involved in a series of relationships occurring between two action systems, each of which is the sum of drives, motives, goals, and all other psychological bases for action. Each individual influences the course of action of another so that each action on the part of one individual is preceded by action on the part of the other. If we let the action system of one individual be represented by a and the action system of another individual be represented by b, then interaction proceeds as follows: b changes to b' as or after a changes to a'. Interaction consists of two sequences: a, a', a'', a''' and b, b', b'', b'''. They are related in that each change in one sequence is determined by a change in the other sequence.

Simmel rejected this common view of interaction, not because it was wrong, but because it did not go far enough. The action systems, according to Simmel, are connected not only by the reciprocity of the two actions but also by an awareness or consciousness on the part of all participants of the relationship. This combination of reciprocity and awareness is sociation.

This special view of interaction is the central focus and most recurrent theme in Simmel's sociology. Interaction among individuals is characterized by unity, and unity is sociation. Simmel's sociation is the focus of investigation, and the forms of sociation are the objects of all scientific inquiry into the nature of society. In translating these views of society into a statement on social groups, we observe that, for Simmel, the nature of social groups can be studied and defined in terms of the forms of sociation which characterize interaction within their boundaries. Nicholas Spykman's (1925:27) interpretation of Simmel's concept of society includes the following definition of the social group:

> A social group consists, in the last analysis, in mental attitudes, or psychological occurrences within the minds of the individuals; but the fact that these attitudes and occurrences are the product of mutual determinations and reciprocal influences creates a dynamic functional relationship between the indi-

---

2. This explanation is based upon a description in F. H. Tenbruck, "Formal Sociology," in Georg Simmel et al., *Essays on Sociology, Philosophy and Aesthetics* (edited by Kurt H. Wolff).

viduals, and that dynamic functional relationship creates and is the unity of the group.

Accordingly, the unity of the social group is determined by the relationships between and among its members, and the study of the social group is directed toward the forms these relationships take.

FORM AND CONTENT

If there is a difficulty in understanding Simmel's view of form and content, it is not in his distinction between the two; although, sometimes Simmel discusses the same subject of investigation, at one point, as form, and, at another point, as content. The distinction is relatively simple: content is not the object of sociological inquiry because it is too variable. Content is different for each relationship and, therefore, not subject to scientific scrutiny. Through his writings, Simmel urges students of the discipline to reject content as their object of study because there is no realistic way in which one can generalize from it.[3]

The difficulty lies in understanding what Simmel meant by forms of sociation. *Social forms* are clusters of elements, abstracted from human interaction, which describe the structure or process characteristic of a given relationship regardless of its content.

Simmel wanted an object of scientific study which was not limited by the personal concerns of individuals or by the substance (content) of the interaction. Simmel wanted an object of study which transcended the immediate interests and expectations which individuals have when they associate with one another in groups. The concept of form eliminates the particulars of any given relationship by describing the way in which individuals interact. The use of form as the object of scientific inquiry frees the investigator from the limitations which the analysis of content or the interpretation of a particular situation places upon him. Donald Levine (1965b:23–24) remarks that:

> This peculiarity of Simmel's writings may be understood in the light of his emphasis on the concept of *form*, which makes the object of his sociological inquiry something that must be abstracted from any given phenomenon or situation.

Simmel would not have been concerned with investigations into particular topics such as the *apartheid* system in Africa or the religious

---

3. Simmel did not intend that these two parts of human associations be considered separate and distinct. Form actually develops from content. Form is that which we abstract from content.

implications of cults. These would have limited him to a specific system and to a specific type of religious organization. Simmel would have been interested in discovering if the *apartheid* system and cult organizations exhibited any specific form or forms in common.

Simmel's method is useful (1) because it allows us to identify the process which characterizes a group relationship even though the content of that relationship may change constantly; for example, in describing the form of family interaction as cooperation, one is able to observe family activity in different settings—at dinner, at play, as a learning environment for the young, and so on; and (2) because by investigating the forms of interaction, two or more groups can be compared and contrasted even though the content of their relationships is by no means of the same order. The large corporation and the family mentioned above are by no means similar in content or in terms of the interests, goals, and expectations of the individuals functioning within each system. However, the form which characterizes both may be the same—that is, superordination—subordination.

Two forms of sociation have been identified in the paragraph immediately above. Simmel identified and discussed a great many others. Let us consider the kinds of processes or structural elements to which the concept of form refers. Since our purpose here is to understand the concept of form and, eventually, to use the concept as a factor in small group analysis, we will present a selected list of forms which are relevant to our present interests. The list will include some forms of sociation with which we are familiar, at least in a general way. Among Simmel's forms of sociation[4] are the following:

Cooperation	Contracts
Competition	Conflict
Imitation	Gratitude
Superiority and Subordination	Conversation
The Division of Labor	The Rendezvous
Partisanship	Mediation
Personal Interdependence	Arbitration
Reconciliation	Nonpartisanship

---

4. Some of these forms are recognizable in more recent sociological analyses as *social processes*. It would appear that the only real difference between the concepts of "form" and "social process" is a semantic one. Joseph H. Fichter identifies cooperation, accommodation, and assimilation as conjunctive positive processes, and conflict, contravention, and competition as disjunctive negative social processes. All these qualify as forms of sociation. See Joseph H. Fichter, *Sociology*, Chicago: The University of Chicago Press, 1957, p. 227.

The importance of these forms of sociation for the study of human interaction in small groups should be obvious. Simmel has described the types of structures or processes which overlay all small group interaction systems. For example, communication networks research (see Chapter Five) is based upon the assumption that cooperation among members and the spatial arrangements of the positions they occupy will influence the performance of tasks, especially in terms of efficiency and time required for the completion of a task. Similarly, the differences observed between primary and secondary small groups are structural differences, that is, differences in form. This last example is particularly relevant since structure elements are devoid of content as are Simmel's forms of sociation (see the section on qualitative aspects of formal and informal groups in Chapter Two). The reader will recall that cooperation was one characteristic of the primary group and contract one characteristic of the secondary group. Both these characteristics are, for Simmel, forms of sociation.

THE USE OF FORM IN SIMMEL'S MICROSOCIOLOGY

Formal sociology has been referred to as pure sociology because forms of sociation are without the specific limitations of content and are the factors in group interactions which force generalizations about the behavior of all social groups. Perhaps the most pure interpretations of group phenomena are to be found in Simmel's analyses of dyads and triads. In these constructions, based on the number of individuals interacting and their positional relationships to each other, Simmel has identified a number of social forms. These numerically based relationships are, for Simmel, forms in themselves, and the social processes which describe them may also be considered forms of sociation.

The selected forms (Levine, 1965a:97–115) and descriptions below have been abstracted from Simmel's writings[5] on the numerical relations of social forms. The selection was made with a view to maintaining continuity with material found in other chapters of this text. The descriptions are divided into two sections. The first section deals with Simmel's use of form in small group analysis. The second section deals with forms which describe quantitative relationships other than those found in the small group.

---

5. In organizing this material, the author used the following sources: Nicholas J. Spykman, *The Social Theory of Georg Simmel*. Chicago: The University of Chicago Press, 1925; and Kurt H. Wolff (ed.), *The Sociology of Georg Simmel*. New York: The Free Press, 1950.

SIMMEL'S USE OF FORM IN SMALL GROUP RELATIONS

Form: Isolation (as a sociological fact)

Group Type: The Individual (psychological interaction with group members)

Description:
- the interruption or periodic occurrence in a given relationship between two or more elements
- interaction between the isolated individual and the group (or society) in terms of:
  - remnants of past relations
  - anticipation of future contacts
  - nostalgia
  - rejection of the group or society
- the isolated individual remains as a group member in the minds of other group members
- the sense of isolation when in a crowd

Form: The Dyad

Group Type: Friendship groups
Monogamous marriage
Love relationships

Description:
- the simplest sociological formation
- the basic scheme for all more complex forms of numerical relations
- variation of members and motives does not change the form of the relation
- the preservation of secrets is a reality *only* between two individuals
- individuals and their relationship to each other are influenced by the imagination of death and, therefore, the loss of the relationship
- the relationship is characterized by affectivity and intimacy
- two-person interactions do not develop a structural identity beyond the awareness the two individuals have of each other[6]

Form: The Non-Partisan (in triads)

Group Types: Family counselor
Labor-management arbitrator

---

6. This characteristic of the dyad is an excellent example of contradictions in Simmel's writings. Groups, for Simmel, are sets of relationships which develop a unity beyond the simple relationships of individuals; a consciousness of the group as a whole. In many passages, Simmel refers to the two-person relationship as a social group. Yet, here, he appears to reject the notion that dyads are social groups since he characterizes the dyadic form as simply a confrontation of two members, without structural identity beyond that confrontation.

Mediator
All third-party intervention into two-party relationships

Description:
- a third party enhances the relationship between two other parties
- a third party produces agreement between the other two parties
- a third party eliminates elements of discord between two other parties
- a third party eliminates the emotional element (affectivity) between two other parties
- mediation requires third-party objectivity; arbitration does not
- a third party functions to perpetuate a two-party relationship
- the function of the nonpartisan third is to resolve conflicts and then to leave the relationship

Form:	The *Tertius Gaudens* (enjoying third)
Group Types:	Triadic relations in families, political groups, business associations and love relationships

Description:
- the *tertius gaudens* is based upon conflict between two of three elements
- characterized by threatened coalition formation (a disruption of a full three-party group relation due to the development of a subgroup)
- characterized by the unity of the weakest member with one of two equal members
- the coalition of one party with another may develop in order to offend or to deny an adversary
- competition for the favor of a third party will result in hostility of the competitors
- the *tertius* (third party) is always in a position of advantage (gain) derived from the relationship of the other parties to each other
- the *tertius'* advantage is lost when the other two parties unite

SIMMEL'S USE OF FORM IN NON-SMALL GROUP QUANTITATIVE RELATIONS

Form:	Numbers (as a basis for the organization of large social groups)
Group Types:	Large corporations All large systems
Description:	• differentiation of members and functions

- complex division of labor
- system interdependence through the approved presence of intermediaries
- high levels of specialization
- group unity results from high specialization and the identity of members with the large system

Form:	The Party
Group Types:	Small private gatherings (approximately fifteen) The "modern ball"

Description:	• the number of individuals which make a party is determined by:
	     • the host's relations to each of the guests
	     • the relations of guests to each other
	     • how individuals interpret the relationships
	 • parties of only a few individuals are characterized by mutual adaptation, intimacy, and relationships of value
	 • as the size of the party increases, adaptation, intimacy, and value decrease
	 • smaller-sized parties facilitate intellectual moods
	 • larger-sized parties facilitate sensuous moods
	 • parties are not characterized by the complete harmony of feelings found in small groups
	 • when unity becomes a relationship of duality (dualism) a party occurs
	 • parties involve a series or relations which are temporary and sporadic
	 • relations are superficial

If the analyses above appear fragmented, it is because the discussions of forms presented by Simmel are little more than fragments which he believed could not be organized or systematized until all the forms of sociation and their implications for human behavior were identified. Even so, the descriptions of small group forms have provided the field of small groups with a wealth of information upon which is built a significant part of the impressive body of research which exists today.

THE SYMBOLIC INTERACTIONISM OF GEORGE HERBERT MEAD

Under the combined influences of such luminaries as Charles Horton Cooley, John Dewey, Henry James, and Wilhelm Wundt, George Herbert

Mead developed a view of the individual as social and a view of the mind as a process having significant social qualities. In developing a symbolic interactionist approach to human behavior, Mead structured a conception of society and of human interaction based primarily upon man's ability to symbolize.

MIND, SELF AND SOCIETY

There are three major elements in Mead's sociology, or, more properly, his social psychology. They are: mind, self, and society.

Mind. Mead saw the human mind as a dynamic entity, as a process. The mind involves the ability of an individual to use symbols as representative of the object world. In using symbols, the mind is able to list a number of options for behaving toward the objects symbolized. This ability of the mind to consider more than one course of action, which Mead called "imaginative rehearsal," is essential to his interpretation of organized group life. Organized group life is possible because human beings can imaginatively think about different lines of action in any given situation. Once such a rehearsal takes place, the individual can then select from the list of alternatives the activity which is most appropriate to a given situation—activity which enhances group integration.

Mead was interested in the development of this mechanism in childhood. Arguing that organized social life is dependent upon the mind's use of symbols as the basis for imagination, Mead asserted that society, as a large collectivity of cooperating individuals, is dependent upon the ability of individuals to symbolize. Once a child is able to use the tools of social interaction (symbols and an understanding of the objects to which they refer), the child recognizes that self behavior forms the basis for determining the behavior of others. The child recognizes that if a specific behavior is directed toward another individual the other individual will behave in a specific way in return. The child, by mentally rehearsing a number of different actions for a given situation, recognizes that if certain actions of self are eliminated in a given situation, the elimination of certain actions from the behavior of others will result.

The very young child, having experienced positive responses from others under conditions in which the child behaved in a specific way, is likely to repeat that action or that kind of action in the future. Similarly, if the very young child elicits undesirable responses from others under conditions in which the child behaved in a specific way, the child is unlikely to repeat such activity in the future.

Life Notes

George Herbert Mead

Unlike Simmel, George Herbert Mead (1863–1931) was not a stranger in the academy. The great majority of his closest friends were colleagues with whom he enjoyed many hours of leisurely discussion about literary works and about the significant elements of social life. These close relationships undoubtedly influenced Mead in his development of a new approach to understanding human behavior.

Mead was born in South Hadley, Massachusetts.[7] In 1870, he moved to Oberlin, Ohio, with his family. His father, a Puritan minister named Hiram Mead, taught homeletics at the Oberlin Theological Seminary. His mother was Elizabeth Shorr Billings, who in later years became President of Mount Holyoke College. After the death of Hiram Mead, the family was forced to sell their home and to live in rented rooms. Though times were difficult, the family remained together and mutually supported each other, emotionally as well as financially.

Mead enrolled at Oberlin College and waited on tables at the college to earn money for his board. After completing the required course of study in 1883, he worked for the master's degree at Harvard College. Following graduate study in Germany[8] where he met Wilhelm Wundt, Mead, with the support of John Dewey, accepted an appointment to the faculty at the University of Michigan at Ann Arbor. There he met and became a close friend of Charles Horton Cooley. The influence of Cooley in Mead's thought is obvious to anyone even vaguely familiar with Mead's theory. In 1894, three years after his appointment to the Michigan faculty, Mead followed Dewey to the University of Chicago where he remained a member of the faculty until his death in 1931. Shortly before his death, Mead had accepted an invitation to join the faculty at Columbia University. During his long tenure at Chicago, two facets of Mead's academic manner became apparent. The first is that Mead's students were split down

---

7. The biographical data and statements about early influences are taken from David Wallace, "Reflections on the Education of George Herbert Mead," *American Journal of Sociology*, 72 (1967), pp. 396-408.
8. It has been suggested that "it is possible he may have listened to an already famous lecturer, Georg Simmel . . . ." See Lewis A. Coser, *Masters of Sociological Thought*. New York: Harcourt Brace Jovanovich, 1971, p. 343.

the middle on the value of his remarks. Some were obviously impressed with him, and others found him difficult to understand, much less accept.

However, Mead preferred to speak rather than write. Except for a very few articles of minor importance, Mead did not put down in writing his most important contributions to an understanding of human behavior. In this regard, it is interesting to note that *Mind, Self and Society* is a statement of Mead's social thought compiled and edited by his students after his death.[9]

Mead considered his approach to human behavior that of a social behaviorist. Today, his name is synonomous with symbolic interactionism, a term originally used by Herbert Blumer (1969:1), student and foremost interpreter of Mead's social thought. There are two schools of thought on symbolic interaction: the Chicago school led by Herbert Blumer, and the Iowa School led by Manford Kuhn (1964). The Iowa school is actually a departure from the Meadian tradition and emphasizes a methodological approach (empirical) different from that of Blumer.

---

9. Mead's important contributions to sociology are found in his *Mind, Self and Society* (Charles W. Morris, ed.). Chicago: University of Chicago Press, 1934. See also, Merritt H. Moore (ed.), *Movements of Thought in the 19th Century*. Chicago: University of Chicago Press, 1936; and Anselm Strauss (ed.), *George Herbert Mead on Social Psychology*. Chicago: University of Chicago Press, 1956.

A child, whom we shall call Helen, learns that selecting the act of extending both arms in the direction of one of her parents elicits a very warm, affectionate response from them. The parent response reinforces Helen's activity and the chances of Helen's repeating the act are greatly increased. If, however, Helen's act is seldom or never responded to positively, Helen will eventually eliminate that behavior from her list of alternatives.

Mead (1934:117−118) explained the mechanism of the mind by pointing out that the mind has a temporal quality which allows individuals to delay completing an act which has already begun. He argued that:

> ... the central nervous system provides a mechanism of implicit response which enables the individual to test out implicitly the various possible completions of an already initiated act in advance of the actual completion of the act.... The higher centers of the central nervous system are involved in ... making possible the interposition between stimulus and response in the simple stimulus-response arc, of a process of selecting one or another of a whole set of possible responses and combinations of responses to the given stimulus.

It is not usual to suggest that any one theory system is based upon one element in that system—an element upon which the entire system stands or falls. It is quite possible, in this case, that all of what Mead called social behaviorism is based upon his interpretation of the functioning of the mind. Without the ability of the individual to symbolize and to consider optional lines of activity, the realities of social life, as Mead saw them, would not be possible. Certainly, as we shall see, the self and society are not possible without Mead's definition of mind.

Self. Mead's position on the concept of self includes the unique ability of individuals to symbolically see themselves as objects. Mead's position is that individuals are capable of having images of themselves as others see them. The self-image originates in the internal definitions which individuals give to the responses of others. In other words, the behavior of another is given a certain meaning in the mind of the acting individual. The meaning given includes a statement of how the other has evaluated the actions of the individual. As a result, the individual develops a concept of himself based upon the interpretations he has given to the responses of the other.

The behavior of an individual B, is the result of that individual's interpretation of the behavior exhibited by individual A. That is, B has internalized and has given meaning to the behavior of A and has responded in terms of the meanings attributed to the behavior of A. If this is so, and if, in organized group situations, there is a sharing of the meanings symbols are said to elicit from interacting parties, then individual A is capable of responding to his own symbols. Individual A will be able to reflect upon his own activity, since the act selected is part of A's imaginative rehearsal, and eventually behave in a manner which A anticipates will fit the behavior of the other, B. In this way, the individual can secure a more positive self-concept since the individual is, by the above mechanism, controlling or limiting the responses of others. The mechanism is a manipulative one in which the behavior of B is, in one sense, determined by the behavior of A, whose behavior is selected as the best possible for eliciting a positive response from B. The reader should note that, in terms of interaction, while this is going on for A, the same mechanism is working for B.

We may conclude from the above comments that, for Mead, the individual as a social entity is constantly in search of means whereby the self-image will be enhanced. When we combine what we already know about the mind (its use of symbols as representations of the object world) and the self (the ability of the individual to view self as an object) two observations are appropriate. The first is that individuals are able to cooperate with each other to achieve the organization and continuity which social life requires. The second is that the individual performs in a manner which optimizes the chance for a positive self-image.

The most important element in Mead's interpretation of the self is the "generalized other." It is that part of the self which results from an individual's taking (internalizing) the attitudes of all other individuals in a social group. The process includes taking on four types of attitudes: (1) attitudes of other individuals to oneself, (2) attitudes of others toward one another, (3) attitudes of others and of self toward the complex of social activity in which the group is engaged, and (4) attitudes of the social group as a whole. When an individual is able to internalize this complex of individual and group attitudes for situations, we say that the development of a self is complete. Mead (1934:154) states that the ". . . organized community or social group which gives to the individual his unity of self may be called 'the generalized other.' The attitude of the generalized other is the attitude of the whole community." Generalized others may be friendship groups, sports teams, families, and all other groups in which individuals hold membership. The generalized other exists in the self in that it is the self which incorporates the complex of attitudes listed above.

Society. Society refers to the complex of patterns of interaction (communication) between and among a large number of individuals (Mead, 1934:253). But the very existence of society is dependent upon mind and self. Mead (1934:227) states: "Human society as we know it could not exist without minds and selves, since all its most characteristic features presuppose the possession of minds and selves by individual members . . . ." When we apply Mead's interpretations of mind and self to human behavior we recognize that society and group life are possible because individuals are able to see each other and to see themselves in terms of the meanings they give to the behavior which each presents to the other.

Recognizing that Mead insisted upon mind and self as prerequisites for social organization of any kind, we may list the following as elements of mind and self which are necessary for society and groups to exist. The two required elements of mind are: (1) the ability of the mind to use symbols as representative of the object world, and (2) the individual's ability to rehearse imaginatively. The self elements are: (1) the ability of the individual to view self as an object, and (2) the presence of the generalized other as part of the self. The above elements combine to form the basis of all social organization including groups as well as the larger society. In the last analysis, for Mead, society—and, at the smaller level of social organization, the group—is a collection of organized patterns of interaction which are controlled and determined by the ability of individuals to behave symbolically toward each other. It is, of course, always more difficult to understand interaction in terms of society simply because of the large size and complexity of the interaction systems which it includes. However, the significance of mind, self, and society is facilitated by applying the principles developed by Mead to the social group. In the arena of group interaction, Mead's thinking is more readily understood.

THE SOCIAL PSYCHOLOGY OF CHARLES HORTON COOLEY

The importance of Charles Horton Cooley's contributions to sociology and to the field of small groups cannot be overestimated. His conceptualizations of the primary group and of the self as a social phenomenon are classic. These have become major themes in the analysis of human behavior and in modern-day interpretations of small group behavior.

THE INDIVIDUAL AND SOCIETY

Charles Cooley's sociology is rooted in his all-embracing observation that the individual and the society are only different aspects of the very same thing. Cooley (1962:5) said: "Self and society are twin-born, we know one as immediately as we know the other, and the notion of a separate and independent ego is an illusion." He argued that the self is social in that it grows directly from the interactions individuals have with each other. Self-awareness is the result of a social process whereby the individual is able to make statements about self based upon an interpretation of the view of others. Cooley developed an interpretation of the individual and interaction similar to that of Mead. It is a view which stresses the interpretive ability of the individual and the individual's constant concern with the opinions and judgments of the self by other selves.

In order to explain the social nature of the self, Cooley developed his brilliant analogy of the looking-glass self. The reflected or looking-glass self has three elements: ". . . the imagination of our appearance to the other person, the imagination of his judgment of that appearance, and some sort of self-feeling, such as pride or mortification" (Cooley, 1964:184). Cooley is suggesting that we see ourselves not as identities separate from those others with whom we interact, but through our imaginations of how others see us and how we imagine they are judging us. Our response to these imaginings is an emotional one, a self-feeling. It is as though we are using the other and the other's behavior as reflections of

Life Notes

Charles Horton Cooley

Charles Horton Cooley (1864–1929) was born in Ann Arbor, Michigan, and seldom ventured beyond its limits and those of the University of Michigan. His father, Thomas McIntyre Cooley, moved from western New York to Michigan, hoping that by moving west he would have a better opportunity to advance himself educationally and to achieve some measure of worldly success. Born the son of a poor farmer, Thomas Cooley was both aggressive and high-achieving. His energies and ambitions were major forces in his becoming a lawyer, college professor, and, finally, a member of the Michigan Supreme Court.

Thomas Cooley had six children. His son, Charles, in ill health throughout most of his childhood and adolescence, developed an early and continuing interest in reading. Cooley was a solitary reader, serious thinker, and daydreamer (Coser, 1971:314). Sociologist Robert C. Angell (Reiss, 1968:1–2), Cooley's nephew, has remarked:

> If Cooley had been a man of action, it would be appropriate to describe in some detail his personal strengths and weaknesses, his ways of playing his roles, his favorite strategies. But he was not a man of action. He was a thinker. Ideas were his instruments, understanding his goal.

Cooley received his doctoral degree from the University of Michigan in 1894. He began his teaching career there two years earlier, remaining a member of its faculty until his death. Cooley's life was the quiet life of scholarly introspection, and his position at the university and in Ann Arbor was a comfortable one. He had no wish to leave the security of his birthplace and refused an offer to join the faculty at Columbia University.

Cooley produced three volumes which showcase his sociological thought: *Human Nature and the Social Order* (1902), *Social Organization* (1909), and *Social Process* (1918). These works reflect his introspection and, more importantly, his need to understand the self and the social world.

115

our own behavior. What we see through our imaginings produces, in Cooley's terms, pride or mortification. Human interaction from the perspective of the looking-glass self is a reciprocation of the imaginings which people have of each other. In this sense the group, as a complex of interaction, is a collection of the imaginings of the participating members and a complex of behavior based upon those imaginings.

In identifying the self as a social fact, Cooley identified the imaginings we have of each other as the solid facts of society. This kind of thinking suggests that Cooley did not want to separate the individual from the social environments to which that individual is exposed. Society and self are, as noted earlier, "twin-born" and exist in the collective imaginings of interacting individuals.

Let us attempt to develop the theme of imaginings from the individual through the social group to the larger society. We already know that the self is the product of our imaginings. In his book, *Human Nature and the Social Order*, Cooley (1964:209) also uses the concept of self to refer to collections of individuals who form groups: "Group self or 'we' is simply an 'I,' which includes other persons." Here Cooley adds other persons to the self and suggests that the group is a psychological fact in that it is the combination of imaginings about oneself and about others in the mind of each individual member. Once he developed the idea that the individual and society are united and function as one in the mind, Cooley (Angell, 1968:10) searched for some mode of analysis which would serve as a connecting link between the two: "It is somewhat ironic that the substantive concept for which he is best known, the primary group, was developed in the attempt to bridge a large gap in his previous thought." (See Chapter Two for an extended analysis of the primary group concept.) If we move upward to the level of society, we find that approaching society either from Cooley's perspective of society as a collection of individuals or from the view that society is a collection of groups of individuals, it is the sum of the imaginings of all its members. Cooley (1964:119) defines society as: ". . . a relation among personal ideas. In order to have society it is evidently necessary that persons should get together somewhere; and they get together only as personal ideas in the mind. Where else?"

---

summary

This chapter presents the theoretical origins of small group analysis and research. A brief biographical sketch of each major theorist, Georg Simmel, George Herbert Mead, and Charles Horton Cooley, entitled *Life*

Notes, was included to make these men more human and to suggest how their lives influenced the development of their social thought.

Georg Simmel, the father of Formal Sociology, presents a view of society which includes the relationships which exist between and among individuals behaving within its boundaries. For Simmel, society is a complex of relationships established among individuals in constant interaction with one another. Society, argued Simmel, is dependent upon the element of sociation: a sense of unity between and among interacting parties, an awareness which derives from the form which the interaction takes. Although Simmel concentrated upon the social elements as important to human behavior, he identified individual awareness as the one psychological element necessary for a full understanding of human social behavior.

Simmel presents a view of interaction which includes the qualities of reciprocity and consciousness. In effect, Simmel argued that individuals must be conscious of the unity which develops within a relationship and, most especially, of the form which the relationship takes.

The object of scientific inquiry into human interaction is the form of social relationships. *Social forms* are clusters of elements abstracted from human interaction which describe the structure (or process) characteristic of a given relationship regardless of its content. By concentrating on the form taken in a relationship, Simmel eliminates the study of content from sociological investigations. The concept of form may be viewed as a fair equivalent of social processes such as cooperation, competition, superordination-subordination, conflict, and arbitration.

In Simmel's discussions of numerical relations he suggests the concept of form as a means of identifying the sociological characteristics present in isolation, in the dyad, and in various types of triadic relationships. For Simmel, the size of the group defines the unity and consciousness of group members. One interesting form of interaction, the party, was also discussed as an example of the variety of human interaction types included in Simmel's interpretations.

The most important elements in the writings of George Herbert Mead which are important to understanding the group phenomenon are found in *Mind, Self and Society*. It was noted that society, according to Mead, was not possible without the self, and neither society nor self were possible without mind. Mead's mind concept is seen as a dynamic entity, a process in itself. The mind involves the ability to symbolize and to list options for behavior choices (imaginative rehearsal). These mental abilities are necessary for organized group life.

The self concept in Mead includes the ability of individuals to see themselves symbolically, that is, the self is capable of having images of self as others view that self. These self/other views originate in the internal definitions individuals give to the responses of others.

The self incorporates the concept of the generalized other. It is that part of the self which allows an individual to internalize the attitudes of others with whom he is interacting. This self process includes: (1) attitudes of other individuals to oneself, (2) attitudes of other individuals toward one another, (3) attitudes of others and of self toward the complex of group activity, and (4) attitudes of the social group as a whole. Self development is complete when internalization of the generalized other occurs.

Mead saw society as a complex of patterns of communication among a large number of individuals. In the last analysis, however, society is possible because individuals are able to see each other and to see themselves in terms of the meanings they give to the behavior present in interaction systems.

When the concepts of mind and self are combined as basic referents for society, the following become prerequisites for society to exist: (1) the ability of the mind to use symbols as representations of the objective world, (2) the ability to rehearse imaginatively how one is going to act, (3) the ability of the individual to view himself as the object of others' behavior, and (4) the presence of the generalized other as part of the self. In summary, society and, therefore, groups may be defined as collections of organized patterns of interaction which are controlled and determined by the ability of individuals to behave symbolically toward each other.

The social psychology of Charles Horton Cooley originates in the view that the individual and society are only different aspects of the same thing. "Self and society are twin-born . . . ." Cooley's explanation of the social nature of the self was developed in a discussion of the concept of the looking-glass self. Using the imagination of an individual as the basis for self-definition, Cooley identified three elements of the self: (1) the imagination of our appearance to the other, (2) the imagination of others' judgment of that appearance, and (3) some sort of self-feeling, such as pride or mortification. From this perspective, human interaction is a combination of the imaginings which people have of each other. The group is a complex of interaction composed of a collection of the imaginings of the participants and a complex of behavior upon which they are based. In the last analysis, the imaginings we have of each other are the solid facts of society.

discussion questions

1. Why does Simmel reject the psychological interpretation of human interaction?
2. Is the individual important to Simmel's view of society?
3. Explain Mead's view of mind, of self, of society.
4. Are Simmel and Mead in agreement on the most basic elements of society?
5. What does Cooley mean by his observation that the self is a social fact?
6. Using the concept of the looking-glass self, describe the teacher-student relationship.

references

Angell, Robert C. "Introduction," in Albert J. Reiss, Jr. (ed.). *Cooley and Sociological Analysis*. Ann Arbor, Michigan: The University of Michigan Press, 1968.

Blumer, Herbert. *Symbolic Interactionism: Perspective and Method.* Englewood Cliffs, New Jersey: Prentice-Hall, 1969.

Cooley, Charles Horton. *Social Organization: A Study of the Larger Mind.* New York: Shocken, 1962.

—————————. *Human Nature and the Social Order.* New York: Shocken, 1964.

Coser, Lewis A. (ed.). *Georg Simmel.* Englewood Cliffs, New Jersey: Prentice-Hall, 1965.

Coser, Lewis A. *Masters of Sociological Thought.* New York: Harcourt Brace Jovanovich, Inc., 1971.

Fichter, Joseph H. *Sociology.* Chicago: The University of Chicago Press, 1971.

Hare, A. Paul. *Handbook of Small Group Research*, 2nd ed.; New York: The Free Press, 1976.

Hare, A. Paul; Borgatta, Edward F.; and **Bales, Robert F.** *Small Groups: Studies in Social Interaction.* New York: Alfred A. Knopf, 1965.

Homans, George C. *The Human Group.* New York: Harcourt, Brace and World, 1950.

Kuhn, Manford H. "Major Trends in Symbolic Interactionist Theory in the Past Twenty-five Years." *The Sociological Quarterly*, 5 (1964): 61–84.

Laurence, Alfred E. "Georg Simmel: Triumph and Tragedy," *International Journal of Contemporary Sociology*, 12 (1975): 33–47.

Levine, Donald N. "Some Key Problems in Simmel's Works," in Donald Coser (ed.). *Georg Simmel*. Englewood Cliffs, New Jersey: Prentice-Hall, 1965a.

——————. "The Structure of Simmel's Social Thought," in Georg Simmel, et al. Trans. and ed. by Kurt H. Wolff. *Essays on Sociology, Philosophy and Aesthetics*. New York: Harper & Row, 1965b.

Mead, George Herbert. *Mind, Self and Society*. Edited by Charles W. Morris. Chicago: The University of Chicago Press, 1934.

Moore, Merritt H. (ed.) *Movements of Thought in the 19th Century*. Chicago: The University of Chicago Press, 1936.

Reiss, Jr., Albert J. (ed.) *Cooley and Sociological Analysis*. Ann Arbor, Michigan: The University of Michigan Press, 1968.

Spykman, Nicholas J. *The Social Theory of Georg Simmel*. Chicago: The University of Chicago Press, 1925.

Strauss, Anselm (ed.). *George Herbert Mead on Social Psychology*. Chicago: The University of Chicago Press, 1956.

Tenbruck, F. H. "Formal Sociology," in Georg Simmel, et al. Trans. and ed. by Kurt H. Wolff. *Essays on Sociology, Philosophy and Aesthetics*. New York: Harper & Row, 1965.

Wallace, David. "Reflections on the Education of George Herbert Mead," *American Journal of Sociology*, 72 (1967): 396–408.

Wolff, Kurt H. (Trans. and ed.). *The Sociology of Georg Simmel*. New York: The Free Press, 1950.

Chapter Five
Interaction Models

Sociologists have been prodigious in their attempts to explain human behavior. The amount of material, both theoretical and empirical, is vast and has spawned numerous subareas of even more intense and microscopic investigation. Such is the case with the study of small groups. The amount of information about small groups, especially in the form of research studies over the last twenty-five years, has been enormous. A. Paul Hare's *Handbook of Small Group Research* (1976) is a recent summary of the major findings in small group research. He reviews the literature on small groups through 1974 by presenting summaries of small group theory and research as well as a complete bibliography of small group research studies. The *Handbook* also places the research into general categories (Group Process and Structure, Interaction Variables, and Performance Characteristics) suggesting a serious and worthwhile attempt at organizing existing research in order to make some sense out of it.

Another way in which we try to make sense out of the research is to construct models which facilitate understanding and which function as pegboards upon which we can hang a number of seemingly unrelated pieces of knowledge in a fairly well-organized and meaningful way. *Model construction* is simply a device for putting information together in a manner which helps us to understand the relationships between and among the elements under investigation. Fortunately, sociologists are avid model builders, and sociologists concerned with small group phenomena are no exception.

The models presented in this chapter have been selected with an eye to variety, interest, and simplicity. There are many other models for organizing small group research, to be sure, and some students will discover these on their own. For those who will not, the models included here are representative and, most importantly, are models which have gained some measure of acceptance in the field.

Why should we concern ourselves with models? We do so (1) to provide the student of small groups with an orderly means for learning about the subject and (2) to familiarize the student with some of the ways in which sociologists like to organize their material. Every individual who has studied small groups seriously has constructed a small groups model or has, at least, a way of thinking about small groups. However, there are some models which stand out from the rest and which appear, from the interactionist's point of view, to merit serious consideration by all students of the discipline.

The models presented here have either withstood the test of time or suggest fresh and interesting approaches to the subject matter. They all focus upon the interaction components of group behavior, as all serious models must, and they all suggest the importance of the communication element in human group behavior. These common grounds do not, however, suggest total consensus or single-mindedness in approaches to the study of human behavior. The Johari model, for example, is framed as an effective model for use in Interpersonal Dynamics and offers a sociopsychological basis for understanding the self in a social milieu. The Newcomb model suggests a frame of reference which is best utilized in sociological research, and which affords a concrete, practical means of organizing and interpreting small group interaction.

The Bavelas model concentrates on the resolution of group tasks and group problem solving. It is important not only because it focuses upon these important areas of group activities, but also because it is a precursor of the new and productive researches into Social Networks. The Homans model is unique in that it crosses the boundaries of numerous disciplines. Although the focus is ideally suited to the interactionist's approach to small groups, it suggests guidelines for understanding human social behavior which are drawn from the fields of economics, psychology, and sociology. The Intra-group Conflict model views the social group as a complex structure moving through continuous conflict situations in order to achieve group goals.

JOSEPH LUFT'S JOHARI AWARENESS MODEL

Considering the importance placed upon (1) the interactive forms taken in a communication framework (cooperation, conflict, competition, and so on) and (2) the meanings which those communicating wish to transmit to each other, the Johari model (Luft, 1969) is, unquestionably, one of the most useful tools for analyzing human interaction as a total communication. By *total communication* we mean the process of transmitting meanings and intentions through the use of verbal, gestural, facial, and other external communication modes.

The Johari model brings together the concepts of the social self and the social other in an interaction setting. It includes the ingredients of transmission, meanings, feelings, attitudes, and behavioral definitions. Such ingredients suggest that the structure of interactive relationships is sociopsychological. The incorporation of such elements as feelings and attitudes suggests a concern for the individual as a functioning unit without destroying the significance of the group as a collectivity. In fact, the model is an ideal construction for understanding the social and psychological implications of dyads and triads.

If there is a flaw in using this model in small group analysis, it is precisely that such a model is not readily applicable to small groups of all sizes. The emphasis upon the individual and the concern with awareness of the total effect of individuals upon each other becomes less meaningful as small groups increase in size. Actually, this is not so much a flaw in Luft's construction as it is simply a limitation upon its use.

According to Luft, the total person, the self, is represented by quadrants. (See Figure 5-1.) These four parts of the individual identify the individual's behavior, feelings, and motivation in the interaction situation. Each quadrant indicates the degree to which behavior, feelings, and motivation is known to the self and the degree to which these elements are known to others. The quadrants are:

1. The *open* quadrant which refers to behavior, feelings, and motivation known to self and to others.
2. The *blind* quadrant which refers to behavior, feelings, and motivation known to others but not to self.
3. The *hidden* quadrant which refers to behavior, feelings, and motivation known to self but not to others.
4. The *unknown* quadrant which refers to behavior, feelings, and motivation known neither to self nor to others.

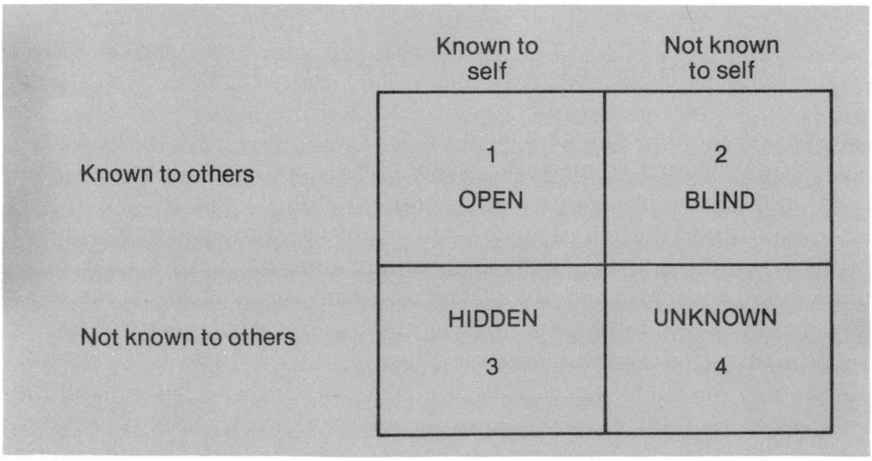

	Known to self	Not known to self
Known to others	1 OPEN	2 BLIND
Not known to others	HIDDEN 3	UNKNOWN 4

Figure 5-1. The Johari Awareness Model (Johari Window)

From *Of Human Interaction* by Joseph Luft. By permission of Mayfield Publishing Company. Copyright © 1969 by The National Press.

According to Luft (1969:6–8) the Johari window has a number of important qualities:

1. Awareness and consciousness are uniquely human attributes.
2. Intrapersonal and interpersonal affairs are inextricably united.
3. The model is essentially content-free.
4. The constructs implicit in each of the quadrants lend themselves to verification.
5. The model can be applied to any human interaction.
6. The model is sufficiently uncomplicated so that it is readily used.
7. The processes inherent in the model guide the reader to important characteristics of human interaction.

We mentioned earlier that the model is particularly useful in groups of very small size. The intensity of interaction in the dyad, for example, is often more difficult to deal with and to understand because, in a relationship between two individuals, the meanings, intentions, and motivations are often private or implied. This is true, most particularly, in dyadic relationships of long duration. The Johari model affords an analytical basis for probing and dissecting such interactions. Hopefully the discussion below will make this point clear.

The relative size of each of the quadrants changes as one interacts with various others and as one interacts with the same other over periods of time in which the individuals' perceptions of each other change. These relationships produce a window, the configuration of which is constantly in flux. We will attempt to express the changing quality of the window through a series of diagrams (Figures 5-2, 5-3, and 5-4) and at the same time integrate some of the information already discussed on small group types.

The language is different, but the implications in terms of group interaction are the same in the Johari Awareness model as in the primary group concept of Charles H. Cooley. (See Chapter Two.) According to the Awareness model, a relationship which is characteristically open involves a large amount of sharing between or among the interacting individuals. Increasing the size of the open quadrant (see Figure 5-2) results in a decrease in the size of the hidden quadrant. Recognizing that all the quadrants are influenced by changes in any one of them we shall, at this point, refrain from complicating the issue by concentrating on the within-self effects between the open and hidden quadrants. Between two individuals who are open to each other as in a long-established friendship, or between spouses, or in a parent-child relationship, the configuration in Figure 5-2 is a realistic possibility.

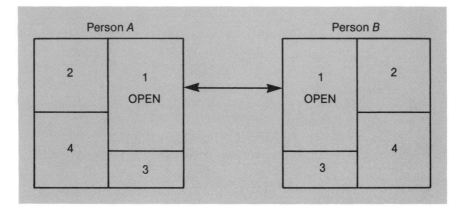

Figure 5-2.   Enlarged Open Quadrant —Primary Relationships

This kind of open relationship is strongly suggestive of relationships which we call primary in type. Being open to others and having the others reciprocate in kind indicates a willingness on the part of both individuals to tell each other much more about themselves than those same individuals might in other kinds of relationships. Being open to others also suggests an intensity of feeling and a desire to share, symbolically, meanings ordinarily kept from the scrutiny of others.

If we move to the opposite end of the primary-secondary continuum, the size of the open quadrant is significantly reduced. (See Figure 5-3.) Being less open to others and having others reciprocate in kind indicates, in this case, a wish to interact within a severely limited area and to use only that information about each other which is absolutely necessary for achieving the limited goals of a secondary relationship. Being less open to others also suggests an absence of self-feeling and little desire to share, symbolically, meanings other than those defined by the relationships. Business relationships and small group relationships within large organizational systems such as the military are examples of the secondary relationtion suggested by a window in which the size of the open quadrant is relatively small.

One question on the applicability of the Johari Awareness model to primary and secondary group types is appropriate here. It is logical to assume that the size of the open quadrant changes in direct relation to where the given relationship is on the continuum of primary and secondary relationships. (See Figure 5-4.)

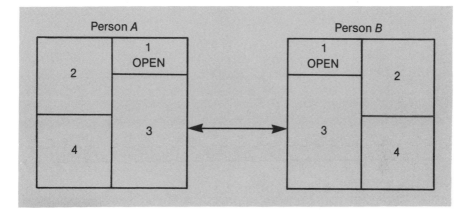

Figure 5-3.   Small Open Quadrant — Secondary Relationships

As mentioned earlier, the applicability of the Johari Awareness model is somewhat limited by the size of the group in which interaction occurs. However, Luft has used the model not only as the basis for understanding groups of very small size, but also as a basic model for intergroup relationships, in psychodrama where the therapy aspects of Quadrants 2 and 4 are best utilized, as a model for the participant-observer, and as a basis for understanding the leadership factors in group interaction.

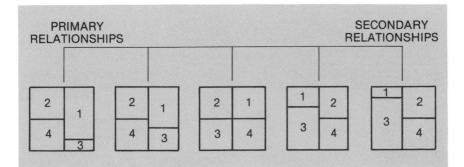

Figure 5-4.   Primary-Secondary Continuum and Size of Open Quadrant

THEODORE M. NEWCOMB'S COMMUNICATIVE ACTS MODEL

Theodore Newcomb based the construction of his communicative acts model (1953:393–404) on the possibility that human social interaction can be studied in terms which the author calls communicative acts. His assumption (1953:393) is ". . . that communication among humans performs the essential function of enabling two or more individuals to maintain simultaneous orientation toward one another as communicators *and* toward objects of communication."

The reader should note, at this point, that "orientation" and "attitude" are equivalents. The *communicative act* is a transmission of information which includes discriminative stimuli from one individual (point of origin) to another (a recipient). The basic model includes three elements: (1) A: an individual transmitting information; (2) B: the recipient of the transmission; and (3) X: the object of the communication. The initial activity in the model is symbolized as A to B re X. Accordingly, Newcomb (1953:393–394) suggests that the minimal components of the A-B-X system are:

1. A's orientation toward X, including both attitude toward X as an object to be approached or avoided and cognitive attributes including beliefs and cognitive structuring.
2. A's orientation toward B, in exactly the same sense. For purposes of avoiding confusing terms, we shall speak of positive and negative *attraction* toward A or B as persons, and of favorable and unfavorable *attitudes* toward X.
3. B's orientation toward X.
4. B's orientation toward A.

The system is designed to fit two-person communication systems, but the elements built into this simple structure are easily adapted to larger-sized small groups. For example, four individuals (A, B, C, D) in a group communicate with each other and about some object (X) in exactly the same manner as does a dyad. The only differences observed would be in the degree of intensity with which each individual views the others and the object of orientation and, of course, the degree of complexity in the interaction within the group setting. The four-person group, as a complex of communicative acts, would appear as shown in Figure 5-5.

Regardless of the group size and the attendant interaction complex to which this model is applied, Newcomb (1953:395) suggests that his model carries the following implications:

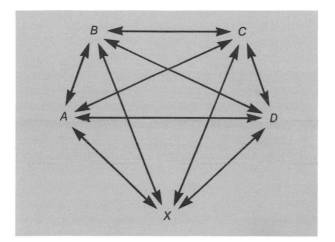

Figure 5-5. The A-B-C-D-X System (Four-Person Group)

. . . that while at any given moment the system may be conceived of as being "at rest," it is characterized not by the absence but by the balance of forces; and that a change in any part of the system . . . may lead to changes in any of the other.

Newcomb's initial concerns about the A-B-X system had to do with the symmetry of orientation in the A to B communication system. He assumes that to the degree that the orientation of A to the object, X, is dependent upon B's orientation to the same object, A's co-orientation to B and to X will be facilitated by the similarity of A and B's orientations to X. The utility of symmetry in the orientations of A and B is suggested by the notion that if A and B have symmetry in their orientations toward X, there is less need for either A or B to have to translate X in terms of the orientation of the other, thus reducing the chance of error in the translations. This assumption requires some translation on our part. What Newcomb is suggesting is that the greater the common meanings between A and B about X, the more effective, or successful, the interaction between A and B about X. Satisfaction (rewards) in the relationship between A and B are more likely when the orientations in the A-B-X system are symmetrical.

Perfect symmetry, of course, is another way of referring to the utopia of human interaction in which the perceptions of individuals about each other and about the object of their relationship are in complete agreement. The questions arises: What can be said about relationships which are asymmetrical? Newcomb presents a schematic illustration of asymmetrical orientation in the *A-B-X* system (Figure 5-6) in which *A* can select any of a number of possible solutions. These solutions range from attempting to achieve symmetry with regard to *X* by influencing *B* toward the orientation of *A* to tolerating the lack of symmetry.

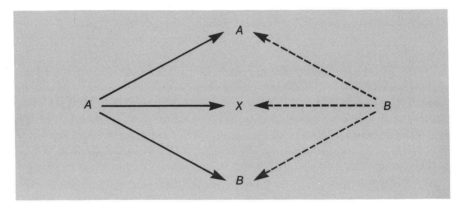

Figure 5-6.   Schematic Illustration of *A*'s Phenomenal *A-B-X* System

The *A* and *B* at either side represent persons as communicators; the *A* and *B* in the center represent the same persons as objects of co-orientation. The broken lines represent *A*'s judgments of *B*'s orientations.

Reprinted from Theodore M. Newcomb, "An Approach to the Study of Communicative Acts," *The Psychological Review*, 60(1953): 393-404. Copyright © 1953 by The American Psychological Association.

In contrast to the Johari Awareness model, Newcomb's model is a strictly sociological system of interaction where the focus is upon the sets of relationships between and among individuals and the objects of their concern. In this sense, the model suggests that human interaction, the communication between *A* and *B*, does not exist in a vacuum but develops and continues within an environment—objects of orientation (*X*)—which ultimately influences the behavior of all members of the social group.

Let us return to the central theme of Newcomb's model—symmetry of orientation. The more consistent the interacting parties are in their co-orientations toward X and toward each other, the greater the chance of success in the communication since there is a corresponding reduction in the need to explain each other's orientation. The need to explain orientations to each other increases the chance of error and possibly failure in the communication. Newcomb's position is a logical one, for it suggests that the presence of common meanings between or among interacting parties as to the object of their orientations increases the chance of successful communication. For example, considering the changing character of sex roles in our society, two women who have been socialized to have career expectations as well as the more traditional female roles will be able to discuss future career choice possibilities (X) with some expectation of consensus about X. In this case, there is no need to explain or translate attitudes (orientations) since common meanings already prevail because of similar early socialization. Similarly, two siblings need not explain in-family activity to each other and can communicate with each other about in-family activity with a storehouse of common meanings derived from socialization within that family. If the same object of orientation is the subject of communication between one of the siblings and a friend, the need for explanation is obvious and the chance of communication difficulty is increased.

The A-B-X system is an excellent model for understanding one relationship which is, at least by implication, a part of most group associations—the helping relationship. The *helping relationship* is defined as one in which a help agent (A) intervenes between a person (B) and that person's problem (X). The individual (B) who may be described in terms of need is one whose present behavior is noticeably different from behavior in past experience. The behavior change is the result of that individual's inability to cope with a problem. The help agent is an individual who intervenes between the other person and that person's problem, the goal of the intervention being a significant reduction or elimination of the problem. The problem may be any circumstance which adversely affects an individual's behavior.

Helping as a form of association is part of both formal and informal group structures. Formally structured relationships, such as those between patients and members of the medical profession, are clearly help-oriented. These include relationships between patients and doctors, nurses, and other personnel who are qualified to alleviate physical and mental problems. The social work profession must be similarly defined. The environment of poverty, for example, often results in problems which, without the help of a professional, become unsolvable. Priests, ministers, and rabbis are all help agents. Members of organized religions often look to these religious functionaries for aid in coping with the stress and guilt which can result from identity with a moral code.

Family systems and friendship systems are constructed upon the principle of support, and it is within such support systems that helping is found. In these informal relationships, helping is an integral part of the larger systems of relationships. The parent-child relationship includes high expectations for helping, as do friendship associations. If there is a point of differentiation between helping in formal and informal associations, it centers around the rewards which helpers in these systems expect. Formal help-oriented relationships carry expectations of profit, whereas in informal systems of help, the rewards which accrue to the help agent are more likely to be associated with the sense of satisfaction one receives from knowing that a relative or friend has been helped.

If the principles of the A-B-X system are applied to the helping relationship, one important consideration emerges. The problem as an object of orientation of both A and B can be understood and coped with most effectively if both A and B are able to develop a symmetrical orientation to it. The medical profession offers an example of the importance of symmetrical orientations to a problem. Illness is viewed by the patient in highly personal terms, but, although concern for the patient on the part of the medical practitioner may be present in treatment, the practitioner may not view the problem in the same way as does the patient. The disparity between the personal perspective of the patient and the impersonal perspective of the practitioner may seriously retard treatment; however, if the practitioner is able to develop an empathetic understanding of the problem as well as of the patient's orientation to the problem, treatment can be enhanced.

The professional role of the nurse, for example, has in more recent years included expectations which refer not only to medical aid procedures but also to consideration of the patient as an individual who must cope and who needs understanding while treatment is ongoing. Nursing colleges are at the forefront of the medical profession in attempting to deal with the role of the medical practitioner in terms of orientations to the patient as well as to the patient's illness. In terms of the A-B-X model, these attempts should result in greater symmetry of orientation to the illness (X) and, hopefully, more effective treatment. There is one difficulty attendant upon the achievement of symmetry of orientation between medical practitioner and patient. The recognition of the patient and the patient's problem in patient terms may result in the development of a relationship between patient and practitioner based upon personal qualities and not medical considerations. It would appear, however, that the effectiveness of treatment which results from practitioner-patient symmetry of orientation to an illness is worth the risk. Serious practitioners are aware of the problems attendant upon establishing primary-like relationships with patients and are usually able to guard against them.

THE COMMUNICATION NETWORK MODEL

There has been considerable activity in communication networks investigation since 1948, when Alex Bavelas (1948) published his research on communication and group structures, and since 1950, when he published material on communication in task-oriented groups. The term, *communication network*, refers to the arrangement of lines of communication which are open between and among members of groups. The specified interests of researchers who are interested in communication networks revolve around leadership emergence, group problem-solving, and group efficiency in production. The research method for studying communication networks includes designing networks in which the lines of communication vary from networks of total and free communication of all group members to networks in which communication lines are restricted both in terms of availability of members to each other and frequency of communication. The network structures produced from the investigations of Bavelas and others (see Figure 5-7) range from the simple wheel $\bigwedge$ and three-person comcon (completely connected) $\bigtriangleup$ to the complex comcon φ and circle $\star$.

The basic argument centers around the assumption that certain established systems of communication channeling are more efficient than others depending upon the goals for which groups are organized. For example, Alex Bavelas was interested in discovering if certain patterns of communication are best suited for specific group tasks. In developing the relation between communication pattern (network) and group task, Bavelas suggested some stable five-person communication networks for task completion including the circle, two types of wheels, and a straight line network in which individuals occupying end positions communicate with only one other member in the network. He argued that the efficient completion of a task is determined not only by the nature of the task and the individuals selected but also by the patterns of communication established for effective interaction.

To include, in this chapter, more than a sampling of the results which laboratory investigations on communication networks have produced

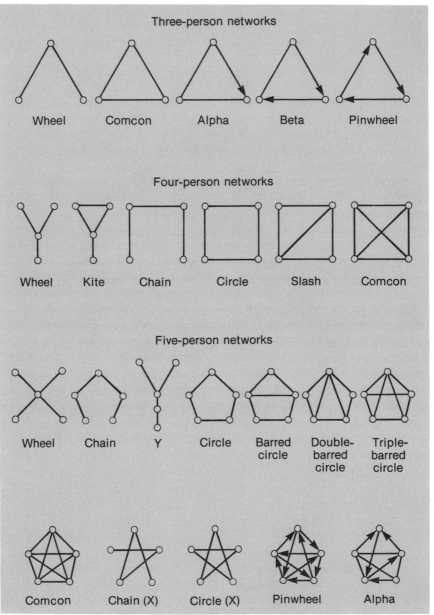

Figure 5-7. Experimental Communication Networks

Communication networks used in experimental investigations. Dots represent positions, lines represent communication channels, and arrows indicate one-way channels.

From Marvin E. Shaw, "Communication Networks," in Leonard Berkowitz, *Advances in Experimental Social Psychology*, Volume 1. New York: Academic Press, 1964, p. 113. Reprinted by permission of Academic Press, © 1964.

would be unrealistic. The following are presented to give the reader some familiarity with the final product of communication networks investigations.

Researcher	H. J. Leavitt (1951:38–50)
Subject	Some effects of certain communication patterns on group performance.
Networks used	Circle, Chain, Wheel, Y. All 5-man networks.
Question	Do different group networks affect group performance?
Task	To identify the symbol all members had in common after each had been given a list of symbols.
Results	Greatest to least agreement as to who functioned as the group leader occurred in ranking the structures in the following order: Wheel, Y, Chain, Circle. Please note that the ordering represents one position from most centralized to least centralized.
	The most centralized position in each structure sent the greatest number of messages while the least centralized position sent the least number of messages.

Researcher	Marvin E. Shaw (1954:211–217)
Subject	Some effects of problem complexity upon problem solution efficiency in different communication nets.
Networks used	Wheel, Circle. Both 3-person networks.
Question	Do communication networks having equal positions (circle) require less time to solve relatively complex problems but more time to solve relatively simple problems than do communication nets having a central position (wheel)?
Tasks	To solve four problems, simple and complex. The two kinds of problems used were the following.
	Simple. Each group member was given cards containing a series of letters. Each group member received one of the cards containing the common letter. The group members were told that at least one card in their possession contained the common letter. The test ended when each group member knew the common letter (E). The following items of information were given each group member:

(1) E A D H
(2) X K L O
(3) J M B E
(4) P U W F
(5) G R E T
(6) N Q S C

Complex. How many trucks are needed for a small company to move four kinds of equipment (chairs, desks, filing cabinets, and typewriters)? The information necessary to answer this question is as follows: the company owns 12 desks, 48 chairs, 12 typewriters, and 15 filing cabinets. One truck can hold 12 typewriters, or 3 desks, or 5 filing cabinets, or 24 chairs. Each group member was given one card stating the problem, and the information necessary to solve the problem was distributed equally among the three group members. Each member was expected to know the final solution in order that the task be considered completed. When the solutions to all tasks were known by each of the three group members, the experiment was ended.

Results   The research generally supported the statement that the circle (equal positions) required less time to solve relatively complex problems and more time to solve relatively simple problems than the wheel (central position). Differences in time required to solve the simple problems in the two nets failed to reach statistical significance.

Researcher   Mauk Mulder (1960:1–14)

Subject   Communication Structure, Decision Structure, and Group Performance.

Networks used   Circle, Wheel. Both 4-man networks.

Questions   (1) Do groups with centralized decision structures give better group task performances? (2) Are the more centralized structures characterized by "vulnerability?"

Tasks   To solve five problems of which the following is an example. How many trucks are needed for a small company to move four kinds of equipment—chairs, desks, filing cabinets, and typewriters? The information necessary to answer this question is as follows: the company owns 12 desks, 48 chairs, 12 typewriters, 15 filing cabinets. One truck can hold 12 typewriters, or 3 desks, or 5 filing cabinets, or 24 chairs. Each group member was given one card stating the problem, and the information necessary to solve the problem was distributed equally among the four group members. Each member was expected to know the final solution in order that the task be considered completed. When the solutions to all five tasks were known by each of the four group members, the experiment was ended.

Results   Decision structures which were more centralized did not significantly perform the task faster. The wheel groups were faster only in the fourth and fifth problems. Centralized interaction structures perform group tasks relatively more slowly during the early part of the experiment. This is true before centralized group structures develop, suggesting early vulnerability.

Researchers (Guetzkow & Dill, 1957) have experimented with communication networks using the nets to examine organizational development and role differentiation in task-oriented groups. Guetzkow's (1960:683–704) experiment dealing with role differentiation, using the group task developed by Leavitt and the Bavelas nets, attempted to demonstrate how role differentiation of group members is related to the development of an organizational structure. He found that: (1) organizational status does not necessarily result from the development of role activity in group task situations which are initially devoid of clear role assignments; (2) the channels for developing an interlocking role system increase when task performances are defined by functional positions and when individual perceptions of role differentiation in the group are more clearly defined; and (3) the development of clearly identifiable leadership-followership roles is also related to clearer definitions of functional positions and individual perceptions of role differentiation. Additionally, there is a tendency for leadership roles to be performed by individuals with high personal ascendency expectations.

For our purposes, the communication network as a group interaction model suggests that the arrangement of group members as an element of group organization and part of the physical environment of the group is a significant factor in the development of the group process. The importance of group arrangement should not be underestimated and may be ranked along with interaction, the individual, symbols and meanings, group norms, and group goals as a significant factor in social group analysis.

The reader should recognize that the model under consideration here is a research model and one which has been developed in laboratory experimentation. The results of such experimentation, however, have gone beyond the limits of laboratory research, allowing sociologists to consider elements of group structure and organization as major elements in the group interaction process.

THE EXCHANGE MODEL OF GEORGE C. HOMANS

George Homans developed an interaction model (1958:597–606) which is framed in terms of situational economics and which incorporates into the interactional analysis such terms as exchange, balance, and profit. In presenting the argument that an exchange of goods is one of the oldest bases for human behavior, Homans is suggesting not only a model for human interaction but a basic human motivation model as well. Central to his thesis are the following propositions:

1. Human interaction is an exchange of material and nonmaterial goods.
2. Human interaction is characterized by mutual reinforcement.
3. The process of give-and-take in terms of costs and rewards in the exchange (interaction) results in a balanced exchange relationship.

Using the idea that interaction is basically a kind of economic exchange suggests that man's behavior in groups can be understood in terms of the rewards and the costs involved in the performance of a social act. One may also infer from the exchange theme that human beings are motivated by a need to maintain some balance in the reward-cost factor in human interaction (see Figure 5-8).

In Figure 5-8, the activity of A in I and B in II is depicted as weighted on a scale. The behavior of both A and B is seen as out of balance since, as the economic exchange model suggests, behavior is cost. When the behavior of each is rewarded by the reciprocal behavior of the other, and when anticipated rewards are actually received by each party, the relationship is depicted as balanced. *Exchange balance* refers to the results of a relationship in which the interacting parties are able to maintain the interaction, having received, and expecting to continue to receive, at least minimally acceptable rewards in relation to the costs involved in the relationship.

The reader should note well that the idea of balance does not suggest that the rewards received by each of the interacting parties are equal. The idea of an equal exchange in terms of rewards is not reasonable since individuals are motivated to behave differentially and to define cost and reward behavior differentially. For example, gossip sometimes centers around the remark, "I don't know why she stays married to him." In some marital dyads the relationship, in terms of rewards, gives the appearance of being totally out of balance: one partner expending all the costly energies, emotional and physical, and receiving little reward for all the effort, and the other expending little or no costly behavior and receiving a great deal of reward. To the third-party observer there is no equitable distribution of rewards in such a relationship. In point of fact, if the relationship continues over an extended period of time, we must assume that it is balanced in that each of the two partners is receiving at least the

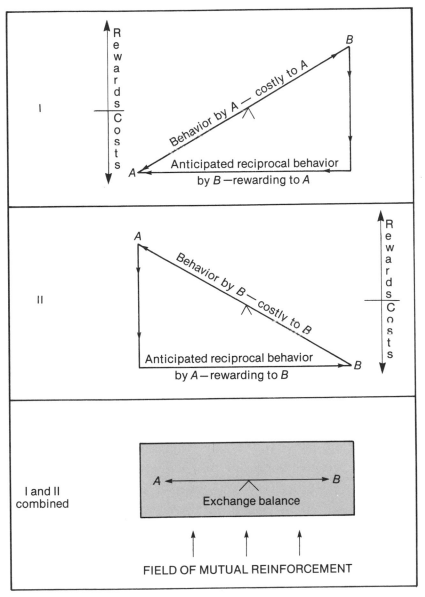

Figure 5-8. Human Interaction as Economic Exchange

minimum rewards anticipated from the relationship even though those
rewards are by no means equal. So, the wife sees enough in him to keep
the marriage intact even though her rewards are much less than those of

her spouse. The relationship is balanced and, in fact, profitable to both. The same may be said of associations based upon friendship, as well as those more limited and formally organized relations such as those between a teacher and student, employers and employees, and business relations based upon contract. Since individual expectations about rewards differ, the balance referred to by Homans suggests that if the expectations of one individual are met by the reciprocal activity of another, the first individual's reward needs have been met and vice versa. The rewards gained by each interacting individual may not be equal but they will be balanced since each individual's expectations have been met.

Homans introduces the term "profit" into his analysis. He (1958:603) states, "If we define profit as reward less cost . . . we have here some evidence for the proposition that change in behavior is greatest when perceived profit is least." The idea of profit suggests that interaction and group activity are defined as worthwhile and should be maintained when individuals view their behavior as resulting in rewards greater than the cost of that behavior. In the remarks which follow, we will consider profit and exchange balance as necessary elements in human interaction. Let us consider the following: If the behavior of individuals in a group relationship results in, at least, the minimum reward expectations (minimum profit) of each, the relation will be conceived of as balanced. Remember that balance in the exchange is not an equal exchange of rewards and that profit forms the basis for continuing the relationship. By way of explanation, we will give numerical values to the cost and reward aspects of an interaction between two individuals. We will place cost (behavior), reward expectations, and actual rewards on a value scale of 1 to 10. Without giving the content particulars for a given interaction, we may argue that one individual (A) initiates an interaction with another individual (B) and that the act performed by A costs (c) 7 units on the $1-10$ scale. A, in acting this way, also expects no less than 8 units of reward (r). So, for A, the activity may be identified as $A_{act} = 8r - 7c$. The other group member (B), in reacting to A, defines activity as being costly, having a value of 5 on the scale, and having reward expectations reaching 9 units on the scale. B's reaction to A may be identified as $B_{act} = 9r - 5c$. If the activity of A actually rewards B at the unit level 9 and if the reaction of B actually rewards A at the unit level of 8, the relationship between A and B is profitable to both and is balanced. The result of A's activity is $A_{act} = 1r$ (profit), and the result of B's reaction is $B_{act} = 4r$ (profit). Both have been rewarded and have profited by the relationship with each other. The relationship is clearly mutually reinforcing and will probably be maintained as long as the balance is maintained. Table 5-1 will present the results of simple two-person interactions as economic exchanges with varying cost and reward levels.

Table 5-1.   Simple Two-Person Exchange using a Value Scale 1 – 10

A (ACT)				RESULT OF EXCHANGE	B (ACT)			
C	R.E.	A.R.	P (+) L (−)		P (+) L (−)	A.R.	R.E.	C
7	8	8	+1	Profit – Balance Mutual reinforcement Continuation	+4	9	9	5
5	6	7	+2	Profit – Balance Mutual reinforcement Continuation	+2	8	7	6
5	7	4	−1	Loss – Balance Mutual discontent Discontinuation	−3	4	8	7
5	9	2	−3	Loss – Imbalance Discontinuation	+2	9	9	7
5	7	3	−2	Loss – Balance Mutual discontent Discontinuation	2	7	10	9
1	9	9	+8	Profit – Balance Mutual reinforcement Continuation	+8	10	9	2

C = Cost   P = Profit
R.E. = Reward expectations   L = Loss
A.R. = Actual reward

Two questions arise at this point: What are the rewards, and what are the costs in the exchange of human behavior? Anything which the individual defines as having some value or which contributes to a sense of well-being is a reward—emotional support, money, friendship, love, help. Anything which the individual defines in terms of giving up something of value or as something which is being lost is cost—energy expended in the performance of activity, time used, emotional drainage, money. How these elements of cost and reward are related will, of course, depend upon the content given the relationship and the needs of the interacting individuals. When profit is added to the reward-cost aspects of social exchange, the "get the most for your money" motto seems appropriate. We are suggesting that, when profit is incorporated into the exchange of social behavior, the major focus of the interaction would have to be a maximization of rewards and a minimization of costs producing the highest possible profit margin.

For some, the harsh economics of exchange in human social behavior is difficult to accept. As it stands, it appears to be a rather inhuman, ultimately rationalistic and materialistic approach to human interaction. To some, there is no room in the model to explain *altruistic behavior*, which, in terms used by Homans, would be defined as the performance of costly behavior to benefit others with little or no expectation of rewards in the exchange. There is this problem in the arguments forwarded by Homans and, clearly, if all behavior is defined as profit-oriented there is no room for altruism. The question is: Should all behavior be defined as profit-oriented? And further, can behavior such as that exhibited by individuals who risk their lives to save the lives of others be defined in terms of profit? Can we explain the high affective behavior of family members toward each other and the willingness of friends to sacrifice for each other in terms of profit? Can we explain philanthropy, religious martyrdom, and humanitarianism in profit-making terms?

A final note on the Homans model in direct relation to group interaction: the model suggests that somewhere in the expressed behavior of the interacting parties, cues are given off which suggest what the reward-cost expectations of each member are. This is important for small group activity since the maintenance of some acceptable system of rewards and costs is required if the group is to survive to realize the goals for which the group came into existence. The ongoing social group will structure some supra-individual system of rewards and costs for each individual which defines the limits within which individuals may behave as elements in the system of exchange within the boundaries of the social group.

THE INTRA-GROUP CONFLICT MODEL

With the body of conflict theory, one of the most telling comments about the basic premise of a conflict model is the following passage by Georg Simmel (Wolff, 1950:59):

> Society asks of the individual . . . his strength in the service of the special function which he has to exercise as a member of it; that he so modify himself as to become the most suitable vehicle for this function . . . the drive toward unity and wholeness that is characteristic of the individual himself rebels against this role. The individual strives to be rounded out himself, not merely to help to round out society . . . this conflict between the whole, which imposes the onesidedness of partial function upon its elements, and the part, which itself strives to be a whole is insoluble.

The intra-group conflict model presents the group as a collection of individuals who are striving for goal achievement against the inevitable conflict which hinders movement toward group goals. The conflict model identifies different bases for conflict within social groups:

1. *Group Differentiation*. Groups are, by definition, conflict-oriented since the inevitable differentiation—for example, leadership-followership or dominance-submission—which occurs within social groups produces conflict between those individuals who occupy the different positions within the group structure. Such conflict is most apparent when, for example, two or more individual group members are competing for a position of dominance. When one individual finally wins and occupies the position of dominance, resentments may develop and are often harbored for long periods of time, resulting in interpersonal relationships within the group which are most conducive to conflict.

2. *Group Expectations*. Individual expectations may differ from the expectations of the group as a whole, and the inability of groups to successfully meet the expectations of all its members often leads to conflict. Individuals enter into groupings with certain needs and expectations which they anticipate will be fulfilled by group membership. This conflict often takes the form of interpersonal conflict between the group leader and one of the follower members. Leaders will bring a personal interpretation of group goals and group activity toward group goals. The expectations of the follower, who also brings personal interpretations to group interaction, will not always be met by the direction given by the leader and conflict ensues. A recent lawsuit brought by a child against his parent for improper and injurious upbringing suggests that the retrospective expectations of the child were, in his view, not met by his parents' socializing efforts. The lawsuit may be seen as an expression of conflict of expectations between parent and child. Members of industrial line organizations, foremen and workers, often experience such conflict of expectations, as do members of small military groups, especially during combat.

3. *Group Limitations*. A social group may function so as to restrict the free movement and thought of its members. Groups sometimes restrict the activity of each member for the good of the whole group. This is so because the absence of controls would lead to: (1) loss of group direction, (2) the development of differing and conflicting goals, and (3) most likely the end of the group as a functioning entity. In order to avoid such dire results, groups impose upon members limitations to their freedom. Assuming that freedom is important to the individual members, the limita-

tions placed upon individuals is seen as a basic contradiction, and conflict results. The socialization of the child, for example, is often a restricting mechanism. It is clearly a system which imposes restrictions on the free movement of the child. It is, of course, necessary for the continued well-being of the family, but parent-child conflict during the socialization period is part of the whole package and is part of the expectations which develop in both parents and their young.

4. *Group Coalitions.* There is, in groups of three or more individuals, the strong tendency for individuals to form into subgroups, and this restructuring of individuals into smaller but more intense and cooperative units often produces intra-group conflict. Conflict occurs when subgroups form as a coalition against the remaining individual or against other subgroups.

In more general terms, the conflict model assumes that all groups are oriented to conflict. The model attempts to identify: (1) the presence of conflict through descriptions of the divisive structural elements within coalitions, and (2) the types and origins of conflict prevalent between group members. The studies below will deal with these two orientations respectively.

The divisive element of coalition formation as a factor in small group conflict has been researched and analyzed best by Theodore Caplow. Working with the triad, he identifies its four properties (Caplow, 1968: 1–5):

1. Every triad has three members.
2. Every triad contains three relationships.
3. There is a tendency for triads to divide into a coalition of two elements against the third.
4. Triads exhibit catalytic effects.

According to Caplow, the most significant property of the triad is coalition formation. This property can be diagrammed as:

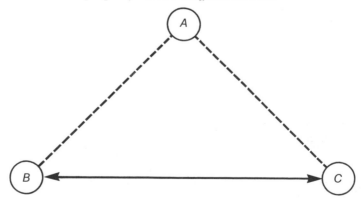

Individuals B and C are in coalition, and individual A becomes the isolate. Keeping the above diagram in mind, let us examine the following example used by Caplow (1968:2) when introducing the subject. The example cited here is a variation of the example cited in Chapter Three.

> Ahab, Brutus, and Charlie are smugglers who divide their goods on a lonely island .... Brutus and Charlie are equally matched. Ahab ... could overpower either Brutus or Charlie ... but could easily be overpowered by the two of them together. Ahab will probably try to form a coalition with Brutus or with Charlie, but neither of them would have any reason to accept him as a partner. The predicted coalition is Brutus-Charlie. If Brutus chooses Charlie, he has a partner who does not threaten to dominate him and who needs him for protection against the superior strength ... of Ahab.

The reader will be able to understand more easily the idea behind coalition formation as a general conflict-producing function of small groups and the example as a particular expression of that function if we perform one simple task. Let us weight the three elements of the triad, Ahab, Brutus, and Charlie, on a scale from 1 to 10. From the example, we know that Brutus and Charlie are of equal strength. Let us assign to each the weight of 3. Ahab, who "could overpower either Brutus or Charlie," requires the weight of 4. The most predictable coalition of Brutus and Charlie can be described as:

$$(B+C) \ > \ A \quad ----\text{Without Weights}$$

$$(3+3) \ > \ 4 \quad ----\text{Weighted}$$

Basic to an understanding of coalition formation in the triad as a form of intra-group conflict is the observation that the strength of the equal member is gained only through the formation of a coalition. When this coalition is, in fact, formed, the power of the strongest single member is reduced to a point well below the newfound combined strength of the other two members. In the above example Ahab is, finally, at the mercy of the other two. We could argue that the final outcome, the distribution of the loot, resulted from the conflict prevailing within the group. We must also be aware that this was accomplished at the expense of the unity of all three members.

Other examples of triads with strong coalition tendencies easily come to mind: the parent-child family coalition, the coalition possibilities in a *ménage à trois*, and in industrial triads involving managers, foremen, and workers. An earlier work by Caplow (1956:489–490) included an examination of triads and the coalitions which form within them. The following assumptions were made about triadic conflict:

1. Members of a triad may differ in strength. A stronger member can control a weaker member, and will seek to do so.

2. Each member of the triad seeks control over the others. Control over two others is preferred to control over one another. Control over one other is preferred to control over none.
3. Strength is additive. The strength of a coalition is equal to the sum of the strength of its two members.
4. The formation of coalitions takes place in an existing triadic situation, so that there is a pre-coalition condition in every triad.

Following Caplow's lead, many others have directed their research efforts to the characteristics and coalition possibilities found in the triad (see Chapter Seven). The high volume of research in this area is not so remarkable in light of the importance of Simmel's earlier efforts and the acceptance of triadic analysis as a central focus in the small groups field.

The research by Blair Wheaton (1974:328–348) suggests a concern with conflict within groups as expressed through interpersonal relations. Wheaton was interested in discovering the relationship between interpersonal conflict and cohesiveness. He studied 102 female roommates. Hoping to discover whether or not conflict has both positive and negative effects upon group cohesion, Wheaton distinguished *principled conflict* and *communal conflict*. Principled conflict is defined as conflict over a basic truth, law, or ethical code. Communal conflict is conflict over how to behave or "the best action for behaving" once principle agreement has been reached. Wheaton was also concerned with the source of conflict— that is, whether the source is external or internal. External sources of conflict include issues which develop from the group's presence in the community or society. Internal sources of conflict include issues which develop out of the behavioral expectations existing at the intra-group level. The types of conflict and types of sources of conflict, when taken together, produce the following combinations: (1) principled-internal, (2) principled-external, (3) communal-internal, and (4) communal-external.

Randomly selecting 102 female roommate dyads from a university residence directory, Wheaton distributed questionnaires on material dealing with 30 issues, 13 of which were internal and 17 of which were external. Each roommate was asked to respond to each issue by indicating:

1. Her own opinion about the issue,
2. Her best estimate of her roommate's opinion,
3. If there have been any arguments or differences of opinion, and
4. If the arguments were principled or communal.

The result of the study supported the two major hypotheses:

1. The degree of conflict itself, unclassified as to type and source of issue, is unrelated to the level of cohesiveness in the dyad, and

2. Principled conflict, without regard to source of issue, has a significant negative effect on cohesiveness, whereas communal conflict has a significant positive effect.

As a model for understanding intra-group conflict, the Wheaton study suggests: (1) that a social group is able to maintain a significant level of integration as long as the members of the group are in agreement as to basic values and norms, and (2) that members of social groups are able to withstand conflict which is basically behavioral and not ideological.

Such reporting is important to our understanding of the intra-group model because it is concerned with the issues of group cohesiveness at the most basic level of principles upon which groups develop, maintain themselves, and move toward the achievement of their goals. In this regard, the research suggests that the degree to which groups have agreement about principles will be a measure of the degree to which they can maintain themselves well. Additionally, once group principles have been established, internalized, and accepted by all members, conflict about the actual behavior can be overcome with little or no effect upon group cohesion.

For our purposes, two points should be made here: (1) the Wheaton research on the dyad is applicable to groups of larger size, and (2) it is applicable to a variety of group types, including marital, business, parent-child, and nonresidence friendship dyads, and relationships requiring more than two members, such as family groupings, committees, and industrial line organizations of supervisor, foreman, and workers.

As suggested in the research reports above, the conflict model has taken a variety of directions but the central focus of intra-group conflict—that there are internal forces at work within all groups which, since they are inevitable, militate against group integration and group maintenance—remains as a way of looking at the group and its members.

<hr>

summary

There are many ways in which the material surrounding small group interaction can be organized. This chapter discusses five interaction models selected for variety, interest, and simplicity. Each of the models has gained some measure of acceptance in sociology or a related discipline.

It was noted that model construction is a device for putting information together in a manner which helps us to understand the relationships between and among elements under investigation. Also, models were defined as necessary because an understanding of the models used in the field provides the student with an orderly means for learning and familiarizes the student with some of the ways in which sociologists like to organize their material. The models presented in this chapter are: (1) the Johari Awareness model, (2) the communicative acts model, (3) the communication network model, (4) the exchange model, and (5) the intra-group conflict model.

The Johari Awareness model, constructed by Joseph Luft, was determined to be a total communication model which identifies the elements presented in the transmission of meanings and intentions through the use of verbal and other external communication modes. The model incorporates the concepts of social self and social other in the interaction setting and is composed of the following elements: transmission, meanings, feelings, attitudes, and behavioral definitions. The model asserts that the social self has four quadrants: (1) open, (2) blind, (3) hidden, and (4) unknown. The model presents a view of the four quadrants as constantly changing in size or in importance as an individual interacts with various others or with the same other over periods of time. In other words, individuals' perceptions of each other are constantly changing. There is, for example, an expansion of the open part of the self in relationships in which there is a high level of sharing between and among interacting parties. The expansion of the open quadrant would result in a shrinking of the hidden quadrant. The use of the awareness model is, however, limited because it is not readily applicable to small groups of all sizes for the following reason: the emphasis upon the total individual and the concern with awareness of the total effect of individuals upon each other become less intense as the size of the group increases. Interpretations of the model center around: (1) the similarity of the model to interpretations of the concept of Cooley's primary group, and (2) the reduced impact of the model as a total self model when applied to the primary-secondary relationships continuum.

Theodore Newcomb's communicative acts model was presented as based upon the assumption that "communication among humans performs the essential function of enabling two or more individuals to maintain simultaneous orientation toward one another as communicators and toward objects of communication." The *communicative act* is a transmission of information, which includes discriminative stimuli, from one individual (point of origin) to another (a recipient). The basic model includes: (1) A —an individual transmitting information, (2) B —the recipient of the transmission, and (3) X —the object of the communication. When these three elements are observed as activity (or interaction) the model is symbolized as A to B re X. The objects of orientation (X) are all the factors which impinge upon the relationship between *A* and *B*. These objects are elements to which *A* and *B* give meaning, and about which effective interaction requires consensus. In this regard, Newcomb refers to symmetry of orientation.

The communication network model has been used in a variety of research siutations. Proven as a research design, a *communication network* refers to the arrangement of lines of communication which are open between and among members of groups. Network designs range from total and free communication to those which are restricted both in terms of availability of members to each other and frequency of communication. The bulk of research using this model assumes that certain established communication channeling systems are more efficient than others depending upon the group's tasks and goals.

The exchange model of George C. Homans argues that the exchange of goods is one of the oldest bases for human behavior. The central elements in the model are: (1) human interaction is an exchange of goods, (2) interaction occurs in a field of mutual reinforcement, and (3) give-and-take in terms of cost and reward in the exchange results in an exchange balance. The model generates interest in the proposition that man's behavior can be understood in terms of rewards and costs in the performance of an act. Interest also centers around the view that human beings are motivated by a need to maintain some balance in the reward-cost results of human interaction (exchange).

Discussion of the exchange model centered around the definition of an *exchange balance*: the results of a relationship in which the interacting parties are able to maintain the interaction, each having received (and with the expectation of continuing to receive) at least minimally acceptable rewards in relation to the costs involved in the relationship. Accordingly, the rewards which accrue to group members do not have to be equal: if the expectations of one individual are realized by maintaining a relationship with another, the individual's reward needs have been met.

The intra-group conflict model identifies group conflict as inevitable and defines attempts to achieve group goals against the background of conflict inevitability. The discussion included the four bases for the development of conflict within groups: (1) *Group differentiation*. Conflict arises between and among those individuals who occupy differing positions in the group structure, especially when two or more group members compete for the same position. (2) *Group expectations*. Conflict arises from the inability of the group to meet the individual expectations of all members and from the differing expectations of individual members in terms of general group expectations. (3) *Group limitations*. Conflict arises from the restrictions (limitations) placed upon individual group members by the group as a whole. Group limitations are necessary for effective goal achievement and group order, but the efficient working of the group toward established goals demands that individuals within accept the limitations placed upon them. (4) *Group coalitions.* Conflict arises from the strong tendency of group members to form subgroups which are more intense, cooperative units. Caplow's presentation of this occurrence is based upon his interpretation of coalition formation in triads. He identified four properties of triads: (1) three members, (2) three relationships, (3) the tendency for triads to divide into a coalition of two elements against the third, and (4) triads exhibit catalytic effects.

Blair Wheaton described group conflict in terms of distinctions between principled and communal conflict. *Principled conflict* is conflict over a basic truth, law, or ethical code. *Communal conflict* is conflict over how to behave once principle agreement has been reached. The sources of conflict were identified as external (the development of conflict which arises from the group's presence in the community or society), and internal (including issues which develop out of the behavioral expectations existing within the group). Wheaton developed a typology of group conflict types by combining the types of conflict and the sources of conflict. The following combinations are produced: (1) principled-internal, (2) principled-external, (3) communal-internal, and (4) communal-external.

---

discussion questions

1. The Johari "window" is a model which describes the self. Why, then, is it a useful tool for sociological investigation?
2. Why is the communicative acts model not influenced by changes in the size of the small group?
3. How do communication networks help explain leadership?
4. Apply the exchange model to the student-teacher relationship. Does the application explain anything about classroom behavior?
5. Is intra-group conflict inevitable?

references

Bavelas, Alex. "A Mathematical Model for Group Structures," *Applied Anthropology*, 7 (1948): 16–30.

Caplow, Theodore. "A Theory of Coalitions in the Triad," *American Sociological Review*, 21 (1956): 489–490.

——————. *Two Against One: Coalitions in Triads*. Englewood Cliffs, New Jersey: Prentice-Hall, 1968.

Guetzkow, Harold. "Differentiation of Roles in Task-Oriented Groups," in Dorwin Cartwright and Alvin Zander (eds.). *Group Dynamics: Research and Theory*, 2nd ed.; New York: Harper & Row, 1960.

Guetzkow, Harold; and Dill, William R. "Factors in the Organizational Development of Task-Oriented Groups," *Sociometry*, 20 (1957): 175–204.

Hare, A. Paul. *Handbook of Small Group Research*, 2nd ed.; New York: The Free Press, 1976.

Homans, George C. "Social Behavior as Exchange," *The American Journal of Sociology*, 63 (1958): 597–606.

Leavitt, Harold J. "Some Effects of Certain Communication Patterns on Group Performance," *Journal of Abnormal Social Psychology*, 46 (1951): 38–50.

Luft, Joseph. *Of Human Interaction*. Palo Alto, California: National, 1969.

Mulder, Mauk. "Communication Structure, Decision Structure, and Group Performance," *Sociometry*, 23 (1960): 1–14.

Newcomb, Theodore M. "An Approach to the Study of Communicative Acts," *The Psychological Review*, 60 (1953): 393–404.

Shaw, Marvin E. "Some Effects of Problem Complexity upon Problem Solution Efficiency in Different Communication Nets," *Journal of Experimental Psychology*, 48 (1954): 211–217.

——————. "Communication Networks," in Leonard Berkowitz. *Advances in Experimental Social Psychology*. New York: Academic Press, 1964, Vol. 1.

Wheaton, Blair. "Interpersonal Conflict and Cohesiveness in Dyadic Relationships," *Sociometry*, 37 (1974): 328–348.

Wolff, Kurt (Trans. and ed.). *The Sociology of Georg Simmel*. New York: The Free Press, 1950.

Chapter Six

Some Perspectives on Small Groups

CHAPTER PREVIEW

There is considerable distance between the theories of Georg Simmel, George Herbert Mead, and Charles Horton Cooley and the mass of research which has sustained the small groups field. The works of men such as Robert F. Bales, Kurt Lewin, Jacob L. Moreno, and George C. Homans give a sense of direction to both theoretical considerations and research efforts by constructing the methods by which hypotheses about small group behavior can be tested in the field or in small group laboratories.

This chapter will review the contributions of the four men mentioned above. The purpose of this review will be to identify the methods these men established for studying group behavior and the results which they obtained when the method was used in laboratory or field settings. Table 6-1 will serve as a preliminary identification of the basic elements used in the construction of the four methods and the areas of investigations to which those methods have been applied.

INTERACTION PROCESS ANALYSIS (ROBERT F. BALES)

The development of the Interaction Process Analysis method (IPA) grew out of Bales' early interest in discovering a theoretical framework for analyzing large social systems such as the society and formal organizations as well as a framework for analyzing small groups such as families, work groups and committees. The basic premise upon which Bales' methodology rests is that *all* social systems must achieve a balance of internal and external forces if they are to maintain themselves and achieve desired goals.

BALES' SOCIOLOGICAL PERSPECTIVE

Unfortunately, the theoretical basis of Interaction Process Analysis (IPA) is often dismissed in favor of a description of the method itself and the interaction categories around which the method centers. In reality, it is extremely difficult to separate the theory from the method since the interaction categories used in experimentation are based upon certain basic assumptions and propositions associated with group balance, group structure, and group interaction. For example, the interaction categories cannot be understood fully without some knowledge of the distinction which Bales makes between two types of problems attendant upon all systems of interaction, and his broader observations about the empirical social world.

Table 6-1. Four Small Group Perspectives

	BASIC THEORETICAL ORIENTATION	METHOD	AREAS OF INVESTIGATION
Robert F. Bales	Groups are systems of internal and external forces which must be balanced. Balance results from the resolution of task and socio-emotional problems.	Interaction Process Analysis (IPA) System for the Multiple Level Observation of Groups (SYMLOG)	Leadership Status and status consensus Group size
Kurt Lewin	Groups are composed of interdependent parts which are subject to field forces from without and from within. These forces propel individual groups toward or away from established goals.	Interpretative analysis of group elements, their interdependencies and the forces determining the direction of individual or group locomotion.	Adolescence Norm divergence Group identity Intergroup conflict
Jacob L. Moreno	The basic fact of all human associations is the affective group bond. This is the foundation for integration in groups, communities and in society.	Sociometric technique	Communities for delinquents Educational groupings Tasks and decision-making groupings
George C. Homans	Group behavior is to be understood as determined by the mutual dependencies between three basic elements: sentiments, activities, and interaction in external and internal social systems.	Interpretation of group behavior through the identification of mutual dependencies of basic elements.	Informal work groups Gangs Family systems

According to Bales, the empirical social world can be observed through the following distinction of types of phenomena: (1) *action or interaction* (observable behavior by interacting parties), and (2) *situational phenomena* (the self, other individuals, and physical environment). If social scientists are to generalize about behavior, the generalizations must ultimately refer to each of these sets of phenomena or to the relationships between them. Figure 6-1 represents the group in terms of the actor and the situations within which interaction occurs.

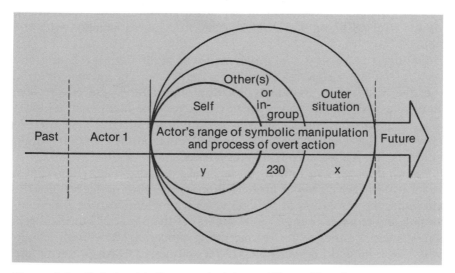

Figure 6-1.   Relationship Between Activity and Group Situations

The balance between internal and external forces which social systems (Monane, 1967) require for systems maintenance and goal achievement can now be discussed in terms of the two types of phenomena mentioned just above. All small groups and all individual action within the group must take into account task and socio-emotional problems. It is these sets of problems which must be resolved if the group is to maintain the balance which goal achievement requires.

Task problems develop out of the relationships which group members have with inner and outer situations. Inner group situations include the self and other group members; outer situations include out-group members, physical, spatial, and temporal environments, and all other factors relevant to the achievement of group goals. The reader may have some difficulty with Bales' incorporation of the self as part of the situations within which the individual group member acts, and may ask how an individual can act toward himself as well as toward others in the group and the group as a whole. The self as a situational element of the actor is understandable when the reader acknowledges the influence of symbolic interaction on Bales' thinking. The self, then, as part of the inner situation, is the actor as an "object" to himself. Socio-emotional problems are those which arise from the relationships members have with each other. Included among socio-emotional problems are interpersonal conflicts, various levels of liking and disliking, and member satisfaction with the group.

Although these two sets of problems occur at different levels of group identity (self, other, and task) they are closely allied. The balance referred to earlier results from the ability which group members have to resolve conflicts associated with each set of problems. The manner in which a system (group) resolves these will determine its survival measured in terms of the level of integration (solidarity) the group is able to maintain within itself as a basis for solving group tasks.

There are serious difficulties associated with the maintenance of a balance in the resolution of each of these two sets of problems. On the one hand, the resolution of socio-emotional problems can be time consuming and requires that group members set their energies in the direction of internal rather than external group concerns. Under such conditions, the time and energy available for solutions to task problems are severely limited, and group maintenance may be lost. On the other hand, solving task problems can immerse group members in concerns which will ultimately destroy the socio-emotional solidarity group maintenance demands. In the last analysis, a delicate balance of internal and external forces must be obtained within which a desired level of socio-emotional integration forms an internal system of identity sufficient to allow for task resolution.

These considerations become important when the data received from the use of the interaction categories are analyzed and interpreted. Bales assumes that the dynamic change (activity) which is observed and recorded is the result of present motivation and the influences on present motivation of the actors. Present motivation describes the bases for activity which originate in the group situation in which the activity occurs. Present motivation is distinguished from prior motivation which, for Bales, includes the actor's orientations to and perceptions of experiences and situations before he enters the situation in which the action to be recorded will occur. Activity also results from structural influences on present motivation. These influences include: (1) the structure of the present outer situation which is the same for all group members, (2) the structure of the culture of the group which is common to all group members, (3) the structure of the differential social relationships between and among all group members, and (4) the structure of pre-existing unique motivational factors in the personalities of group members (prior motivation). These elements are not observable, they are inferred. Such inferences are necessary in order to explain the similarities and differences in the observed interaction.

In constructing a theoretical basis for the IPA method, Bales is describing a dual set of concepts, one of which is functional, the other structural. In explaining the relationship between these two conceptual areas, Bales (1950:127) observes that ". . . the social structure and culture of groups can be understood primarily as a system of institutionalized solutions to various functional problems which arise in the course of action." There are four classes of functional problems to which group structures and cultures provide solutions: (1) the implementing of needs and desires which for any reason are active in the members as organized personalities and as biological organisms, (2) the adaptation of activities to the situation external to the social system, (3) the integration of activities within the social system itself, and (4) the expression of emotional tensions created within the personality by changes in the situation. Bales' theoretical orientation is an attempt to identify the relationships between these two areas of conceptualizations. The development of interaction categories is a logical result of this orientation to the nature and development of social groups. For Bales, IPA is the study of interaction as a complex functional element of the group (or, more particularly, the regularities in the distribution of types of interaction) which results in identifying generalizations about the social structure of the group.

THE IPA METHOD

Bales' method was designed to analyze and interpret interaction in small groups. His definition of the small group reflects his interest in using the unit of action as the basis of observation and in identifying interaction as the framework for making generalizations about the dynamics of small group behavior. According to Bales (1950:33), a small group is defined as:

> . . . any number of persons engaged in interaction with each other in a single face-to-face meeting or a series of meetings, in which each member receives some impression or perception of each other member distinct enough so that he can, either at the time or in later questioning, give some reaction to each of

the others as an individual person, even though it be only to recall that the other was present.

Although Bales sets no size limits to the small group, he does identify certain characteristics which distinguish groups from nongroup social activity. Direct interaction, propinquity, distinct member impressions, member awareness of presence of all other members, and member ability to react to each other member as an individual are all requirements for a collectivity to be considered a small group.

The definition is specifically designed to determine the groups to which the IPA technique can be applied. Meetings in which interaction occurs on a face-to-face basis are necessary for the application of the interaction categories to specific group situations. These categories were designed to observe, analyze, and interpret the "structure and dynamics of interaction" in all small groups which fit the above definition.

The twelve interaction categories (see Figure 6-2) are at the center of Bales' Interaction Process Analysis method, and they form the bridge between Bales' theoretical considerations and empirical experimentation. The distinction between task and socio-emotional activity in groups is reflected in the organization of the categories into positive and negative socio-emotional activity and task activity. Categories 1 through 3 identify units of interaction which enhance group integration and which contribute to the solution of problems of a socio-emotional nature. Categories 10 through 12 indicate units of interaction which lead to the development of socio-emotional problems and hinder the development of group integration. Units of interaction which fall into the remaining categories (4 through 9) contribute to the solution of task problems (sometimes called instrumental problems) which face the group. Categories 4 through 6 include interaction units which occur in response to questions which are included in categories 7 through 9 (Bales, 1950:9).

Below are lists of functions for each set of categories. These should help the reader keep the categories and the functions of each in their proper places and should facilitate understanding of the relationships between the sets.

Positive **socio-emotional** **categories**	**Negative** **socio-emotional** **categories**
Shows solidarity	Shows antagonism
Shows tension release	Shows tension
Agrees	Disagrees

Task categories	Task categories
(Questions)	(Answers)
Asks for orientation	Gives orientation
Asks for opinion	Gives opinion
Asks for suggestion	Gives suggestion

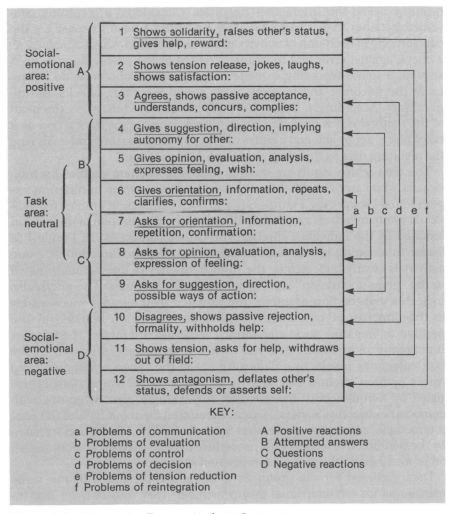

Figure 6-2.   Interaction Process Analysis Categories

Reprinted from *Interaction Process Analysis* by Robert F. Bales. By permission of The University of Chicago Press. Copyright © 1950, The University of Chicago Press.

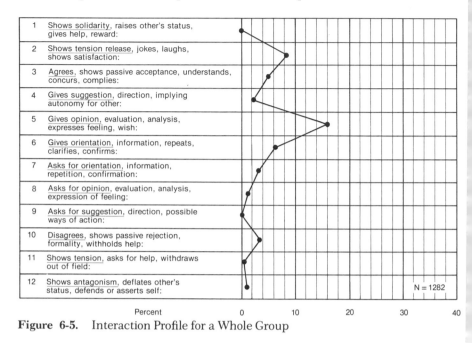

| | | Percent | 0 | 10 | 20 | 30 | 40 |

Figure 6-5.   Interaction Profile for a Whole Group

these indicators point toward a cooperative effort in member attempts to achieve higher levels of integration.

In experimental group sessions, data are gathered for each group member. This information can be combined as in Figure 6-5 or kept separate in order to develop interaction profiles for each group member. In analyzing small groups by examining individual interaction profiles, Bales argues that the experimenter is able to develop a sense of the social relationships of each individual group member. In one study conducted in the small groups laboratories at Harvard University, a five-member group was observed during a chess problem-solving experiment. The interaction profiles were prepared for each group member, and the analysis of these profiles prompted the experimenter to make the following observations about each group member. Since our purpose at this point is to suggest the kinds of results which the IPA method yields and not to discuss or analyze the profiles themselves, we will not show the five interaction profiles upon which these results are based.

There were few similarities found among the five profiles, but there were strong indicators of role differentiation and emerging group structure. The group members had accepted and were carrying out clearly different roles and occupied different positions within the group structure. Member 1, identified as the group leader, performed 46% of the total units of activity recorded, and his interaction profile closely approximated the profile for the whole group. The activity of Member 1 was so dominating that it shaped the profile of the entire group. Member 2 was tagged as a leader reinforcer because of the high frequency with which she agreed with the group leader. Bales (1950:152) noted that ". . . without her to provide a continuous 'green light' Member 1 might have slowed down considerably." Member 3 was continually giving suggestions which were invariably rejected by the leader. Member 3 scored unusually high on giving suggestions and relatively low on agreement. The profile of Member 4 indicated extremely low levels of any kind of participation at all in the activity of the group and, therefore, was not a significant factor in the group process. Member 5, similarly uninfluential, was, however, consistently more in agreement than disagreement with other group members.

The use of the IPA method, which included the development of the interaction profiles, resulted in the belief that these impressions of the social relationships among group members were reasonable. From the impressions, hypotheses were developed not only for the experimental group but for all small groups. The following hypotheses will serve as examples (Bales, 1950:153):

> (1) As particular functional problems . . . become more acute, pressing, or continuous, more demanding in time and effort, strains are created toward the definition of special social roles, differentiated in terms of particular persons, who are given the implicit or explicit responsibility of meeting and solving the specific functional problems as they arise . . .(2) As the felt advantage of a particular person in the distribution of access to resources increases, strains are created toward an increase in his generalized social status. Conversely, as the advantage of the particular person decreases, strains are created toward a decrease in his generalized social status.

The hypotheses are not only applicable to the experimental group and all small groups but to large social systems as well. In an interesting adaptation of the research to large social systems, Bales observes that one's understanding of the small group and its structure can be enhanced by abstracting those structural aspects from the larger society which are found in small groups as well.

At the large system level, the interconnections are those "chains of events" or "series of strains" which are in opposition to each other. One chain of events involves adaptation to the outer situation (goal-directed behavior involving division of labor, changes in property distribution, and so on). The other includes concerns about integration and the need for solidarity. Bales concludes that the large societal system tends to vacillate between these two chains of events. Theoretically (Bales, 1966:128), failure to balance the two forces results in ". . . optimum adaptation to the outer situation at the cost of internal malintegration, or optimum internal integration at the cost of maladaptation to the outer situation."

SMALL GROUP RESEARCH

We observed earlier that Bales' definition of the small group was designed to include those kinds of groups which could be studied through the use of the IPA method. The groups to which the definition applies are identified by Bales. Included in the list are discussion groups, therapy groups, counseling, planning, and training groups, and experimental teaching groups. Policy-forming committees, boards, panels, and diagnostic groups can also be studied through the use of the Bales method. Additionally, problem-solving groups, teams, work groups, and family groups, as well as adolescent gangs, children's play groups, and social and recreational clubs are included in the list. There are, of course, many other groups which lend themselves to the IPA method, but the listing above should suffice as an index of the variety of groups which can be approached with Bales' method. Bales indicates that the method can also be used on dyadic associations (therapist/patient, teacher/student, interviewer/interviewee). Bales conducted a large portion of his investigations with the IPA method in the laboratory and attempted to measure a variety of small group factors. These include investigations into the great man theory of leadership, status, status consensus, and group size.

The Great Man Theory of Leadership. Although the many studies of leadership in small groups have yielded questionable results, these investigations by Borgatta, Bales, and Couch (1954:755–759) are an exception. Conducting 166 sessions of three-man Air Force personnel groups (N=126), Bales set out to test the "great man" theory of leadership in terms of performance within groups.

Arguing that a great man would have to possess the qualities of task ability, individual assertiveness, and social acceptability, Bales wished to test the following hypotheses: (1) great men will tend to remain great men over a series of sessions, (2) sessions in which great men participate will have a higher product rate of suggestion and agreement, (3) sessions in which great men participate will have lower time rates of showing tension than those in which they do not participate, and (4) sessions in which great men participate will have higher time rates of showing solidarity and tension release than those in which they do not participate. In order to test these hypotheses, the subjects were told that they were to be observed in groups in order to discover how small groups work and that role playing was involved. Each subject participated in four sessions with two different co-participants (each session was 24 minutes long). Great men were chosen on the basis of their performance in a first group session. In all, only eleven such subjects were selected as great men on the assumption that only about one-tenth of the total number would be able to satisfy the criteria established for "great man" performances.

The initial question posed by the research design—identified in Hypothesis 1—bears on whether a great man chosen in a first group session will remain in that position throughout further sessions. Bales' evidence strongly supports the initial hypothesis. Of the eleven chosen after the first session, eight remained in the top ranks through the second and third sessions. Seven remained in the top rank after the fourth session ended. These consistent performances were defined as exceptionally stable, and the pattern established was significant beyond the .001 level.

In testing the second hypothesis, Bales also found that the first sessions in which great men participated had significantly higher production rates (task ability) than found for the nongreat men sessions, and that the subsequent group sessions in which great men were included were characterized by higher production rates than those subsequent sessions in which great men did not participate. These rates were measured by frequency of activity in IPA Categories 3 (agreement) and 4 (gives suggestion).

The third hypothesis is supported by the data. First sessions from which great men were selected and subsequent sessions in which great men participated consistently showed less tension than in those sessions in which great men did not participate.

The fourth hypothesis is also supported by the data. First sessions and subsequent sessions in which great men participated were consistently rated higher in IPA Categories 1 (shows solidarity) and 2 (shows tension release) than sessions in which great men did not participate. The consistency with which high rates of activity were reported in the two categories measuring positive affect within the group is strong support for the fourth hypothesis.

In conclusion, Bales observed that groups which include great men can be expected to have higher rates of productivity and, over time, increasingly higher rates of productivity than groups without great men, and that great men groups will function more smoothly and respond in a less inhibited manner and with less anxiety than groups in which great men do not participate.

Status Consensus in Laboratory Groups. Heinecke and Bales (1953:7–38) reported on the development of status consensus from data gathered from ten groups each composed of five or six members. The groups met for either four or six sessions. After each session the group members were asked to rank each other in terms of who produced the best ideas and who was most effective in leading the group discussions. Using this variation of the sociometric technique, Heinecke and Bales developed a framework for measuring status consensus.

The researchers then separated the groups on the basis of high or low degrees of status consensus and found that when agreement on status was high, the three top-ranked group members shifted their positions while those members who ranked fourth and fifth maintained their positions. In those groups which were low in status consensus, shifts in positions occurred at all levels, and shifts occurred with greater frequency.

Heinecke and Bales found some interesting relationships between status consensus and other group characteristics. For example, both high-and low-consensus groups were consistent in their status rankings of group members over several sessions. Also, member satisfaction was also greater in high than in low consensus groups. High-consensus groups scored consistently higher as effective problem-solving agents than did low-consensus groups. Low-consensus groups were less effective in solving problems in the socio-emotional area and were characteristically argumentative about status consensus rankings and other decision-making and problem-solving areas of group interaction. In terms of Bales' discrimination of task and socio-emotional problems which all groups face and their need to achieve some balance between the two problem areas, the results of this study are not surprising. Low-consensus groups, having difficulties in the socio-emotional areas, could not be expected to have high scores in problem-solution or high frequency rates in those IPA categories which reflect group member attempts to resolve task problems.

These research findings support the view that high status consensus is an important factor in the development of group solidarity. When groups having high status consensus among its members are found to perform tasks consistently at a higher level than low status groups and to score low in maintained levels of socio-emotional conflict, the relationship between status consensus and solidarity is reinforced. As a final note, it might be suggested that high status consensus as an indicator of group structure is a factor in group organization which functions to facilitate the task-socio-emotional balance necessary for goal achievement. In these experiments, high status consensus resulted in effective problem-solution and a minimum of socio-emotional difficulties. It is certainly possible that the incorporation of member agreement (which high status consensus reflects) into the system of group interaction is a crucial element in maintaining effective group organization.

The Effect of Group Size on Interaction. Bales was also interested in the variations in group interaction patterns which result from variations in the size of the group. In an extended laboratory experiment (Bales & Borgatta, 1966:493–512), Bales and his research team studied male students obtained from the university employment office. Each student group met for four sessions. In each session, the group memberships remained the same. There were four groups of each size from two through seven. At each group session the members were given the task of discussing a human relations problem and making recommendations for a solution. Different but similar problems were used for each session for each group.

Employing the IPA method, Bales was able to indicate the variations in interaction which accrue to groups of different size. The amount of data produced during the two years over which 96 student sessions were held is extensive. The following is a summary of the major findings.

(1) *As the size of the group increases*:
 Showing tension release increases emphatically
 Giving suggestion increases emphatically
 Showing solidarity increases somewhat
 Giving information increases (if dyads are excluded from this category)
 Showing tension decreases emphatically
 Showing agreement decreases
 Asking for opinion decreases
 Giving opinion decreases (if dyads are excluded from this category)

 EXPLANATION: Each group member is under increasing pressure to maintain appropriate relationships with an increasing number of group members. There are more relationships to maintain and increasingly less time in which to do so. The effects of the pressure of time and increasing numbers are reflected in the above-noted changes in IPA category frequencies.

(2) *Special characteristics of dyads*: The findings indicate that the dyad is unique. In the report, the unique features of the dyad are associated with the impossibility of a majority forming except by unanimity.
Notably high rates of showing tension
Uniquely high rates of asking for orientation
High rates of giving orientation
Uniquely high rates of asking for opinion
High rates of giving suggestion
Low rates of showing disagreement
Low rates of showing antagonism
Lower than average rates of giving opinion

EXPLANATION: The above rates for the listed IPA categories result from: (1) the lack of influence which comes from majority pressure, (2) the absence of public opinion or group sanctions, (3) no third party to mediate differences, and (4) a necessary softening of the dominant-submissive distinction between the two members in order to reduce the possibility of group breakdown.

(3) *Differences between odd- and even-sized groups*:
Even-sized groups (4 and 6 members):
Higher rates of showing disagreement
Higher rates of showing antagonism
Possibly higher rates of solidarity
Possibly lower rates of agreement
Lower rates of asking for suggestion

EXPLANATION: Groups of any even size are able to subdivide into two equal parts without the possibility of a majority influence. Under this condition, conflict (higher rates of disagreement and antagonism) is understandable. Odd-sized groups are more likely to divide into unequal-sized subgroups and reach a decision sooner, thereby avoiding the conflicts which characterize even-sized groups. (It is interesting to note that these results are consistent with much earlier interpretations offered by Georg Simmel [see Chapter Three] in his discussions of two- and three-party relations.)

Bales and Borgatta (1966:503) report that "... all categories show a tendency toward greater variability for each individual's performance as the size of the group increases." Also, the authors observed increased variability among members in the "tension release" and "giving suggestion" categories as the size of the group increases, and variability among individuals decreases in the "showing agreement," "disagreement," and "showing tension" categories.

The IPA method is useful in measuring a host of factors which are believed to be significant determiners of group interaction. We have looked at the factors of leadership, status consensus, and group size. Theodore M. Mill's (1967:33) summary of the IPA method lists others for which the Bales method is useful for gathering the necessary data:

> . . . the kind of problem the group is working on; the personalities of the members, taken individually and as a figuration; the size of the group; sex, age, and social class of members; age of the group; relation of the group to other groups, and its relation to the observer.

SYMLOG—1979

Most recently, having coordinated the IPA method with a self-analytic method for use by members of small groups (Bales, 1970), Bales has developed, along with Stephen P. Cohen (Bales & Cohen, 1979), a SYstem for the Multiple Level Observation of Groups (SYMLOG).

SYMLOG is a complex method of small group observation but may be identified simply (Bales & Cohen, 1979: 8 & 9) as an observational technique that results in the description of ". . . all behavior and content in the interaction of a group . . . by reference to a concept of a three-dimensional space." The central focus of the many scoring and rating methods which SYMLOG encompasses are the three dimensions of behavior identifiable in small group interaction. Described by adjectives, they are: 1) Dominant vs. Submissive, 2) Friendly vs. Unfriendly, and 3) Instrumentally Controlled vs. Emotionally Expressive. These three dimensions, when conceptualized in terms of physical space and location, have the following spatial referents: 1) U—Upward–Dominant, 2) D—Downward–Submissive, 3) P—Positive–Friendly, 4) N—Negative–Unfriendly, 5) F—Forward–Instrumentally Controlled, and 6) B—Backward–Emotionally Expressive. (See Figure 6-6.)

Bales and Cohen are aware of the complexity of the SYMLOG system and suggest that its effective use requires serious study and preparation. Since it is not the purpose of this discussion to describe the entire methodology but to introduce the reader to the most recent development derived from Interaction Process Analysis, the following example of one rating method will suffice. Members of a small group may use the SYMLOG Adjective Rating Form. Through a simple procedure of adding the ratings and diagraming them, the group members will be able to develop

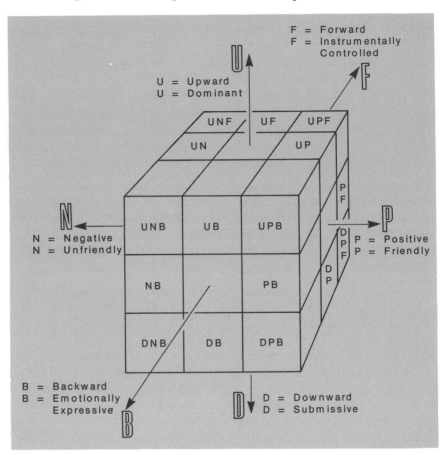

Figure 6-6. The SYMLOG Cube

The three spatial dimensions of SYMLOG may be depicted as located on the six planes of a cube with the two opposing constructs in each dimension (U-D, P-N, and F-B) placed on opposing faces on the cube. When each face on the cube is divided into nine cells, combinations of the dimensions can be identified as cells within the cube. The combinations number 26 with the 27th or centermost cell not applying to the combinations.

Reprinted with permission of Macmillan Publishing Co., Inc. from *SYMLOG: A Manual for the Case Study of Groups* by Bales, Cohen, and Williamson. Copyright © 1979 by The Free Press, a division of Macmillan Publishing Co., Inc.

guidelines for improving group interaction and for assisting the group toward the achievement of stated or implied goals. The rating form includes 26 items corresponding to the 26 combinations of the three dimensions discussed above. Some examples of the adjectives used in the rating form are: "active, dominant, talks a lot," "unfriendly, negativistic," and "passive, introverted, says little." The reader should note the similarity of these items to items suggested in the IPA categories.

FIELD THEORY (KURT LEWIN)

It should be clear at this point, that the field of small groups and the interactionist approach are strongly oriented to a social-psychological view of human behavior. Such a view combines the psychologist's interest in the individual as a discrete, functioning unit and the sociologist's interest in the group as a social system. Before the development of the field theory approach to the study of social groups, there was little cooperation between these two disciplines. Psychologists argued that the only true reality is the individual, and some sociologists were convinced that only the social group was real. As the spokesman for those psychologists who had begun to recognize the importance of social forces on individual human behavior, Kurt Lewin (1948:74) argued that ". . . the behavior of individuals as well as groups depends upon their situation and their peculiar position in it," and that ". . . it is possible to give a clearly detailed description of the peculiar structure of a concrete situation and its dynamics in scientific terms."

The basic social-psychological framework within which Lewin was to develop his field theory is one in which the separate disciplines were to combine their knowledge and work together in order to fully understand the individual as developing within a social milieu and the social group as a special collection of individuals. Framing these early interests in terms of the problems facing social psychology, Lewin (1939b) listed the difficulties inherent in this new approach to the study of human social behavior. We present a partial list of relevant difficulties here not only because it identifies some pervasive small group problems, but also because it points to the elements which combine to form the theoretical basis of Lewin's field theory:

1. The handling of both historical and systematical problems.
2. The handling of problems related to groups as well as to individuals.
3. The handling of all "sizes" of objects or patterns (social psychology has to include problems of a nation and its situation, as well as of a play group of three children and their momentary struggle).
4. Problems of "atmosphere" (such as friendliness, pressure, etc.).
5. Experimental social psychology will have to find a way to bring the large-size patterns into a framework small enough for the technical possibilities of experimentation (Lewin, 1939b:870).

CONCEPTS IN FIELD THEORY

Lewin's field theory is built upon a view of social groups as "sociological wholes," the parts of which are interdependent. Group behavior is to be understood as goal-oriented. Groups (and individual members) have *life-spaces* which refer to the situations in which groups and individuals are found. Life-spaces have *boundaries* which limit freedom in that they define the lines across which *locomotion* is prohibited. The concept of life-space includes three separate *regions*: (1) regions in which movement is entirely free, (2) regions in which movement is entirely prohibited, and (3) regions in which movement is intermediate between freedom and prohibition. Intermediate regions refer to social situations in which activities are not formally prohibited but which produce a sense of restriction for the group or the individual. *Life-space*, then, refers to situational regions within which behavior (group or individual) is free, prohibited, or intermediate between freedom and prohibition.

It is within a life-space that a social group moves in the direction of regions which carry *positive valences* (forces which are attractive to the group's goal orientation) and away from regions which carry *negative valences* (restrictive, prohibitive forces which work against the group's goal orientation). *Valences* are equivalents of group forces which influence goal-related activity, and the direction taken by a group in relation to these forces is called the *vector*.

The terminology used by Lewin is adapted from the physical sciences. Lewin argued that the behavior exhibited by members of groups and by groups as sociological wholes can be described in purely scientific terms. Behavior exhibited by groups and their members can be measured with greater facility and precision by adapting the physical scientist's terminology and technique to social situations in which these groups are striving to achieve defined goals.

Terms such as life-space, valence, and vector are only a few of the terms employed by Lewin to help explain social groups. Recognizing the importance of the individual within group boundaries, Lewin incorporates the concepts of *individual needs*, *human aspiration*, and *emotions* as systems within the individual which help determine individual response to group forces. Drawing on sociological research and analysis, Lewin also uses concepts such as *group decision making*, *group atmosphere* and *"we-feeling."* Lewin's consideration of this last concept provides an excellent example of his use of sociological terminology. In differentiating the effects of autocratic and democratic group atmospheres on elementary-school-aged children, Lewin (1939a:27) observed significant differences in levels of "we-feeling": "Statements which were 'we-centered' occurred twice as often in the democracy as in the autocracy, whereas far more statements in the autocracy were 'I-centered' than in the democracy."

METHOD AND ANALYSIS

Unfortunately, there is no single source which presents a complete statement of Lewin's field theory and method. Lewin preferred writing articles and monographs on specific group types and group problems, and it is within these writings that his methodology is to be found. Included among these are his studies dealing with intergroup conflict and group identity (Lewin, 1935:175–187), and conflict in small groups (Lewin, 1940:Chapter IV). Lewin was interested also in culture and its effects upon behavior and produced a number of interesting reports which include a comparative analysis of the United States and Germany, and interpretations of cultural change and normative divergence (cultural re-education).

THE PROBLEM OF ADOLESCENCE

In his introduction to the problem of adolescence and the influences which surround adolescent behavior, Lewin (1939b:872) discusses the relationship between his method and the problem at hand:

> The field-theoretical approach is intended to be a practical vehicle of research. As is true with any tool, its characteristics can be understood fully only by the use of it in actual research. Therefore, instead of stating general methodological principles *in abstractum*, I prefer to discuss the problem of adolescence . . . as an illustration.

Lewin's approach to the problem of adolescence integrates the basic elements of his field theory with the typical difficulties apparent in adolescent behavior. The analysis is a complicated one and is best presented here in the form of an outline summary.

Typical Problems of Adolescent Behavior

THEMES: 1. Adolescence is a period of transition which involves significant changes in behavior.

         2. Group environments to which the adolescent belongs are the basic influencers of perception, feeling, and activity.

PROBLEM 1: *Adolescence involves a change in group-belongingness.* The adolescent does not consider himself a child, nor do others.

Changes in group belonging take on a greater or lesser degree of importance depending upon how central group belonging is to the individual adolescent. However, any shift in group belonging must be considered "social locomotion"; that is, the position of the individual shifts. Shifts in group belonging change the individual's perception of reality since surrounding regions must be viewed from a completely different perspective.

PROBLEM 2:   *The shift from the group of children to the adult group involves "locomotion" to an unknown position for the adolescent.* Adult-oriented perceptions indicate that the adolescent is entering an unknown environment in which there are new rights, privileges, and taboos not part of the environment of the child. During the period of adolescent transition the individual is confronted with broadening his childhood space of free movement to that of the adult world, a field of activity which is unknown. Lewin suggests that, for the adolescent, the adult world is a cognitively unstructured environment—unfamiliar and uncertain.

PROBLEM 3:   *Change in adolescent perception of his physical self.* The adolescent's knowledge of his body is seriously challenged by the fact of sexual maturation, and the individual may be disturbed by these changes. Lewin considers the body part of the individual's life-space which, during adolescence, becomes strange and unfamiliar. For some adolescents, bodily changes can result in unstable feelings and attitudes about the total environment in which the adolescent functions. This view of the adolescent's perception of his changing body may result in uncertainty in behavior and psychological and social conflict—in some cases, aggression.

PROBLEM 4:   *Radicalism as a characteristic of adolescence.* Adolescence is a time in which the individual is in the process of moving from one region to another (here Lewin uses the term "region" as an equivalent of group). Because of the transitional nature of adolescence, the individual is more formative, more pliable. The adolescent is in a psychological environment in which radical behavior and radical ideologies do not appear as extreme as they do to members of the adult world. If one considers ideologies as regions, shifts from one to another by the adolescent in his cognitively unstructured environment, do not assume the significance placed upon them by adults whose life-space is already cognitively structured and clearly differentiated. Put simply, the political "right" and the political "left" are only shades of the same color for the adolescent. Lewin points out that the lack of a well-developed psychological system of cognitive differentiation is possibly the basis for behavioral and ideological extremes being manifested during the period of adolescence.

PROBLEM 5:   *Adolescence, as a widening of the life-space of the individual, involves changing perceptions of the time dimension.* Adolescents are influenced by the manner in which they view the future. Since future time influences present behavior, it must be considered part of the present life-space. During adolescence, the scope of time is increased and perceptions of time change from days, weeks, and months to years. The vague ideas about future plans, specifically occupational plans, must now be replaced by a more clearly differentiated perspective about real and unreal expectations about the future. This involves the differentiation of ideal expectations and the realities of present and future possibilities. The difficulty associated with adolescence in this regard is that these new perceptions of time must occur in a cognitively unstructured environment and about a field (the adult world) which is relatively unknown.

PROBLEM 6:   *The problem of adolescence is one of marginality.* The transitional quality of adolescence suggests that the position and life-space of the individual is marginal to childhood and adulthood. The adolescent has rejected childhood and, wanting to enter the world of the adult, is aware that adult acceptance is by no means complete. This places the adolescent on the boundaries of both groups, belonging to neither of them. With reference to the concept of the "marginal man" as found in the literature on minority groups, Lewin suggests that the position of the adolescent is sociologically the same as for marginal members of minority groups. Characteristically, then, the adolescent is emotionally unstable and sensitive and exhibits tendencies toward unbalanced contradictory behavior.

Adolescence, when viewed from the field theory perspective, becomes a time in human development in which the stereotyped characteristics of adolescent behavior (shyness, sensitivity, and aggressiveness) are found to result from the insecurity of the adolescent's tenuous position between his childhood group and the adult group. The lack of cognitive structure during the marginal time of adolescence produces the changeable character of the period in regard to values and ideologies. It is the tension produced by the adolescent's marginality which results in the insecurities of the individual's emotional life and the ease with which the adolescent accepts and then rejects radical extremes. Although the analysis appears to concentrate only on group forces as elements in the determination of adolescence, Lewin insists that these group forces produce the traditional results only when the individual adolescent is receptive to them. A crucial element in the adolescent field is the individual who, if emotionally and socially stable, will be less subject to the unsettling influences of surrounding regions. This last observation is important because it reinforces Lewin's social-psychological interpretation of human behavior which views group life and human interaction as systems of interrelated individual and group forces.

GROUP ATMOSPHERES

Since Lewin was concerned with the interrelations and total effect of all the elements in the situations within which groups and individuals function, it is not surprising that he commented on Ronald Lippitt's (1939: 26–49) study of democratic and autocratic group atmospheres in task-oriented clubs composed of ten- and eleven-year-old boys and girls. The subjects were chosen from volunteers from two school classes for a mask-making club. One group of subjects was given a democratic leader and the other group an autocratic leader. The leaders attempted to create appropriate atmospheres by following certain rules. For example, in the democratic group, policy was determined by the entire group, while for the autocratic group all policy determination became a function of the leader; in the democratic group members were free to work with whom they chose and were given freedom to divide the tasks as they chose, while in the autocratic group the leader usually determined who should work with whom and what function each member should perform.

Using techniques similar to those of Bales' IPA, observers recorded the number of actions per unit of time and determined that autocratic leaders were approximately twice as active as democratic leaders over the same time period. Democratic leaders performed more submissive actions than did autocratic leaders, but both leaders were less submissive than the average member. The same results occurred for objective, matter-of-fact actions. The autocratic leader initiated activity 118% more than other group members, and the democratic leader initiated activity only 41% more than other group members.

Our interests here are in Lewin's interpretation of group atmospheres. Therefore, we will concentrate upon his interpretation of Lippitt's data. In his report on the Lippitt study, Lewin (1939a:26–28) remarks on the influence of the total situation upon the members of the two groups and identifies the autocratic leader and the situation which develops around autocratic leadership as forces which direct the individual group member toward induced goals. *Induced goals* are those given the group member by the leader to replace a goal accepted by the group member, and, in this case, Lewin argues that the induced goal becomes a barrier against the free movement of the member toward the achievement of that member's goal (in field theory terms, induced goal barriers limit or reduce the space of free movement or locomotion). Democratic leaders were found to aid locomotion by reinforcing the direction taken by the group member toward the realization of the member's own goal. Goal achievement resulted from creating an atmosphere in which barriers toward the realization of goals were eliminated through the cooperation of leader and group member.

The different group atmospheres had significant effects upon the relationships between group members. The autocratic group atmosphere generated much higher rates of hostile domination among group members, a higher frequency of demands for attention, as well as more criticism than was found in the democratic group. As noted earlier in this chapter, the emergence of integrative elements within the democratic group was apparent in the frequency with which members made statements which were "we-centered." Democratic group members made such statements twice as often as did members of the autocratic group.

Lewin also interpreted Lippitt's data to indicate that: (1) children were less matter-of-fact, less cooperative, and more submissive to the leader in the autocratic group than to the democratic group leader; (2) democratic group members exhibited more individuality than did autocratic group members; and (3) subgroups developed spontaneously in the democratic group, while in the autocratic group, subgroups organized only under the direction of the leader. Lewin's interpretation also emphasized the importance of group atmospheres in the Lippitt study by identifying the changes in behavior of two children whose group memberships were switched during the series of meetings. Before the switch, the two children exhibited the characteristics of the groups to which they belonged. After the switch, the children adapted to the new group atmosphere and group leader and began to exhibit characteristics of their new memberships. The autocratic child who entered the democratic group changed his behavior from less friendly and more dominating to more friendly and less dominating. The same turnabout in behavior occurred for the democratic child who entered the autocratic group. That child became less friendly and more dominating. Lewin's argument is that the behavior exhibited by individuals in specific group settings is not determined only by personality and other forces which individuals bring to the group. These are important, but individual differences are offset by the force with which the group atmosphere influences the behavior of group members.

Although Lewin was an early advocate of the group influence perspective, he also concerned himself with the individual who must behave within the group setting. Lewin wanted to account for the motivational factors which influence behavior and argued that motivation must be viewed as a process of tension production and reduction which facilitates goal achievement. Individuals organize systems of tension which form a motivational basis for behavior. When the behavior of the individual results in the achievement of an individual or group goal, the tension is finally reduced. In a study by Helen B. Lewis (1944:113–126) two subjects worked cooperatively at the completion of a task. Lewis found that when one of the two subjects completed a task, the other behaved in exactly the same manner. After the series of task completion sessions, subjects were able to recall fewer uninterrupted tasks regardless of which subject had completed that specific task. The evidence indicates that when individuals identify as group members, they do not have to reach a desired goal themselves to have a sense of task completion. For both individuals in the study, satisfaction with the completion of a task by one or the other resulted in tension release by both. The experiment highlights the interdependence of individuals and the groups to which they belong. In the study, the distinction made between individual and group goals is less clear when, through cooperation, individuals develop a strong sense of group identity.

Finally, Lewin's thinking about the group and the relationship of the group to the individual member is clear in his observation that a social group is best defined in terms of the interdependence of its parts, and that the properties of a group such as group structure, goals, and norms are different but connected to similar properties of individuals.

SOCIOMETRY (JACOB L. MORENO)

In 1953, Jacob L. Moreno wrote *Who Shall Survive?* in an attempt to present the origins, methodology, and applications of the field of sociometry. Initially, Moreno viewed sociometry as a separate field of investigation. Sociometry was presented in the text (1953) as a technique for reorganizing not only social groups, but communities and, in an effort to change the existing larger social order, society as well. The sociometric technique was officially introduced at the convention of the Medical Society of the State of New York in April, 1933, when early sociograms were exhibited which suggested those social forces which influenced human behavior.

The two decades which followed were disappointing to Moreno because he felt that the use of his technique as a means of reorganizing groups, communities, and societies had been largely ignored. More disappointing was the complete rejection of the philosophy behind the development of the technique. Moreno wanted to develop a new positive religion which would incorporate the insights of the world scientific community. In effect, Moreno's concerns were more properly those of community integration based upon member creativity, mutual sharing, love, faith in fellow man, and the organization of a "superdynamic" community based upon scientific techniques.

Moreno developed the sociometric discipline as the means to realizing the construction of a fully integrated world community. His first sociometric principles were:

> The sequence of "proximity" in space established a precise order of social bonds and acceptance, the sequence of giving love and attention is thus strictly preordained and prearranged, according to a "spatial imperative". . . . the sequence of proximity in time establishes a precise order of social attention and veneration according to a "temporal imperative." The here and now demands help first, the next in time to the here and now backward and forward requires help next (Moreno, 1953:xx).

Since the 1950s, Moreno's contributions have been limited to the use of his sociometric tests to measure the affectivity factor in group relationships. Small group researchers have adapted the Moreno technique in order to measure interpersonal attraction and sentiment. The purpose, in most cases, is the spatial rearrangement of group members in order to facilitate interpersonal behavior and goal achievement. The argument in favor of the use of the sociometric technique is as follows: Goal achievement and interpersonal relations are facilitated by spatial arrangements which take into account the sentiments and interpersonal attractions which prevail among group members.

The technique is used to reduce or eliminate elements of group disorganization or disruption which derive from member dissatisfaction or patterns of dislike among group members. Used in therapeutic groups to reduce tension and to increase the ameliorative results of these groups, the sociometric technique is also effective in increasing group efficiency in task performance through increased cooperation among group members.

THE SOCIOMETRIC TECHNIQUE

Although the history of the development of the technique suggests a complex and difficult method for group restructuring, the technique is simple to apply and to interpret. Members of a group are asked to participate in the reorganization of the group by identifying other group members whom they like and dislike or group members with whom they would prefer working and those with whom they would not want to work. In classrooms, for example, students are asked to choose other students next to whom they would prefer to sit. The answers to these questions form the basis for the construction of a sociogram. The *sociogram* depicts preferred associations based upon feelings and interpersonal attractions among group members, or upon some specific criterion such as preference of a partner for the performance of a task or some other goal requiring cooperation.

The sociogram is constructed by indicating, symbolically, each member of the group and their preferences according to some stated criterion. For example, if the criterion for identification is work partner preference, a sociogram might be designed (see Figure 6-7) which indicates answers to the question: Which group members would be your first choice and your last choice as work partners?

In studying Figure 6-7 it becomes clear that if interpersonal attraction is expected to enhance the achievement of a work goal, then subgroups *AB* and *EF* should perform more efficiently than any other combination of partners. The third combination, *CD*, would not be expected to perform as efficiently as the other two subgroups since they did not choose each other as partners.

The use of the sociometric technique is based on the assumption that when interpersonal conflicts within groups are reduced or eliminated there results an increase in the morale of group members. Increased morale and the integration which ensues promote greater efficiency in the achievement of group goals.

An early study by Moreno (1953) established the relationship between sociometric restructuring of groups and increased morale. The investigation was conducted at a home for delinquent girls near Hudson, New York. The residents, numbering between five and six hundred, were housed in sixteen cottages, each of which was presided over by a housemother. Moreno attempted to reorganize the cottage memberships using

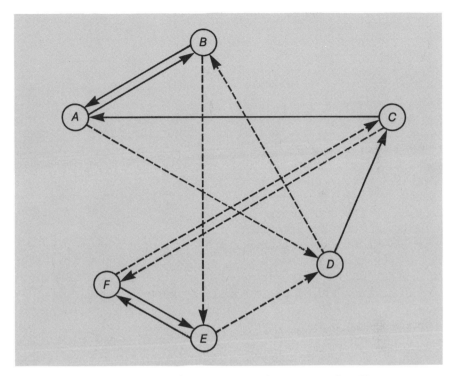

Figure 6-7. Example of Simple Sociogram Indicating Member Choices

Symbols: The circles symbolize group members; unbroken arrows, first choices; broken arrows, last choices; reciprocal unbroken arrows, interpersonal attraction; reciprocal broken arrows, interpersonal repulsion.

sociometric choices of each resident. The criterion on which the choices were made was each cottage member's like or dislike for others in the community as cottage residents. Moreno concluded that the cottage reorganization resulted not only in increased morale—which Moreno noted in the reduction of psychological and social tensions—but also in the reduction of problems of discipline.

In a study by John G. Jenkins (1948) on developing morale among naval air personnel, sociometric choice tests were administered in which members of an air group were asked to choose two men to fly wing in combat and two men least desired to fly wing in combat. Contrasting two squadrons, Jenkins found that the sociogram produced for one squadron supported the generally held view that it was one of high morale, good combat effectiveness, and low combat fatigue. By way of contrast, the sociometric choices in a second reinforced common opinion that it was a low-morale squadron.

Once morale is established in a group through sociometric choice procedures, the prevailing view is that effective goal achievement, such as the completion of a task or effective group performance, is a logical outcome. Moreno's restructuring of work groups in the delinquent home indicated that mutually attracted pairs were more efficient in their work production. Marvin E. Shaw and Lilly M. Shaw (1962) reported similar results but only during the initial performance periods. They studied second-grade students who were asked to identify three other students as desirable study companions and three students as the least desirable study companions. When study groups were organized along the lines of recorded sociometric choices, the initial study period produced high correlations between cohesiveness resulting from sociometric choices and performance. However, during the second study period, these high performance rates were not maintained.

There is clearly a strong relationship between groups organized along lines of sociometric choice and group morale, but it would appear that sociometric choice as a factor in the development of morale is only one of many determiners of high levels of group productivity and performance. When groups are determined by sociometric choice there may be some misinterpretation by those making the choices. In the study by Shaw and Shaw, it is possible that student choices were made not according to the established criteria of desirable study partners but according to liking, which carries more social than work connotations. This might explain the reduction in performance during the second study session. The zeal of the first session, which resulted in high performance rates, may have been redirected in the later session to the pleasant experience of being with others whom one liked.

The development of the sociometric technique by Moreno adds a singularly unique dimension to the understanding of behavior in group settings. Rather than accept the limitations which group controls and group pressures exert upon individual behavior, Moreno sought to identify the importance of individual feelings and emotions as important elements in group organization. The sociometric technique, as the studies cited above indicate, offers a method which allows groups to function more effectively by restructuring them along lines more closely allied with the emotions and interpersonal needs of individual group members.

THE PSYCHODRAMA AND SOCIODRAMA

The psychodramaturgical method of therapy was defined by Moreno as the science which explores truth through the use of drama. In the psychodrama, Moreno constructed a therapeutic environment which includes the five major elements of dramatic presentation: the stage, the subject or actor, the director, the staff, and the audience. As the actor, a patient is expected to use the tools of stage acting freely and spontaneously in order to explore life experiences and deep personal involvements which are to be transferred, eventually, to the audience. Members of the audience then relate to the patient their feelings about the performance. In the performance, the actor is expected to relate life incidents and feelings about them. The audience reacts to these. The expected result is a group catharsis. Through the sharing of experiences, the patient is able to understand the dynamic forces which control behavior. In a sense, the performance is an acting out through free association the elements which contributed to the need for a therapeutic experience. Interestingly, the key to the effectiveness of psychodrama as therapy is not derived from the patient alone or from others in the dramatic situation, but from the interaction between the actor and the audience.

The concentration of the actor on feelings and emotions, and the responses of the audience at the same level, are typical of Moreno's perspective on human social behavior. Communication is not therapy if the communication is only surface interaction, that is, interaction at the verbal symbolic level. For success, verbal communication must be combined with other communication forms such as body language, bodily contact, and, most especially, with the communication of feelings, which join the patient and the audience into a functioning whole. Moreno considered the relationship between the patient and the audience absolutely necessary in order for the patient to share feelings and experiences. In the psychodrama, sharing becomes the basis for successful therapy.

Moreno's psychodramatic technique began a tradition in group therapy and analysis clearly different from any other. From the sociological perspective, psychodrama is a technique which uses interaction between an individual and a collection of others, but at a level of emotional sensitivity rather than at the level of symbolic meanings. The level of sensitivity used in psychodrama is roughly equivalent to the counselor's understanding of second-level communication. In both these levels, communication is believed to occur between or among individuals through a communication of feelings. However, symbolic interaction deals with intentions and meanings through the use of verbal symbols established under consensus of interacting parties.

The Johari Interpersonal Relations Model discussed in Chapter Five is closest to the concepts of psychodrama. All quadrants might be subject matter for the psychodramatic performance. The common therapeutic qualities of the psychodrama and the Johari Model suggest that the information in each window may be used in the dramatic performance. The following interpretation translates each quadrant into material used in the patient's relationship to the audience:

1. Open quadrant—   The information results from common day-to-day experiences members of the psychodrama audience have with the actor/patient. Ordinarily, the information in this quadrant would provide the audience with a pre-performance point of reference.

2. Blind quadrant—   The information results from pre-performance and during-performance interpretations which the audience imposes upon the actor/patient and results from audience members "reading," through expressed behavior by the actor/patient, feelings and motivation of which the actor/patient is not aware.

3. Hidden quadrant—   The information results from knowledge which the actor/patient chooses to keep from the audience. However, during the performance by the actor/patient the dynamic effect of the situation may function as a basis for releasing the content of this quadrant. Information released becomes part of the content of the open quadrant.

4. Unknown quadrant—   This quadrant might be identified as the true psychiatric quadrant. Neither the actor/patient nor audience is aware of the content of this quadrant. As in the third quadrant, however, the performance dynamic may function to release information stored here, in which case the psychodrama becomes a situation reaching psychiatric proportions.

Moreno developed the psychodrama as a technique for placing the patient in an objective environment which, he argued, is necessary for the resolution of deep mental conflicts. The technique is one which uses interaction in terms of interpersonal relations in order to explore the private worlds of the actor/patient.

The Sociodrama. Moreno (1953:87) defined the sociodrama as ". . . a deep action method dealing with inter-group relations and collective ideologies." It is briefly discussed here because of Moreno's unique identification of the social group as patient and, in the sociodramatic situation, as the actor. In the group sessions, the members interact in order to achieve the goal of conflict resolution, not of individual group members, but of the group as a whole.

The sociodrama is based upon the assumption that there is a set of roles which the culture imposes upon individuals. When the role sets of individuals are not in agreement with those established by the culture, it is necessary to resolve the differences and to establish an order within the group (and the society) which is more in keeping with the expectations established by the culture.

Moreno's hopes for the sociodrama were far reaching. The technique was constructed to reach large groups of people through the use of electronic media of mass communication. It was believed that through the use of the media, the sociometric technique could reduce intercultural tensions in neighborhoods and communities everywhere and reduce the possibilities of riots or other forms of conflict in these areas.

Moreno's entire system of thought about human group behavior was underscored by concern with the affective bonds which develop among members of social groups. The sociometric technique as well as the more therapeutically oriented psychodramatic and sociodramatic techniques were developed as means by which the scientific community could achieve a deeper understanding of the emotional structure of human relations. Moreno also saw these techniques as helping mechanisms for achieving a level of integration within the group which would be based upon the spontaneity of human association and the creativity of the actor.

If there is a flaw in Moreno's theory of affective bonds in human groups and in his development of techniques for understanding them, it lies in the limitations which restrict all psychological attempts to understand social behavior. There is no place in Moreno's thinking for consideration of activity and interaction patterns which direct the group toward the achievement of task-oriented or decision-making goals. Moreno simply did not recognize that while the deeper, more affective life of a group is a necessary component for group integration and maintenance, its worth must be measured against the effectiveness with which the group functions at the social level of act and interact, and the efficiency with which member behavior contributes to the achievement of personal and group goals.

SYSTEM THEORY (GEORGE C. HOMANS)

George Homans wanted to develop a sociological theory which explained group behavior as a system of mutually dependent elements. Accordingly, the relationships among these elements are viewed as determiners of group development and maintenance.

CONCEPTUAL ELEMENTS

There are three basic elements in Homans' scheme. They are: sentiments, activities, and interaction. *Activity* refers to the observable acts which individuals in groups perform. For example, a student enters a classroom shortly before class is to start and begins talking to another early-arriving student. The student has performed an act. When the professor enters the class and begins the lecture, the professor is performing an act. The two acts are not connected but each is an observable act. The student acted and so did the professor, and both acts occurred in the same environment but at different times.

Interaction refers to the relationships or patterns of communication which connect members of groups to each other. Interaction is a combination of acts which occur in a time frame and which are related to each other in much the same way as are any two co-dependent objects. The examples given above for activity are useful here. The student and the professor were not interacting with each other, but they were establishing, through their acts, an interaction situation. In the example involving two students, each student will respond to the activity of the other. They are communicating, or interacting, with each other. The professor, upon entering the classroom and beginning the lecture, is performing activity directed toward the class. When students respond to the activity of the professor and patterns of communication are established between the professor and the students, an interaction is occurring and can be observed as such.

Activities and interaction are the observable elements in group systems. Sentiments are more difficult to identify and are usually inferred from activities and interaction. *Sentiments* refer to feelings, emotions, needs, and attitudes of group members toward each other. In the example of the two students, their feelings can be known to the observer through attempts to interpret how each is behaving toward the other. In order to identify sentiments it is necessary to define interaction situations by giving them some value or meaning. If the two students are arguing, the meaning given their acts and the interaction between them is quite different from the meaning their acts and interaction would be given if the situation were defined as a friendly exchange of confidences.

Homans used these three elements as the basic components of his analysis of groups as systems, but these elements are important only in that they are interdependent elements. Much of Homans' presentation is concerned with the way these elements are connected to each other, that is, with their interdependencies.

In his book, *The Human Group* (1950), Homans presents the three elements of group behavior as parts of both the external and internal systems of social groups. The total social system of the group is made up of these two component systems, and, in turn, each system is composed of sentiments, activities and interaction (see Figure 6-8).

THE EXTERNAL SYSTEM

Individuals are motivated to associate with others and to form, eventually, a system of group interaction for a great variety of reasons. For example,

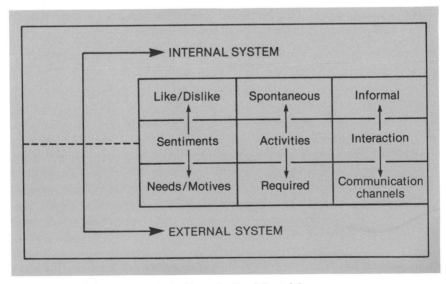

Figure 6-8. Components of the Group's Total Social System

individuals may have special skills which they want to use constructively, or may need money and so apply for a job. From the Homans perspective, a job is a complex of activities. Since, in most job situations, activities are coordinated and require the cooperation of occupants of both the same and different work positions, interaction results. Interaction in the external system might here be described in terms of the formal communication network which is established for the efficient coordination of work activities in, for example, an industrial plant or business office.

In observing the relationships between and among the three basic elements in the system, Homans argues that, if there is a change in sentiments or a change in activities, there must develop a different form or pattern of interaction. The relationships between the three elements in the external system can be stated as follows: sentiments determine activities upon which interaction is based.

THE INTERNAL SYSTEM

The line of separation between the external and internal systems is clearly delineated by Homans (1950:110):

> . . . think of the external system as group behavior that enables the group to survive in its environment and think of the internal system as group behavior that is an expression of the sentiments towards one another developed by the members of the group in the course of their life together.

Interpretations of the three elements which form the internal system of group behavior shift from the need/motive → required activities → communication channels type of scheme found in the external system to a scheme which can be represented as follows: feelings (for example, like/dislike) → spontaneous activities → informal patterns of interaction. The distinction being made here is roughly equivalent to the distinction between formal and informal group structures found in Chapter Two. In effect, the development of the internal system follows and develops out of the relationships among elements within the external system.

MUTUAL DEPENDENCIES

Homans was not concerned with the straightforward analysis of each of the three conceptual elements of sentiments, activities, and interaction. Their importance lay in their mutual dependencies. Group systems are whole systems characterized by the relationships between parts. The foundation of group behavior in terms of the dependency of elements is sentiment. Activities result from individual sentiments, and activities combine to form both external and internal systems of interaction.

In order to develop generalizations about the mutual dependencies which relate the three basic elements of group behavior, Homans reanalyzed five studies of social behavior. Through this reexamination of reported facts, he developed a series of generalizations in the form of testable hypotheses. One of the five studies reexamined is the study of workers at the Hawthorne Works of Western Electric Company (see Chapter Nine). This study will serve as an example of the use of the case study to develop hypotheses which surround the three elements central to Homans' theory. Each of the hypotheses developed indicates a relationship between two of the three basic elements and derive from interpretations of the behavior observed, for example, within the internal system which developed among workers while on the job.

Homans noted that workmen in the Bank Wiring Observation Room were required to interact with each other frequently because of the requirements of connecting job functions. With some exceptions, the friendliness which developed was widespread throughout the worker population. The observations resulted in the development of the following hypothesis: Persons who interact frequently with one another tend to like one another (Homans, 1950:111). This hypothesis reflects two facts about basic elements and group systems. The mutual dependency is between interaction and sentiment, but the interaction is part of the external system and the sentiments which developed are part of the worker group's internal system. Throughout the analysis, Homans indicates that the mutual dependencies between elements include all possibilities within and between the external and internal systems.

The Bank Wiring Observation Room workers developed a system of informal relationships in which all members participated, though to varying degrees. One facet of the informal character of these on-the-job relationships was helping. Even though the company forbade employees to help each other in the performance of their jobs, the practice was a common one. The development of a pattern of helping other workers was noted by Homans (1950:118) and formed the basis for his observation that

> . . . persons who feel sentiments of liking for one another will express those sentiments in activities over and above the activities of the external system, and these activities may further strengthen the sentiments of liking.

Work efficiency defined in terms of output was observed to be the basis for the development of subgroups within the worker population. Those who were less productive developed stronger informal ties to each other than did those whose production was greater. The hypothesis developed from these observations indicated the relationship between activity and interaction within across-system lines:

> . . . persons who interact with one another frequently are more like one another in their activities than they are like other persons with whom they interact less frequently (Homans, 1950:135).

Homans' efforts are, in the view of most, impressive. Along with his interpretation of human behavior as exchange (see Chapter Five), he has developed a system approach to understanding human groups which accounts for the relationships between human motivation, human activity, and the patterns of interaction which develop from these basic elements. The criticism that Homans' concerns are about the most apparent elements of group behavior does not reduce the significance of his conclusions about their mutual dependencies. Until their actual presentation in the form of the above and many other hypotheses in 1950, these interrelationships were by no means apparent in the literature except in the most general sense. And further, the use of field studies as the basis for the development of these hypotheses is, by no means, the chosen environment of most researchers for investigating the small group phenomenon. While refusing to criticize laboratory experimentation, Homans suggests a different arena for research which, to this date, has seldom been used. In the last analysis, both laboratory experimentation and field research are necessary. Past laboratory experimentation has yielded considerable information about the small group, especially about its formation and the emergence of such factors as group norms and leadership. It remains for those who are interested in our understanding of the field to follow Homans' lead and to discover the forces which prevail upon individuals not only while they are forming their group identities and establishing group norms, but also while they are maintaining them in systems of small group interaction.

---

summary

The four major perspectives on small groups discussed in this chapter are: (1) Robert F. Bales' Interaction Process Analysis, (2) Kurt Lewin's

Field Theory, (3) Jacob L. Moreno's Sociometry, and (4) George C. Homans' System Theory.

Robert F. Bales believed that all generalizations about human social behavior must ultimately refer to two types of phenomena: action or interaction phenomena and situational phenomena. All groups and individual action must take into account task and socio-emotional problems. These problems must be resolved if the group is to maintain the balance of internal and external forces necessary for goal attainment.

Interaction Process Analysis (IPA) is a method designed to analyze and interpret interaction in small groups. The IPA technique involves the application of twelve interaction categories to specific group situations. The categories are divided into neutral task area categories, and positive and negative socio-emotional categories. In experimentation, every unit of activity must be recorded by an observer who places them in one of the twelve categories. Interaction profiles result for individual group members and for whole groups. The experimenter is, then, able to develop a sense of the social relationships of group members and of the group as a whole. The task and socio-emotional forces which influence group behavior are, through an interpretation of the interaction profiles, identified, and determinations can be made as to the direction in which the group is moving. The use of the IPA method facilitates leadership studies and laboratory experiments on status consensus and the effects of group size on behavior.

Kurt Lewin believed that it is possible to use the scientific method to give a detailed description of the unique structure of concrete interaction situations. Field theory is built upon a view of social groups as sociological wholes, the parts of which are interdependent. All group behavior is viewed as goal-oriented in that there are forces which propel individuals and the groups to which they belong toward or away from established goals.

Using such concepts as life-space, positive and negative valences, locomotion, boundaries, and regions, Lewin developed a mode of analysis which identified forces in the life-space of individuals and groups. One excellent example of the use of Lewin's field theory is his study of adolescence as a transitional period in which the elements of bodily self-identity, radicalism, time perceptions, and marginality are understood as forces in the development of the individual to maturity.

The sociometric technique of Jacob L. Moreno developed from his belief in a new, positive religion which would incorporate the insights of the scientific community. Moreno was concerned with community and group integration based upon member creativity, mutual sharing, love, and faith. Moreno envisioned a discipline of sociometry which would eventually form the basis for restructuring the world community. This was not to be. Moreno's contributions have been limited to the use of sociometric tests to measure the affectivity factor in group relationships. The intent is to measure interpersonal attraction and sentiment. The premise upon which the use of the sociometric technique is based indicates that goal achievement and interpersonal relations are facilitated by spatial arrangements which take into account the sentiments and interpersonal attractions of group members. In practice, the technique is used to reduce or eliminate elements of group disorganization, to reduce tension in therapeutic groups while increasing the possibilities for successful therapy, and to facilitate task and decision-making group processes.

The psychodramaturgical method was designed by Moreno as a therapeutic device which incorporates the elements of a stage drama in which the patient performs or acts out life experiences and deep personal involvements in the presence of an audience, which results in the development of a special form of interaction between the patient and the audience. The interaction between patient and audience is the key to successful psychodrama since, through establishing a meaningful relationship between the two, group catharsis results. The sociodrama is an extension of the psychodrama and is viewed as a technique which uses the group as actor and which helps resolve inter-group conflict.

The system theory of George C. Homans attempts to explain group behavior as a system of mutually dependent elements. The three conceptual elements in Homans' scheme are sentiments, activities, and interaction. The mutual dependencies among these forms a basis for the determination of group development and maintenance. Activities and interaction are observable group elements. Sentiments are less so and are inferred from activities and interaction patterns. These three elements are present in both the external and internal systems of groups. The external system refers to the formal requirements placed upon group members in order that a task be performed, a decision reached, or a problem solved. The internal system is a collection of sentiments, activities, and interactions which develops as a result of the external system behavior of group members. Essentially, the internal system refers to the development of informal relationships based upon interpersonal attraction and the resulting spontaneous activities of which informal patterns of interaction are composed.

The underlying assumption in Homans' system approach to groups is this: Group systems are whole systems characterized by the relationships between parts. These relationships, or mutual dependencies, form the basis for making generalizations about specific groups in specific settings.

In order to develop generalizations about these mutual dependencies, Homans reexamined five studies of social behavior, among which was the famous study of workers in the Hawthorne Works of Western Electric. By applying his method to the study, Homans developed hypotheses based upon the mutual dependencies found between the basic group elements. Homans' analysis concentrates on the internal systems of groups in which he observes the development of relationships which accrue from external system expectations placed upon group members.

discussion questions

1. If the IPA method were used to develop profiles of members of a delinquent gang, do you think the results would be the same or different from those for a highly integrated college student friendship group?
2. Using the mode of interpretation developed by Kurt Lewin, describe your "locomotion" as a member of a student club or sports team.
3. Assuming that your class is small enough to develop group identity, describe the group atmosphere.
4. If the sociometric technique were applied to your class, do you think learning would be enhanced? Why, or why not?
5. Can you distinguish the sentiments which result in an individual's decision to marry from those which develop in the marital relationship?
6. What are the external and internal systems of an American nuclear family?

references

Bales, Robert F. *Interaction Process Analysis: A Method for the Study of Small Groups*. Cambridge, Massachusetts: Addison-Wesley, 1950.
_____. "Adaptive and Integrative Changes as Sources of Strain in Social Systems," in A. Paul Hare, Edgar F. Borgatta, and Robert F. Bales (eds.). *Small Groups: Studies in Social Interaction*. New York: Alfred A. Knopf, 1966.
Bales, Robert F. *Personality and Impersonal Behavior*. New York: Holt Rinehart & Winston, 1970.

Bales, Robert F.; and Borgatta, Edgar F. "Size of Group as a Factor in the Interaction Profile," in A. Paul Hare, Edgar F. Borgatta and Robert F. Bales (eds.). *Small Groups: Studies in Social Interaction*. New York: Alfred A. Knopf, 1966.

Bales, Robert F.; and Cohen, Stephen A. *SYMLOG: A System for the Multiple Level Observation of Groups*. New York: The Free Press, 1979.

Borgatta, Edgar F.; Bales, Robert F.; and Couch, Arthur S. "Some Findings Relevant to the Great Man Theory of Leadership," *American Sociological Review*, 19 (1954): 755–759.

Heinecke, Christopher M.; and Bales, Robert F. "Developmental Trends in the Structure of Small Groups," *Sociometry*, 16 (1953): 7–38.

Homans, George C. *The Human Group*. New York: Harcourt, Brace and World, 1950.

Jenkins, John G. "The Nominating Technique as a Method of Evaluating Air Force Group Morale," *Journal of Aviation Medicine*, 19 (1948): 12–19.

Lewin, Kurt. "Psycho-sociological Problems of a Minority Group," *Character and Personality*, 3 (1935): 175–187.

———. "Experiments in Social Space," *Harvard Educational Review*, 9 (1939a): 21–32.

———. "Field Theory and Experiment in Social Psychology: Concepts and Methods," *American Journal of Sociology*, 44 (1939b): 868–896.

———. "The Background of Conflict in Marriage," in Moses Jung (ed.). *Modern Marriage*. New York: F. S. Crofts, 1940.

Lewin, Kurt. *Resolving Social Conflicts*. Edited by Gertrud E. Lewin. New York: Harper and Brothers, 1948.

Lewis, Helen B. "An Experimental Study of the Role of the Ego in Work: 1. The Role of the Ego in Cooperative Work," *Journal of Experimental Psychology*, 34 (1944): 113–126.

Lippitt, Ronald. "Field Theory and Experiment in Social Psychology: Autocratic and Democratic Group Atmospheres," *American Journal of Sociology*, 45 (1939): 26–49.

Mills, Theodore M. *The Sociology of Small Groups*. Englewood Cliffs, New Jersey: Prentice-Hall, 1967.

Monane, Joseph H. *A Sociology of Human Systems*. New York: Appleton-Century-Crofts, 1967.

Moreno, Jacob L. *Who Shall Survive?* Beacon, New York: Beacon House, 1953.

Shaw, Marvin E.; and Shaw, Lilly M. "Some Effects of Sociometric Grouping upon Learning in a Second Grade Classroom," *Journal of Social Psychology*, 57 (1962): 453–458.

PART 3

SMALL GROUP RESEARCH AND ANALYSIS

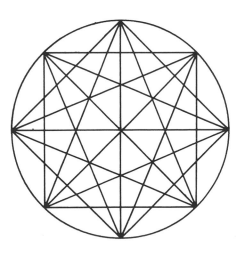

Chapter Seven

Research Directions in Small Groups

CHAPTER PREVIEW

THE NATURE OF SMALL GROUP RESEARCH

The most frequently used setting for small group research is the experimental laboratory. Although participant and non-participant field observation and interview techniques are used to some degree, the dominant method for obtaining information about small groups is experimentation in a laboratory environment. This method enables the researcher to control the group by eliminating unnecessary variables from the group environment and to concentrate upon the specific interests of the given experiment. Laboratory experiments are contrived, and they are not necessarily a reflection of the actual conditions in which individuals perform group functions. However, they do afford researchers the opportunity to concentrate on the impact of only one or two variables which are believed to influence group behavior. For example, if we are interested in the effect of seating position upon individual behavior in task-oriented or decision-making groups, we can control the seating arrangement and observe the behavior which results. In the same testing situation, we can change the seating arrangement and again observe the behavior which results. After a series of tests, we can note changes in behavior in relation to changes in seating positions. Manipulation of this sort is difficult, if not impossible, in natural group settings.

Research, especially in the small groups laboratory, has covered a variety of specific topics relating to the small group. Each study is designed to help us understand the group interaction process. Studies of interpersonal choice (Albert & Brigante, 1962), sometimes called interpersonal attraction, have attempted to identify degrees of liking and disliking among group members through the use of rating procedures. Studies of interpersonal choice help in attempts to structure the group membership and to identify the structurally based positions of individuals within the group. The methodological basis for studies in this area has come from Jacob L. Moreno's development of the sociometric technique discussed at length in Chapter Six.

Behavioral expectations, identified as social roles, have been studied as a major factor in the development of the gang, as evidenced in William Foote Whyte's *Street Corner Society* (1955). Researchers have concentrated on small family groups (Aldous & Straus, 1966) as well as on therapy groups (Talland, 1957). Since the performance of a task is the action counterpart of an individual's social role, a significant amount of research has been conducted in task-oriented groups whose structure is more formal and where there is a clearer definition of the social role of each member. For example, sociological research in factories has often distinguished the formal and informal roles and activities of workers (Burns, 1955).

Studies of group controls and the formation of group norms have attempted to identify the importance of behavioral standards on performance within groups. Much of the research is concerned with the conformity of individuals to group norms (Costanzo, 1970) and the effects of changing group norms on individual behavior (Levine & Butler, 1952). Researchers have concentrated on these and other areas of group behavior and structure such as group decision making, the group process, and task-oriented behavior. The subject matter is clearly diverse, but all researchers have one common concern: to understand the small group as a unit of human interaction.

This chapter will cover four areas of research which are indicative of important directions in the small group field. These areas are: (1) social space and personal distance, (2) leadership, (3) coalition formation, and (4) group size. The space factor was selected because it represents, in this writer's view, a somewhat neglected subject area which holds strong possibilities for future research interests. Leadership, always a problem area for sociologists and psychologists as well, has been selected to highlight some of the problems researchers encounter when investigating areas difficult to research. Coalition formation, unlike space and leadership, is a small group concept with a tradition dating back to the writings of Georg Simmel. The research on coalition formation has been continuous over the last thirty years. From the outset, this area of investigation has been orderly and is the best example of legitimate research rooted in a strong theoretical tradition. The size factor is included here for two reasons: (1) it has proven to be of major importance as a determiner of group structure and is of value in our attempts to understand group interaction, and (2) failure to review investigations into group size would be an unforgivable oversight considering the subject of this book. Finally, the choice of these four subjects is compatible with material discussed throughout these chapters.

SOCIAL SPACE AND PERSONAL DISTANCE

A photograph once viewed by this writer depicted two *gauchos* greeting each other for the first time on an Argentine *pampas*. These two men embraced each other in a manner which can only be described in "bear hug" terms. Americans might well describe the meeting as one between two very close friends who had not seen each other for many years; or possibly two brothers reunited after a long separation. The photograph depicted a greeting quite different from the handshake common among Americans when they first meet.

A past acquaintance of this writer was in the habit of using the phrase "get out of my face" when individuals whom he did not know well would get too close to him. Clearly, he did not like the discomfort which resulted from being physically close to someone he did not consider a friend.

These two examples suggest that one very important factor which influences how we behave with others is the factor of distance or, more inclusively, space. The first example identifies the cultural variations which define the individual's use of space and distance. The second example suggests that individuals within a common cultural setting perceive space and distance differently.

Do our perceptions of space and distance influence our behavior? What are the effects on behavior which result from changes in the amount of space available for an interaction? What happens if there is a change in the distance between individuals who are interacting with each other? These questions have been asked by anthropologists, psychologists, and sociologists for many years. Although our present interests are neither anthropological nor psychological, we will look at some of the interpretations of the spatial factor from these nonsociological perspectives.

EARLY INFLUENCES

In Chapter Three we discussed space and distance as parts of the physical environment and noted the importance of Edward T. Hall's book, *The Hidden Dimension*. In one sense, Hall's work is a popularization of the anthropologist's many years of work on space and distance as variables in human cultures. The sociological interpretations of these variables derive, in part, from the earlier researches of anthropologists as well as from research performed by experimental psychologists. We will consider these early sources only briefly.

The Hidden Dimenion is an extended report on the concept of *proxemics*. Hall (1966:1) coined the term and uses it to refer to "the interrelated observations and theories of man's use of space as a specialized elaboration of culture." Citing the works of such notables as Franz Boas, Edward Sapir, and Benjamin Lee Whorf, Hall puts forward the view that individual perceptions of space and distance vary cross-culturally and that behavior between and among individuals changes as the spatial factors change. The author reports on cultural variations and differential perceptions of space and distance elements. The following will serve as an example of Hall's (1966:144) cross-cultural approach to proxemics:

> Americans in the Middle East are immediately struck by two conflicting sensations. In public they are compressed and overwhelmed by smells, crowding, and high noise levels; in Arab homes Americans are apt to rattle around, feeling exposed and often somewhat inadequate because of too much space!

Although many sociologists are prone to reject animal experimentation as a basis for understanding human social behavior, Hall (1966:7) argues that, "By restricting our observations to the way animals handle space, it is possible to learn an amazing amount that is translatable to human terms." Accepting that there is a bridge between animal experimentation and human behavior, Hall (1966:Chapters 2 & 3) proceeds to discuss experiments conducted on a population of Sika deer (a study of stress caused by overcrowding within a limited space) and on a population of Norway rats (a study of radical behavioral changes brought about by stress from beyond-normal crowding in four specially constructed pens). These and other similar research studies have produced interesting findings on the relationship between overcrowding and stress.

Experimentation such as this is, at best, only intriguing to the sociologist. Although the idea of building research bridges between animal and human experimentation is foreign to many, it is clear that such early investigations into the effect of space and distance factors on social behavior are an important source of contemporary interest on the subject.

Research in the small groups field does not concentrate on cross-cultural variations in spatial perception or on effects such as overcrowding. Small groups research efforts are regularly directed toward an understanding of the relationship of spatial elements in the environment to group interaction. For example, sociologists are interested in discovering if there is a relationship (1) between proximity and interpersonal choice, (2) between seating arrangements and leadership, and—since we consider controlled contact a spatial element—(3) between contact and interracial relations. We will discuss three areas of small group research concerned with space and distance factors: seating arrangements, proximity, and interracial contact.

SEATING ARRANGEMENTS

Leadership (Rosenthal & Delong, 1972; Heckel, 1973), task-oriented behavior (Felipe, 1966; Batchelor & Goethals, 1972), attraction of interacting parties (Cook, 1970), and informal conversation (Hare & Bales, 1963) are some of the interaction factors which have been identified as being influenced by seating arrangements.

A. Paul Hare and Robert F. Bales (1963), working with data from thirty-one group sessions conducted in a small groups laboratory, found that interaction patterns among participating members of task-oriented groups were predictable in terms of seating positions and distance among group members. Using Bernard P. Cohen's (1953) results on the same data, it was found that in informal sessions with no central task focus individuals were more likely to talk to other members who were seated next to them. The results of the social sessions were interpreted in terms of group members turning away from the group in order to participate in informal or more intimate conversation. The differences observed between task and social sessions suggest that spatial elements can be used to predict interaction patterns when individuals, functioning as members of a group, are required to cooperate in the performance of a group function or task, or when the task requires a group decision. At the risk of overgeneralization, seating positions and distance between interacting parties are factors which determine interaction patterns in group situations which tend to be formal and rigidly structured in type and which carry expectations beyond those imposed on the interaction by each group member. Studies of leadership and seating arrangements tend to reinforce this view.

Research conducted during a mental health workshop (Heckel, 1973) in which fifty-five professionals participated suggests that there is some evidence to support the view that there is a relationship between perceived leadership and voluntary seating choice. The assumption made was that leaders in groups usually occupy one or another end of a table or some other position which would force interaction. It should be noted that individuals who voluntarily select one of these positions are very likely indicating a desire to perform a leadership role. Also, when individuals choose positions at one or another end of a table, others in the group situation perceive those individuals as occupying seating positions which carry leadership expectations. Although the correlation between the group's leadership ratings and voluntary seating choice was low, Heckel (1973:142) argued that such results are encouraging:

> Considering the many problems which exist in attempting to take such measurements in a naturalistic setting, the results are encouraging. Had this been done in a laboratory setting where each individual who would choose a "head" seat had 100% opportunity to do so it is felt that the outcome would have been clear cut.

Heckel's argument in favor of a higher correlation is acceptable. In the natural setting, individuals may arrive late for reasons beyond their control, or, in the moments before the session is to begin, they may find themselves out of position to select the appropriate leader or nonleader seat. When experiments are performed in a laboratory, unforeseen circumstances such as these do not occur because the experiment is controlled. This writer organized 18 classroom conferences in which eight students were allowed to choose a seat before the start of each conference. In 17 sessions, a student who chose an end seat at the rectangular table was elected the conference leader. In each case, participating students stated that seating position influenced their vote. In the one session in which a leader was chosen from a nonleader seating position, students explained privately that the two students who chose the end seats were unpopular with their classmates and had little chance of becoming an elected leader no matter where they sat. Although popularity, or interpersonal attraction, may have little to do with leadership ability, apparently, in this one case, popularity was an important factor in leader selection. In these sessions, the classroom was used as a small groups laboratory in which the participants were given directions on how to proceed; the experiment was controlled.

Robert Pellegrini (1971) reports on the halo effect which results from the occupancy of certain seats at a rectangular table. Using photographs of five college students seated at a table (four students occupied side positions at the table and one student occupied the head position), subjects were asked to rate the students so depicted on the following ten-point scales: Quiet-Talkative, Not Persuasive-Persuasive, Dominant-Submissive, Follower-Leader, Self-confident-Self-doubting, Not Intelligent-Intelligent. The researcher (Pellegrini, 1971:890) reports that ". . . the mean ratings for the occupant of the head position were consistently higher than the mean ratings given for occupants of side locations on all scales." The occupant of the head position was also chosen more often as the individual who most likely contributed most to the group interaction. Since the highest ratings were given consistently to the occupant of the head position at the table, Pellegrini suggests the halo effect, which characterizes occupancy of the leader seat.

Robert Sommer (1962) reports that individuals prefer sitting across from one another rather than side-by-side when involved in conversation. Two exceptions to this rule were found:

> . . . when the distance across is too far for comfortable conversation, and secondly, when the distance across exceeds the distance side-by-side. When the two distances are equal, or when the distance side-by-side exceeds the

distance across, people strongly prefer to sit opposite one another . . . (Sommer, 1962:115).

The author notes the importance of considering the environment in which the interaction takes place. The study was conducted in a large (46′ × 48′), attractively furnished room. Considering the size of the room, Sommer concluded that the closeness of chairs varies inversely with the size of the room. In other words, the larger the room, the closer people sit for comfortable conversation. This observation was prompted by observations that smaller residence conversation areas usually include seating arrangements in which chairs are positioned approximately eight feet apart. This distance contrasted considerably with the one- to five-feet distances used in the experiment.

PROXIMITY

Proximity (propinquity) refers to the physical distance between and among individuals who are interacting with each other. Studies which investigate proximity as a determiner of human behavior concentrate upon the relationship between physical distance and interpersonal attraction (liking). The basic proposition regarding propinquity has been clearly stated by Theodore M. Newcomb (1956:575): " . . . other things being equal, people are most likely to be attracted toward those in closest contact with them." Before we discuss Newcomb's research, the phrase "other things being equal" should be explained. One criticism of the proximity-attraction proposition suggests that proximity only provides the physical basis for attraction and is not a direct determiner of it. Proximity makes it possible for individuals to discover things about each other such as feelings, interests, and abilities. Recognizing this interpretation of the proximity factor, Newcomb (1956:575–576) argues that the concern is "with . . . something that is made possible, or more likely, with decreasing distance." Newcomb identified the something as interaction.

In his research at the University of Michigan, Newcomb rented a house near the campus and offered 17 male transfer students who did not know each other free rent if they would agree to cooperate in the research project. Newcomb assigned rooms to the 17 students but did not further control their activity within the house. Students were free to associate with whom they chose and were able to determine cooking and cleaning arrangements on their own. Interest centered around the assumption that roommates would develop stronger and more frequent interpersonal associations than nonroommates. Newcomb was also interested in discovering if similarities developed in the interpersonal attraction complex.

Similarity was viewed as common liking of an individual by two or more others and agreement of attitude.

Newcomb found that roommates were more attracted to each other than they were to nonroommates. The students were housed on two floors, and it was discovered that students who lived on the same floor were more attracted to each other than students living on different floors. Students reported liking others whom they perceived liked them. It was found that student perceptions of liking were accurate. In other words, students who were perceived as liking the responding student actually reported liking that student. Finally, Newcomb found that students who liked each other tended to be in agreement about other students they liked. Students who liked each other also tended to agree on items of value which were unrelated to their common housing experience. For example, students who liked each other were in agreement on such subjects as sex, politics, and money. This last result was found to be of less significance than the results suggesting proximity and attraction as meaningful correlates of each other.

A similar study by Festinger, Schachter, and Back (1950) identifies proximity as the crucial factor in the development of friendships among married couples who, as college students, resided in a student housing environment. Having been assigned to housing quarters in the order in which they applied for them, married couples developed friendships with other couples who had been placed in quarters next door to them. Those couples who were given end-of-the-line quarters did not develop friendships nearly as frequently. The study suggests that there is a significant relationship between interpersonal attraction and residential proximity.

The results of other studies support the proposition that proximity and interpersonal attraction are related. College students sitting next to each other in classrooms are more likely to become acquainted (Byrne & Buehler, 1955); physical proximity significantly affected the rate of interaction between workers, and the increased rate of interaction resulted in the development of interpersonal attraction (Gullahorn, 1952); and individuals who sat near each other in the cafeteria of a mental hospital interacted with each other more frequently than did persons seated at greater distances from each other (Sommer, 1959). The results of a study of students in a large, French boarding school supported the proposition that proximity and interpersonal attraction were related (Maisonneuve, 1952).

There appears little question that attraction is associated with the physical distance factor. In consideration of the suspicion that proximity only facilitates the emergence of factors more directly associated with the promotion of interpersonal attraction, further studies are needed which will indicate with greater clarity whether proximity is a primary or secondary source of interpersonal attraction.

INTERRACIAL CONTACT

Ordinarily, interest in interracial contact is directed toward contact between large, racially distinct populations. Sociologists have identified the various processes which result when large populations from different racial origins come into contact with each other. The processes range from conflict to integration. Assimilation, pluralism, and segregation are other social processes involved in interracial contact. Such interpretations are ordinarily macrosociological in nature and are framed as integral parts of the sociological subfield designated as Race Relations or Intergroup Relations.

Interest in interracial contact of a more personal nature and, therefore, more in keeping with the limits of the small groups discipline developed in the aftermath of World War II. Research on the attitudes of white soldiers (Info. U.S. War Dept., 1952) to military decisions to attach a number of black rifle platoons to white companies produced interesting results concerning the relationship between increased interracial contact and the reduction of racial prejudice. The results are presented in terms of the percentage of white soldiers who indicated strong disagreement with and dislike of the desegregation arrangement. Sixty-two percent of 1,450 respondents who were in military field units which did not have black platoons attached to white companies expressed strong dislike of the procedure. Twenty-four percent of 112 respondents who were in the same division but not the same regiment as black soldiers expressed strong dislike. Twenty percent of 68 respondents who were in the same regiment but not in the same company as black soldiers expressed strong dislike, and only seven percent of 80 respondents who were in a company with a black rifle platoon expressed strong dislike of the procedure.

The classic research conducted in two integrated interracial housing projects in New York City and two segregated biracial projects by Morton Deutsch and Mary Evans Collins (1951) investigated the effect of prolonged, intimate, interracial contact on racial attitudes and relationships between individuals of different races. One hundred white housewives from each of the four housing projects were interviewed. The results indicate that there was a higher incidence of friendly contact between members of the two racial groups who had been housed in the interracial housing projects. In these projects there occurred a more frequent verbalization of positive stereotypes and a less frequent verbalization of negative stereotypes. A much larger percentage of those interviewed indicated that they had undergone a most favorable attitude change regarding their relationships with blacks and that the attitude change was a result of their experiences in the interracial housing project. This last observation indicates that those interviewed believed that increased contact with members of another race was a major factor for change in the direction of increased favorable attitudes and less discriminatory behavior.

Other studies support the view that increased and close contact between members of different racial groups is a major factor in the reduction of negative attitudes and discriminatory behavior. For example, one study indicated that white department store employees who worked with blacks in the past were willing to do so again. Whites who had not had the same past experience were less willing to work with blacks (Harding & Hogrefe, 1952). The same results were found in research conducted in university classrooms using sociometric choice procedures (Mann, 1959). In an early study conducted by F. Tredwell Smith (1943), an experimental group of forty-six students and a control group of the same number of students from Teachers College of Columbia University were selected and given attitude tests. Shortly after testing, the experimental group of students was taken on a four-day tour of Harlem. They spoke with black residents and attended lectures. Tests administered after the tour indicated that students in the experimental group had developed significantly more favorable attitudes toward blacks than those held before the tour. No attitude changes were indicated among control group students. The interracial contact was relatively short in duration, but it was intense and clearly the significant factor in attitude change.

Some studies indicate that favorable attitude changes result from factors such as the proportionate size of the interacting racial populations as well as from proximity or contact. Marvin E. Shaw (1973) found that the frequency of interactions between black and white elementary school students in the fourth, fifth, and sixth grades was related directly to the proportion of black students in the class. This means that the greater the proportion of black students in any one class, the less frequent the interactions of students across racial lines. On this point, Shaw (1973:143) points out that a "relatively low proportion of minority members appears to be most effective in improving racial relations." These results suggest that a factor other than the proximity of students of different races is important in determining the frequency of interaction.

However, Shaw also found that black students rejected white students significantly less frequently, and white students rejected black students significantly less frequently than could be expected by chance. These observations suggest that the proximity factor was at work and did, in fact, influence the total interaction complex within the interracial class. Shaw (1973:156) concluded that ". . . equal status association may not eliminate the cleavage between races, but it may eliminate much of the hostility between races that has been fostered by unequal status association."

Shaw's research, and studies similar to his (Stein, Hardwick & Smith, 1965), are important because they suggest that there are factors other than proximity or contact which promote an increase in positive cross-racial attitudes and, more generally, interpersonal attraction. Researchers concerned with proximity and contact have never rejected the idea that there are other determiners of interpersonal attraction. Theodore Newcomb's investigations in the mid-fifties recognized that many factors combine to determine the basis for interpersonal attraction.

Two important observations remain. The first is that further research is necessary to identify the other determiners of interpersonal attraction, and the second is that, although some sociologists view proximity as only a facilitator, its importance and the importance of other elements of the physical environment in which human interaction occurs should not be underestimated. With regard to this last point, Donn Byrne (1961:69) has remarked that ". . . the influence of propinquity on the formation of classroom relationships is a stable and predictable phenomenon."

LEADERSHIP

There are some distinct difficulties associated with the study of leadership. There is an enormous amount of research on the subject, but the findings are unclear and have produced no indicators as to the direction research on leadership should take. There is no consensus on what leadership is or on which individual qualities and group forces determine an individual's ability to lead. The majority of leadership research is centered around the physcial characteristics, abilities, and personality traits of individuals who are leaders and who, in the many laboratory experiments, occupy leadership positions or emerge as leaders. This kind of research has not been especially productive since the findings indicate that the correlations between leadership and individual factors are consistently low. Hare (1976:278), in reviewing the literature on leadership and personality traits, observes that: "While correlations between 'good' personality traits and leadership are generally positive, they are rarely large."

For the most part, researching leadership has been the responsibility of psychologists and social psychologists who have marked the subject with their particular emphases and orientations. Unfortunately, sociologists have not been as interested or as prolific in dealing with leadership as a function of the group structure and as an important element in the group process as one might expect. As a result, there is a void in the research material which has severely limited our understanding of leadership as a group phenomenon.

However, researchers have devoted a great deal of time and energy to the study of leadership and have attempted to isolate the qualities which determine a leader. Investigations center around the identification of three basic types of leaders: authoritarian, democratic, and laissez-faire. There is some discussion about leaderless groups in order to discover factors which contribute to leader emergence (Bass & Wurster, 1953). Leadership research also attempts to identify the qualities necessary for leadership maintenance and the functions of leaders in varying group situations. Other concepts associated with a leader and leadership functions, such as authority and power, can be found in the literature, and there are some references made to the factor of social or group controls.

If we approach leadership from the symbolic interactionist point of view, the leader and the leadership position can be viewed as symbolic representations of the norms established by the group or as the authority symbol necessary for the attainment of group and individual goals. However, the utility of the interactionist approach lies in a consideration of the relationship between leaders and followers. Ralph M. Stogdill (1974:354) makes the following observation in this regard:

> The leadership hypothesis is often stated to imply a one-way flow of effects from leader to follower. The interaction hypothesis implies a two-way flow of effects. The leader's behavior conditions the response of the followers and the follower's behavior conditions the response of the leader. This latter appears the more realistic assumption.

One key to a sociological understanding of leadership is the simple fact that the role of leader is a reciprocal of the role of follower. Leaders are important only in terms of those who follow the leader's direction and who, in fact, accept the leader and the position he occupies as controls over their behavior. It is impossible to consider leadership as a sociological fact without consideration of those with whom the leader must interact.

The approach to the subject should include attempts to understand the structure of group roles and relationships. If we are to understand the role of a parent, we must understand the role of the child; if we are to understand the role of a friend, we must understand the role of those who return the friendship. Included in the list of roles and their reciprocals are the following relationships: employer-employee, teacher-student, lawyer-client, doctor-patient, and many others. These observations are based upon the basic principle that every role is a reciprocal of some other role. Certainly, this principle holds true for leaders and their followers.

We want to emphasize the importance of leader-follower interaction to offset the rather commonly held view that personal traits (Stogdill, 1948), including physical characteristics, individual ability, and skill, are the basic determiners of leadership. Individual traits and abilities have some effect upon who becomes a leader. As noted earlier, the degree of significance of any one trait or combination of traits must be questioned.

DEFINITIONS OF LEADERSHIP

Cecil Gibb (1954:880–884) has discussed the elements which are usually included in the many definitions of leadership. These elements give consideration to the leader: (1) as an individual in a given office, (2) as the focus for the behavior of other group members, (3) as the individual identified by sociometric choice of group members (as one who exercises influence over others through sociometric choice), (4) as an individual who occupies a headship position (appointments in leadership positions in large structures), (5) as an individual who influences group effectiveness, (6) as one who engages in leadership behavior, and (7) as a set of functions which must be carried out by the group and not by one individual (distributed leadership).

Ralph Stogdill's (1974) review of leadership definitions identifies leadership: (1) as the effect of special personality characteristics, (2) as the art of inducing compliance, (3) as the exercise of influence, (4) as behavior which directs group activity, (5) as a form of persuasion, (6) as an instrument of goal achievement, (7) as an effect of group action, (8) as a differentiated role, and (9) as the initiation of structure.

These considerations, as attempted definitions, are selected from the many studies and discussions on leadership. For example, in a study conducted by Ferenc Merei (1949) in two day-nurseries, the child selected as leader was the one whom the researchers defined in terms of personal traits. The leader was older, domineering, frequently imitated, aggressive, and had initiative. Krech and Crutchfield (1948:437) distinguished leaders from nonleaders in terms of ". . . the urgency of certain kinds of needs . . . dominance, prestige and power." More recently, Marvin E. Shaw (1976:447) defined leadership as ". . . a process in which one group member exerts positive influence over another group member."

The influence, or inducement, theme can be found in a definition offered by W. G. Bennis (1959:296): "Leadership . . . is viewed as a tripartite concept involving means control over rewards (power), an agent who manipulates these rewards, and an influence process." I. Knickerbocker's (1948:26) concern with group and individual goals resulted in the following definition of leadership: "The functional relation which is leadership exists when a leader is perceived by a group as controlling means for the satisfaction of their needs." These and the many other definitions present in the literature are useful in that they examine leadership as a function of a particular characteristic of some importance to understanding group process. However, there is little in these considerations which suggests change in the leader, the group situation, the spheres of influence within the group, or the group goals. Beyond this lack of a dynamic quality in leadership analysis, there is also a clear absence of consideration of the follower and the follower's response to leadership.

However, the reader should be impressed with the variety of definitions and interpretations of leadership and with the apparent lack of agreement to be found among them. It is not surprising that this should be the case. Definitions are offered which usually serve the purpose of the writer and which reinforce the particular perspective which is taken on a given subject. For example, if we are interested in giving a profile of a leader, we might tend to use personality, ability, and skill factors as descriptive of group leaders. If, however, we are concerned with group control, we might want to direct attention to the elements in leadership which function to control or limit the behavior of other members of the group. If we are interested in leadership as a part of the democratic process, we might want to define leadership in terms of considerations which are less authoritarian and less suggestive of the control elements others might require in their definitions, and which concentrate on permissiveness and group decision making.

The following list of characteristics which are commonly associated with definitions of leadership may facilitate understanding and may help the reader to focus interest in one or another direction. Leadership definitions usually include one or a combination of the following:

1. Personality traits
2. Individual ability and skill
3. Sociometric choice of group members
4. Occupancy of office or group position
5. Leadership as a group function
6. Embodiment and interpretation of group norms

7. Dominant influence on group goal achievement
8. Central focus for and dominant influence over the behavior of other group members
9. Central agent of group organization, group control, and group order

Reviews of the research upon which these considerations are based are complete in the separate works of Stogdill, Hare, and Gibb. These works have been cited earlier in this chapter and are the most important compendia of research on the subject of leadership.

Our present interests are with the small group and small group interaction, so we will proceed along somewhat specific line of analysis. However, we will feel free to cite particular studies which become relevant as our discussion of group leadership unfolds.

Unfortunately, the list of leadership considerations presented above includes interaction as a factor in leadership only by implication. Interaction is implied when, for example, leadership is viewed in terms of group function and when the leader is defined as the central agent in group organization or in group control. Such considerations only suggest that leadership is in some way or other tied up with the interaction going on within a group. However, suggesting that interaction is a necessary condition for describing leadership is not the same as defining leadership in terms of interaction.

From the point of view of the interactionist, four principles of group activity and structure must be employed in arriving at a definition of leadership. They are:

(1) *All group behavior is a process.* That is, group behavior is in a constant state of flux or change. Part of any sociological consideration of leadership must consider this dynamic quality of group behavior.

(2) *All group structures are differentiated.* Group structures are composed of hierarchical positions, the occupancy of which necessitates variations in the amount of influence individuals have over each other. This is true of both formal and informal groups. In this sense, leadership is to be considered in terms of degrees of influence.

(3) *Situational environments influence the behavior of group members.* Leadership, as well as other group elements, is a response to the situation which characterizes a given group at a given time.

(4) *Leadership positions are positions of authority.* Individuals who occupy these positions use authority in a variety of ways. Some leaders

are authoritarian, some are democratic, and others are characteristically laissez-faire.

These four principles of group activity and structure are combined to produce the following definition. *Leadership* is a group process in which an individual, in a given situation, is able to direct and control group interaction more influentially than any other group member.

When we approach leadership from the interactionist point of view, we are able to eliminate the nonproductive position that leadership is a static group phenomenon. Studies which approach leadership in terms of personality traits (Smith & Cook, 1973; Hanawalt, Richardson & Morris, 1943) and personality types (Lippitt & White, 1958) are often subject to interpretations which do not explain the dynamic qualities inherent in the concept of leadership.

The definition, as stated, is broad enough to include interpretations of leadership in informal groups as well as in the more frequently researched formal organizational systems. There is a great deal of information on leadership in formal systems such as the military and industrial bureaucracies (Roff, 1959; Pelz, 1951; Stouffer, 1949) but, since individuals are most often appointed to positions of leadership in these systems, there is a strong tendency to view leadership only as part of the from-top-to-bottom system structure. Our interests are only partially in formal systems. More realistically, we are concerned with small groups, formal and informal, and with the emergence of leaders and the maintenance of leadership within all these groups.

The phrase, "in a given situation," is a necessary part of any definition of leadership. Cecil Gibb (1954:901) has remarked that "Leadership is always relative to the situation," and he has noted frequent leadership shifts as situations change in small, traditionless groups (Gibbs, 1947). In discussing symbolic interaction (Chapter One) we discussed the social, physical, and cultural elements present in every situation. When these situational elements change, so must the behavior of group members. Individuals who are capable of functioning as effective leaders in one group situation are not necessarily capable of functioning as a leader in another group situation. We are all aware of the shifting of leadership activity from the mother to the father, and back again, in family activities. These shifts in the use of family authority are not arbitrary; they are determined by corresponding shifts in the situations in which the entire family interacts. Similarly, leader shifts occur in friendships, and these shifts are based upon the situational needs and expectations of the membership.

When we incorporate the situational factor into leadership analysis, we are accepting a basic assumption about all social groups: that is, that they are in a constant state of change. If this is so, changes in the elements which compose group situations require changes in the leadership of the group unless the leader is able to maintain effectiveness in a great variety of situations or at least in those situations which confront the group. Stogdill's (1974:63–64) insight is appropriate here:

> . . . leadership must be conceived in terms of the interaction of variables which are in constant flux and change. The factor of change is especially characteristic of the situation, which may be radically altered by the addition or loss of members, changes in interpersonal relationships, goals . . . .

The most important contribution to understanding leadership is the belief that leadership is co-dependent upon followership. If we are to understand leadership, we must understand the influence of leadership upon the other group members and the reactions of group members to their leaders. Interaction is the one element which gives a truly dynamic character to the concept of leadership. Stogdill (1974:64) discusses the importance of interaction and frames his argument in terms of group situations: "The evidence suggests that leadership is a relation that exists between persons in a social relationship."

GROUP STRUCTURE

The definition offered in the previous section emphasized that leadership is a function of social groups. It is difficult to understand leadership if the phenomenon is approached from a purely psychological perspective, that is, as a function of personality attributes. Nor can we hope to understand leadership if we insist upon definitions which concentrate on ability and skill. Leadership is a group process and must be understood in terms of the structural and functional elements which prevail in social groups. The following discussion suggests some of the important group factors which must be considered when attempting to understand the concept of leadership.

In Chapter Two we distinguished between formal and informal types of group structures. If we place these two types of group structures at endpoints on a continuum, we have a basis for differentiating groups according to the degree that their structures exhibit formal and/or informal characteristics. It is clear, for example, that small groups such as boards of directors or ad hoc groups which are organized to resolve a difficulty or to perform an explicit task are more formally structured than are either the informal associations which often develop within larger, formal organizational systems or of relationships which are characteristically informal, such as friendship associations. If we are able to understand that group structures can be so variable, it follows that leadership roles which emerge in these groups are just as variable. The organization of leadership positions within groups is consistent with the types of structure prevalent within those groups. It would not be worthwhile to consider that formally structured groups develop leadership roles in the same way that families and friendship associations do.

The emergence of the leader in formal, as opposed to informal, groups can be distinguished in terms of the procedure used for leader selection. In formal organizational systems, individuals are delegated as leaders or they are appointed to leadership positions by others who already occupy even higher positions and who have the right of delegation or appointment. In groups which are informally structured, individuals usually emerge as leaders through election by the membership or through the very informal procedure of silent acclamation. By silent acclamation is meant the acceptance of a group member as a leader without open acknowledgment of the fact.

Figure 7-1 illustrates the selection of leaders in formal and informal groups by identification of the differences in the sources from which leaders emerge. In the formal system, the leader is chosen from above and is presented to those who will be in subordinate positions. The leader may or may not be chosen from the ranks of subordinates. In any case,

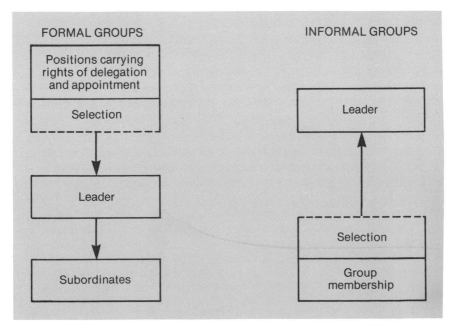

Figure 7-1.   Procedure for Leader Selection in Formal and Informal Groups

the decision to appoint is not made by those over whom the leader will have authority.

In the informal group, the leader is chosen by and from the group membership and needs no presentation since the membership is, in most cases, aware of the potential, if not actual, ability of their leader. Figure 7-1 also suggests a very important distinction between leadership in these two types of groups. In the formal organizational system, the individual who is selected by the customary means is in a middle position and must consider not only the impact of leadership performance upon those who will be subordinate, but also upon those who made the selection. In informal groups this is not the case. Ordinarily, individuals who are selected by group members need only concern themselves with how well they are able to lead the follower population to goal achievement. This difference in the concerns which are imposed upon leaders in contrasting group structure settings may be an important determiner of how the individual who occupies the leadership position will behave. In the formal group, the additional element of concern over the evaluative possibilities of higher authorities will seriously influence the performance of anyone who occupies an appointed or delegated leadership position.

There are many factors which contribute to leader emergence in groups. For example, J. C. Gilchrist (1952) has identified success as a major factor in the selection of a leader. In experimental groups of four members each, both the successful individuals and individuals who failed in a given task tended to choose other successful individuals as partners for future task situations. The study suggests that when an individual group member is reinforced, that is, is successful, that individual is more likely to be viewed by others as a leader than others who are unsuccessful.

Dominance as a personal characteristic has been identified as a significant factor in leader emergence (Megaree, 1969); seating position studies suggest that individuals who are leadership-oriented have a strong tendency to sit at the head of the table (Sommer, 1961); leadership is often determined not by the characteristics which leaders or potential leaders exhibit but by the characteristics exhibited by followers. In a report by A. Zander and A. Havelin (1960), it was observed that experimental group members have a tendency to be more attracted to others who have competence levels similar to their own.

The factors outlined above are not sufficient in themselves as explanations of leader emergence. This is true, especially here, since our concern is with understanding leadership as an element in group organization. There are group factors which influence the emergence of leaders such as group structure and group size. In discussing these, we are able to understand leadership as contingent upon the kind of group requiring the leadership and the type of leadership required by groups of different size. The development of a role structure in which there is leader-follower differentiation has been found to be a necessary requisite for the effective performance of group tasks (Borgatta & Bales, 1953). When a group lacks effective leadership, activity remains undirected, and the achievement of task-oriented goals is not possible. In reporting on problem-solving groups, J. R. French (1941) found that although the members of groups with leaders and leaderless groups became frustrated in attempts to solve unsolvable problems, groups with leaders were less prone to split into subgroups or factions as a result. These and other similar studies indicate that the simple differentiation of membership along leader-follower lines is sufficient and necessary to activate the group membership in the direction of effective goal- and task-directed behavior.

Along somewhat different lines, the distinction made earlier between formal and informal structures has been the subject of research in leadership emergence. In the classic research by Stouffer (1949), it was found that discussion orientation groups produced more rewarding experiences for group members when the leaders were chosen by them. Stouffer also reported that participants in the orientation groups felt more positive toward leaders whom they liked and respected them. These leaders were always better educated than the group members. Quite simply, acceptance and trust of leaders by those who follow is present when the leader is chosen by the followers rather than appointed by nongroup members. Leadership differences are observable in groups with different structures. This was evident in an observation made by James E. White (1950:55–56): "Informal and formal leadership are not closely related to each other; they are simply different."

GROUP SIZE

There is a clear relationship between the size of the group and opportunities for a group member to emerge as a leader. Research to date suggests that there is an inverse relationship between group size and the possibility of leader emergence. One report by B. M. Bass and Fay-Tyler Norton (1951) indicates that, as the size of the group increases, there is less chance for any one member to perform leadership functions. A. Paul Hare (1952) found that leaders were more influential in groups of small size, and, in an interesting report by J. K. Hemphill (1950), it was found that group members are more tolerant of control by a leader and demand more effective control from leaders as the size of the group increases. The formalization of the leader-follower relationship in this last report indicates that the movement to the upper limits of small group size foreshadows the loss of the group's informal character. Clovis Shepherd (1964:4) has commented on the relationship between an increase in group size and the development of a formal group structure: " . . . as a small group increases in size it reaches some upper limit where the group seems to become altered so that its members establish formal rules and regulations and the group becomes more like a formal organization than a small group." In terms of leadership and leader performance, we may paraphrase Shepherd and observe that, as the size of the group increases, an upper limit is reached where the performance of the leader becomes altered so that behavior directed toward group members is more formalized and more highly structured. Further understanding of leadership rests in an increase in research efforts by sociologists who will be able to place leadership in a group perspective.

COALITION FORMATION

In Chapter Nine we will discuss coalition formation in terms of the traditional conflict view and in terms of the future possibilities for understanding coalitions as a process which may also enhance group integration and goal achievement. Research dealing with coalition formation has never considered the enhancing effects of coalitions but has concentrated upon the more traditional interpretation. This is understandable since the theoretical base upon which the research is constructed presented a view of group member realignment in terms of group conflict. Because of this limitation, the research discussed in this section will treat only non-enhancing, conflict-oriented small group coalitions. The title of Theodore Caplow's volume on triads, *Two Against One: Coalitions in Triads* (1968), clearly identifies the central thrust of research into coalition formation. The view that a group of three individuals will divide into two members against the third is indicative of the established conflict frame of reference which surrounds coalition research.

The reader should refer back to Chapter Three and recall the discussion on triadic relations in which triads were distinguished according to their interaction configurations: separation, unification, and coalition formation. It was noted that in coalition formation analysis, the three-member group exhibits all the possibilities for variation between and among group members. In this regard, the variations suggested were based upon Caplow's eight types of triads. The reader should recall, also, that one common assumption about coalition formation in triads is that the development of a coalition is the most likely possibility, and that although integration, that is, the absence of coalition activity, is a realistic possibility, it is not the most prevalent one under conditions of long-term association.

Serious investigations into coalition formation in triads were initiated in the mid-fifties. Investigations from then to the present have been well organized, and serious attempts have been made to incorporate the theoretical discussions found in Georg Simmel's writings. For these reasons, we are able to present the review of this research in chronological order. The reader should note that much of the research, particularly during the earlier years, is in some way connected and includes attempts to integrate theory and research on the subject. The results of a study by Theodore M. Mills (1953:356; 1954) confirmed Georg Simmel's argument that "the threesome tends to break up into a pair and another party." He discovered further that fear of a third party by a dyad is not a necessary factor in the development of a group coalition. In an attempt to refine the earlier principles of Georg Simmel, Mills suggested two propositions: (1) solidarity between two members in a triad is the most threatening development to the position of the third group member, and (2) solidary bonds between two members intensify in the presence of a common object of opposition, a third member.

Mills' report was an early influence[1] on the direction to be taken in coalition research. Theodore Caplow (1956) attempted to structure a theory of coalition formation in small groups by presenting six types of triads using a differential power relations model. The development of these triadic types was based upon four assumptions: (1) members of a triad may differ in strength and a stronger member can control a weaker one and will attempt to do so; (2) each member of the triad seeks control over others with preference for control over two others; (3) strength is additive—coalition member strength is equivalent to coalition strength; and (4) there is a pre-coalition condition in every triad. A stronger member's attempt to coerce a weaker member into joining a non-advantageous coalition will promote the formation of an advantageous coalition to oppose the coercion. Having argued that many types of social groups cannot be based upon the assumption that there is an equal distribution of power, Caplow (1956:490–491) constructed six types of triads in which the initial distribution of power is known:

---

1. This writer believes that the work of Theodore Caplow in 1956 was the major impetus for continuation of research in coalition formation in triads. However, earlier studies produced before 1956, such as the following, are worthy of note: Fred L. Strodtbeck, "The Family as a Three-Person Group," *American Sociological Review*, 19, 1954, pp. 23–29.

(1) $A = B = C$ • Three parties have equal strength. Any coalition is possible.

(2) $A > B$
$\quad\; B = C$
$\quad\; A < (B+C)$ • One member slightly stronger than other two who are of equal strength. Most likely coalition is $B + C$. Strongest member becomes weakest.

(3) $A < B$
$\quad\; B = C$ • One member weaker than the other two members who are of equal strength. Most likely coalitions are AB and AC. Either coalition strengthens A's position.

(4) $A > (B+C)$
$\quad\; B = C$ • Little possibility of coalition formation since any coalition will do nothing to strengthen or weaken the position of any member.

(5) $A > B > C$
$\quad\; A < (B+C)$ • Strength of any two members combined is greater than the strength of the third member. Most likely coalition possibility is BC.

(6) $A > B > C$
$\quad\; A > (B+C)$ • Few, if any, coalitions are possible.

In structuring these triadic types, Caplow successfully demonstrated: (1) that prediction of coalitions is possible when the initial distribution of power is known; (2) the possibilities for groups to develop in which there is differential power distributed among the members are many; (3) that there is a theoretical basis for understanding the relationship between power distribution in three-person groups and chances for coalition formation; and (4) in terms of continuing research, the construction of a coalition theory for three-person groups is a legitimate basis for laboratory studies.

W. Edgar Vinacke and Abe Arkoff (1957) constructed a series of three-person group experiments in order to test Caplow's hypotheses. Using 90 male college students in a laboratory experiment, 30 groups were formed. The students were asked to participate in a game situation in which a modified Parcheesi board was used. Students, through a balanced equal-chance procedure, drew counters which determined differential power for each player for each game. Vinacke and Arkoff concluded that Caplow's initial interpretation of coalition possibilities was confirmed by the Parcheesi game experiments.

In Type I triads the prediction that all three coalitions are possible was supported by the game results. Similarly, as Caplow hypothesized, the BC coalition in Type II triads formed significantly more frequently than the other two coalition possibilities. For Type III triads, the predicted coalitions, *AB* and *AC*, occurred more often than coalition *AC*. The Caplow prediction that few coalitions would form in a Type IV triad was supported by the findings. The predicted *BC* coalition outcome for a Type V triad was also supported. The Vinacke/Arkoff experiment also reinforced the prediction that few coalitions would be formed in the Type IV triad.

Caplow's (1959) six types of triads were extended by him in a report which added two new types of triads. The two new formations were presented as: $A > B > C$, $A = (B + C)$ and $A = (B + C)$, $B = C$. In both types, the most likely coalitions are *AB* or *AC*. The *BC* coalition is not possible since it is not able to control the triadic situation. Realistically, the *BC* coalition can do no more than block *A*'s possible domination of the group.

Sheldon Stryker and George Psathas (1960; Kelley & Arrowood, 1960) were the first to attempt to integrate coalition formation theory and research. Their report, in one sense, coordinates the theory of Georg Simmel, the hypotheses of Theodore Caplow, and the Vinacke/Arkoff experimental study. The following example will serve as an indicator of the manner in which the authors relate the material of Simmel, Caplow, and Vinacke/Arkoff. Working with Caplow's Type III triad ($A < B$, $B = C$), it was determined that this type is equivalent to Simmel's *tertius gaudens* or the enjoying third (see Chapter Three). Approaching coalitions from a strictly rational view, Vinacke/Arkoff, the authors note, argue that in Type III triads, among others, any coalition is likely and the winning coalition should divide the rewards equally between the two members:

> This is true because . . . anyone failing to enter a coalition cannot win against any combination of the two others. Any player must presume that, should he attempt to remain aloof, the two others will form a coalition and defeat him . . . any player threatened with omission from a coalition should be willing to grant another at least half the spoils in order to share in these (Stryker & Psathas, 1960:218).

Caplow's predictions do not agree with the equal sharing suggested by Vinacke/Arkoff. Caplow indicates that in a weak-strong coalition (for Type III, coalitions between *A* and *C* or between *A* and *B*) the stronger member would, in fact, improve his pre-coalition position and at the same time remain more powerful than *A*. Simmel's interpretation of the *tertius gaudens* includes the observation that the weakest member in the triad (Type III) can acquire maximum profits when the relationship between the other two members is one of contention.

Stryker and Psathas proposed five hypotheses in order to test the above predictions and findings. Stryker and Psathas proposed: (1) a higher frequency of occurrence of weak-strong coalitions; (2) in weak-strong coalitions, less than half the prize will go to the weak member; (3a) more coalitions will form which include the weak member, and (3b) larger parts of the prize will be obtained by the weak member when the weight of the weak member increases in relation to the two stronger members; (4) contention between the two stronger members of a triad will result in larger parts of the prize for the weak third member; and (5) weak-strong member contention will result in the weak member's receiving smaller parts of the prize.

Using a 12 × 12 Latin Square (a procedure for randomizing experimental tests), twelve triads composed of male undergraduates were assigned at random to play twelve games. Stryker and Psathas found that the test results did not support Hypothesis (1). The findings indicated that weak-strong coalitions occurred exactly as could be expected by chance. Hypothesis (2) was supported; weak-strong coalitions divided the prize in a way which gave the weak members less than 50%. Hypothesis (3a) was not supported; increases in the weight of the weak member in relation to the two stronger others did not result in more coalitions which included the weak member. Hypothesis (3b) was supported; when a coalition is formed which included a weak member, the weak member tended to receive larger proportions of the reward as his weight increased. Hypothesis (4) was supported; when the two stronger members were in contention, larger proportions of the reward were received by the weak member. Hypothesis (5) was generally supported with the conditional observation that the absence of constraint on the weak member was beneficial only when the other two stronger members were in contention with each other.

Two important facts emerge in consideration of the report by Stryker and Psathas: (1) the predictions suggested by Simmel and Caplow are, for the most part, supported by continuing research into coalition formation; and (2) the research into coalition formation is enhanced by researchers maintaining an orderly and integrated approach to continuing investigations. The use of propositions based upon Simmel as well as the use of the more recent Caplow material has served to strengthen efforts resulting in generally clearer research directions.

A report by William A. Gamson (1961) is an excellent example of attempts to build upon previous activity into coalition formation. The author outlines a coalition theory based upon the view that coalitions, as temporary alliances, are means-oriented and include little value consensus. Coalition members remain tacitly neutral on noncoalition matters. Gamson's premise is that the pursuit of power itself is an ideal basis for the formation of coalitions since it is a form which can be instrumental in achieving a wide range of goals. The author's view of coalitions becomes clear in the following observation:

> Two members may realize their mutual goal antagonisms but such decisions lie in the future and the present alliance may make both between able to achieve a wide range of goals not all of which will be incompatible. Power is the currency of politics (Gamson, 1961:374).

The Gamson coalition theory includes the following conditions which are necessary for a full-fledged coalition situation to occur: (1) a decision is necessary and the decision involves more than two social units attempting to maximize their rewards, (2) no single reward will maximize the rewards for all members, (3) no one member has dictatorial powers, and (4) no participant has veto power. The theory applies to all coalition situations which reflect the following assumptions:

1. All participants have the same information about initial resource distribution and about the payoff given to a coalition.
2. Participants do not distinguish between payoffs in the same payoff situation.
3. Every participant has a rank ordering of nonutilitarian preferences for joining with the other players.

Gamson's general hypothesis can be stated as follows: Any participant will expect others to demand from a coalition a share of the payoff proportional to the amount of resources which they contribute to a coalition. Gamson compared his hypothesis with Caplow's (discussed earlier) and found that predicted coalition outcomes were identical in both cases with only one exception. Gamson's report is important not only because it provides an enrichment of our understanding of coalitions but also because it serves to strengthen the earlier theory and research upon which it was built.

The approach to coalition formation developed by Caplow was based upon the premise that coalition outcomes can be predicted if precoalition power distributions are known. Peter Nacci and James Tedeschi (1976) suggest that this structural approach to coalition formation, while effective when considering the role of power in coalition formation, cannot account for the influences of interpersonal relations upon coalition formation. These authors were concerned with the effects of liking upon coalition formation and the differential effects of liking, by sex, of group members. Using the Parcheesi game, 36 male and 43 female introductory psychology students were asked to read a description of the game. The results indicate that when one disregards the sex of group members, coalition partners are chosen on a random basis. Power and attraction (liking) had no effect upon choice.

However, male subjects showed no preference for a coalition partner, but they did indicate an awareness of the power distribution in the three-member groups. Female subjects made choices based on presumed attraction of precoalition members and also predicted that attracted members would form coalitions. Females did not choose coalition partners at random, and they did not choose partners in terms of power distributions.

GROUP SIZE

When a group changes its leader, group members must be alert to changes in other parts of their structure and to changes in expectations about defining their behavior. When coalitions develop within groups, members accept that the patterns of association previous to the formation of the coalition have changed. Changes such as these are obvious to all group members, and most individuals are ever alert to such possibilities. However, changes in the group process which are brought about by an increase or decrease in the size of the group are more subtle. Individuals are less aware of changes produced by variations in group size. In some families, increases in the number of children are met with the observation that another one won't make a difference. An uninvited guest at the dinner table is just one more mouth to feed, and college fraternities consistently maintain their brotherhoods and sororities their sisterhoods at size levels well beyond reasonable limits.

The effects of an increase in numbers upon the group process are many. There will be an increase in the number of interactions within the group (see Chapter 2) which, in turn, will reduce the frequency of individual activity. An increase in group size will make more people available from which a leader can be selected and will provide additional human resources for a broader distribution of group tasks. Increased size will also provide the group with a greater number of individuals from which to draw necessary abilities and skills.

There is early evidence of concern over the size of groups, particularly among preschool children. The findings of Jean Piaget (1932) have formed the basis for decisions in the field of child development and among educators concerning the cooperative potential of preschool children. Piaget found that there is a clear pattern in the development of preschool children in their play habits. Initially, children play alone with no regard for others who may be about. Children then move to a point where they will continue to play individually, but in parallel. At this point in development, preschoolers tolerate the presence of other children, but they are unwilling to cooperate by sharing the objects of their interest or by entering into concerted effort to achieve a common play goal. Finally, the preschooler will enter into cooperative play with one other child and then proceed to participate in play activities in increasingly larger groups.

SIZE VARIATION AND GROUP STRUCTURE

John James (1951) reported on the average size of three types of small groups: (1) *informal groups* which included shopping, conversational, play, and walk groups, (2) *simulated informal groups* which included groups of individuals acting in stage plays, in movies, and performing in a radio broadcast, and (3) *work groups* which included buying, construction, and repair groups. The mean group size for informal groups was determined to be 2.41, for simulated informal groups, 2.37, and for work groups, 2.35. The mean of the mean group sizes for all three types of small groups is 2.37. By way of contrast, James also reported on formally structured groups including U.S. Senate and House of Representatives subcommittees, judiciary boards, state committees and boards, and subgroups in officer and board of director organizations of four large corporations. The mean group size for Senate subcommittees was 5.4, for House of Representatives subcommittees, 7.8. The mean group size for judiciary boards and other state bureaucratic substructures was 5.7, for state committees and boards, 4.7, and for corporate boards of directors, 5.3. The mean of the mean group sizes for the five group types was 5.7.

James argued that if small groups are thought of as collections of individuals who interact functionally and continuously toward a goal, then the size of the group is a significant factor in determining the range and complexity of the interaction structure. His findings (James, 1951:477) suggest that when the interaction is face-to-face and spontaneous, groups "tend to gravitate to the smallest size, that is, 2—to the point of the least number, that is, 1, of relationships required for interaction." However, in small groups which are characteristically formal and in which individual behavior and units of interaction are not spontaneous but determined, the group does not gravitate to the smallest possible number of individuals and the least number of relationships, but to a size consistent with established group goals. The results of James' investigations support these observations. Although the findings result from a preliminary investigation, there is little doubt that the evidence and thinking in the small groups field is consistent with them.

As the size of the group increases, it becomes increasingly more difficult for group members to develop interpersonal relationships. Evidence suggests that as the size of the group decreases, there is an increase in the intensity of affective bonds established by the members (Kinney, 1953). Recalling James' observation that the tendency in such informally constructed groups is to reduce to size two, we can argue that the most intense bonds which individuals can establish and maintain are in two-person group relationships.

Strong, affective, personalized relationships require groups which are small enough to permit members to respond to one another frequently in a personal way and without distraction. With increasing size, a number of elements enter into the group process which are counterproductive of the quality and quantity associated with interpersonal relationships. Individual group members often feel threatened and withdraw from frequent, active participation in larger-sized groups (Gibb, 1951), and the experience of participation in groups of increasingly larger size is found to be less satisfying to individual group members (Lundgren & Bogart, 1974). A. Paul Hare (1952) found that individual group members have fewer chances to speak in larger-sized groups. The amount of time required by each group member in order to establish relationships which are, in effect, primary in type is significantly reduced as the size of the group increases. Frederick Huff and Thomas Piantianida (1968) found that as the size of the group increases, there develops an increasingly more complex interaction structure in which any one member is less able to participate effectively. As the interaction structure increases in complexity, there develops a pattern of increased role differentiation within the group. The more informal associations of smaller groups in which the interaction system is less complex give way to a situation in which some group members increase the frequency of their participation and others reduce the amount of time spent in active participation (Bales, Strodtbeck, Mills & Roseborough, 1951).

Earlier it was pointed out that group size is a factor in distinguishing groups in terms of formal and informal structures. When groups increase in size and role differentiation becomes more apparent, the group is becoming more formally structured and is adapting to a pattern of leader emergence. Those individuals whose participation increases as group size increases are establishing a position of control or domination over others in the group. In a study of leaderless discussion groups, Bernard M. Bass (1954) found that those group members who talked most frequently tended to emerge as the discussion group leaders. As mentioned in the discussion on leadership, Hemphill (1950) found that members of larger-sized groups are more tolerant of control by a leader than members of groups of smaller size. The presence of a feeling of threat and decisions to withdraw from participation, a reduction of satisfaction, a decrease in opportunity to participate, the development of a complex interaction structure, the emergence of leadership as a control, and tolerance of leader control are all elements which develop as part of the group process in groups of increasing size. In light of the above, it is clear that group size is a significant factor in the determination of the group process and of individual behavior within the group.

summary

The great majority of small group research projects are conducted in laboratories and are designed to enable the researcher to control the subjects by eliminating all unnecessary variables from the environment. Although laboratory studies do not reflect actual conditions in which individuals perform group functions, they afford researchers the opportunity to concentrate on one or two variables which are believed to influence group behavior. This chapter reviewed four research areas: (1) social space and personal distance, (2) leadership, (3) coalition formation, and (4) group size.

SOCIAL SPACE AND PERSONAL DISTANCE

Early researches by anthropologists and experimental psychologists on the subject of space and personal distance were discussed. Edward T. Hall's *The Hidden Dimension* was identified as an important source book for studies conducted on the subject. Additionally, his reporting on *proxemics* (the interrelated observations and theories of man's use of space as a specialized elaboration of culture) defined the cross-cultural variations in space and distance perception and concentrated on the distances of man discussed in Chapter Three.

Three specific areas of space and distance research were reviewed: seating arrangements, proximity, and interracial contact. Research indicates that seating arrangement is a factor which influences patterns of group leadership, task behavior in groups, interpersonal attraction, and informal conversation. Hare and Bales found that interaction patterns of members in task-oriented groups were predictable in terms of seating arrangements and distance between group members. Other research presents evidence to support the view that there is a relationship between perceived leadership and voluntary seating choice. A study by Pellegrini indicated that the individual who occupies the head of the table was chosen more often as the participant who contributed most to group interaction. Sommer's report on the distance for comfortable conversation supported the view that individuals prefer sitting across from one another rather than side-by-side when conversing informally.

Proximity refers to the physical distance between and among individuals. Many students of proximity concentrate on the relationship between physical distance and interpersonal attraction. Newcomb's study of college students in a small dormitory concluded that individuals are most likely to be attracted toward those in closest contact with them. A report by Festinger, Schachter, and Back supported Newcomb's results and indicated that proximity was the crucial factor in the development of friendships among married couples in a student housing environment. Other studies indicated that college students sitting next to each other in classrooms were more likely to become acquainted and that proximity significantly increased the rate of worker interaction which resulted in the development of a system of interpersonal attraction.

This research strongly supports the belief that there is a significant relationship between proximity and interpersonal attraction. One important criticism associated with this research area involves the suspicion that proximity may function as a facilitator of the emergence of other factors more directly associated with the promotion of interpersonal attraction.

Interest in interracial contact at the personal level developed after World War II with research on the attitudes of white soldiers toward integration of blacks into the armed forces. Results indicated that past integrated military experiences resulted in more favorable attitudes toward integration than past segregated military experiences.

In a study of two integrated and two segregated biracial housing projects the results indicated a much higher incidence of friendly contact among the members of the two racial groups who resided in the interracial housing projects than among biracial residents of the segregated housing projects. Research is strongly supportive of the view that increased and close contact between racial groups is a major factor in the reduction of negative attitudes and discriminatory behavior.

LEADERSHIP

The enormous amount of research on the subject of leadership has produced findings which are inconclusive. There is no consensus as to what leadership is or which individual qualities or group forces determine leadership. Characteristic of the findings is an observation by Hare in which he notes that while correlations between personality traits and leadership are generally positive, they are rarely large.

Leadership research has been the concern of psychologists and social psychologists, but sociologists have not been prolific in presenting findings on the subject. When viewed from the perspective of group interaction, interest in leadership centers around the leader-follower relationship. Stogdill's remarks indicate that the more realistic assumption about leadership involves an understanding of it as a two-way flow of effects rather than as a one-way flow: the leader's behavior conditions the response of the followers, and the follower's behavior conditions the response of the leader.

Leadership definitions usually include one or a combination of elements which focus upon individual characteristics and traits, member choice, occupancy of a given group position, leadership as a function of the group, as a symbol and embodiment of group norms, dominance, and influence, and as the central agent of group organization.

It was noted that an interactionist interpretation of leadership should include the following elements: group behavior as process, structural differentiation, situational influences, and authority. *Leadership* was defined as a group process in which an individual in a given situation is able to direct and control group interaction more influentially than any other group member. When group structures are viewed as formal or informal, the procedure for the determination of a leader moves from the appointment of a leader by those in positions which carry the rights of delegation and appointment to the selection of a leader by the group membership.

One of the most important questions associated with leadership research centers around those factors which contribute to the emergence of group leaders. Gilchrist identified success as a major factor in leader emergence. Megaree identified dominance as a personal characteristic conducive to leader emergence, while others have noted proximity and the characteristics of the followers as important factors. Zander and Havelin observed that experimental group members tended to be more attracted to leaders who have competence levels similar to their own. French found that problem-solving groups with leaders were less prone to split into subgroups or factions when frustrated in attempts to solve unsolvable problems. The influence of group members on leadership and leader emergence was noted by Stouffer, who found that orientation groups produced more rewarding experiences for members when they chose their leaders and when they liked and respected them.

Group size was discussed as a factor in the emergence of a group leader. Research indicated that there is an inverse relationship between group size and the possibility of leader emergence. Bass and Norton observed that as the size of the group increases, there is less chance for any one member to perform leadership functions; Hare found that leaders were more influential in groups of small size; Hemphill found that group members were more tolerant of leader control and demanded more of leaders as the size of the group increased.

COALITION FORMATION

Studies of coalition formation were found to be orderly and began with investigations conducted in the mid-fifties. Rooted in the theory of Georg Simmel, early studies, such as one by Theodore M. Mills, confirmed Simmel's argument that "the threesome tends to break up into a pair and another party." This writer views the early research of Theodore Caplow as a most important contribution to the development of coalition research. Caplow constructed six types of triads (1956) and increased the number to eight (1959). These triadic types demonstrated that the prediction of coalitions is possible when the initial power distribution is known. They indicated: (1) that the possibilities for groups to develop in which there is differential power distributed among the members are many, (2) that there is a theoretical basis for understanding the relationship between power distribution and changes for coalition formation, and (3) that the construction of a coalition theory for three-person groups is a legitimate basis for laboratory studies.

Research by Vinacke and Arkoff tested Caplow's hypotheses and confirmed his interpretations of coalition possibilities. Research by Stryker and Psathas reported that the predictions of coalition possibilities by both Simmel and Caplow were supported by laboratory investigation. Gamson's research was included as an excellent example of a successful attempt to build upon previous research. Gamson outlined a coalition theory based upon the view that coalitions as temporary alliances are means-oriented and include little value consensus. He noted that coalition members remain tacitly neutral on non-coalition issues.

GROUP SIZE

Group size was identified as having a subtle effect upon the group process. Individuals are less aware of changes produced by variations in group size, as suggested in the commonly used phrase, "one more won't make a difference."

Group size increases the number of interaction possibilities within a group and these, in turn, will affect the frequency of individual activity. As the size of the group increases, more members are available from which a leader can be selected. An increase in group membership provides additional human resources for the performance of group tasks. The larger number of individuals will provide a tool from which additional abilities and skills can be drawn.

Early research by Jean Piaget indicated the importance of group size in child development. He noted that there is a pattern to the play habits of preschool children. Children play alone, then in parallel, and then cooperatively. The child proceeds, at that point, to participate in play activities in groups of increasingly larger size.

John James reported on the average size of three types of small groups. The informal group (shopping, conversational, play, and walk groups) had a mean size of 2.41 members. Simulated informal groups had a mean size of 2.37, and work groups a mean size of 2.35. James also reported that formally structured small groups had a mean size of 5.7. The report concluded that the size of a group is a significant factor in determining the range and complexity of the interaction structure: when group interaction is spontaneous and face-to-face, there is a tendency for groups to gravitate to the smallest size; groups which are formal and determined tend to gravitate to a size consistent with established goals.

Research indicates that the development of interpersonal relationships is restricted by increases in group size. Kinney reported that as the size of the group decreases, there is an increase in the intensity of affective bonds established by the members. Also, individuals feel more threatened and withdraw from frequent, active participation in larger-sized groups; experiences in larger groups were found to be less satisfying. There were fewer chances for individuals to speak in groups of larger size, and in such groups there developed an increasingly more complex interaction structure which reduced the chances for individuals to participate effectively in group activity.

discussion questions

1. What does Hall mean when he says that observations of the way animals handle space are helpful in understanding how human beings handle space?

2. Is proximity a factor in the development of interpersonal relations between and among individuals of different backgrounds and interests?
3. Can you explain the low correlations found between leadership and personality traits?
4. Are there characteristics common to leaders in both formal and informal groups?
5. Why is an individual less active in large-sized groups?

references

Albert, Robert S.; and **Brigante, Thomas R.** "The Psychology of Friendship Relations: Social Factors," *Journal of Social Psychology*, 56 (1962): 33–47.

Aldous, Joan; and **Straus, Murray A.** "Social Networks and Conjugal Roles: A Test of Bott's Hypothesis," *Social Forces*, 44 (1966): 265–270.

Bales, Robert F.; **Strodtbeck, F. L.**; **Mills, T. M.**; and **Roseborough, M. E.** "Channels of Communication in Small Groups," *American Sociological Review*, 16 (1951): 461–468.

Bass, Bernard M.; and **Norton, Fay-Tyler.** "Group Size and Leaderless Discussions," *Journal of Applied Psychology*, 35 (1951): 397–400.

Bass, Bernard M.; and **Wurster, C. R.** "Effects of the Nature of the Problem on LGD Performance," *Journal of Applied Psychology*, 37 (1953): 96–99.

Bass, Bernard M. "The Leaderless Group Discussion," *Psychological Bulletin*, 51 (1954): 465–492.

Batchelor, James P.; and **Goethals, George R.** "Spatial Arrangements in Freely Formed Groups," *Sociometry*, 35 (1972): 270–279.

Bennis, Warren G. "Leadership Theory and Administrative Behavior: The Problems of Authority," *Administrative Science Quarterly*, 4 (1959): 259–301.

Borgatta, Edgar F.; and **Bales, Robert F.** "Task and Accumulation of Experience as Factors in the Interaction of Small Groups," *Sociometry*, 16 (1953): 239–252.

Burns, Tom. "The Reference of Conduct in Small Groups: Cliques and Cabals in Occupational Milieu," *Human Relations*, 8 (1955): 467–486.

Byrne, Donn; and **Buehler, J. A.** "A Note on the Influence of Propinquity upon Acquaintanceships," *Journal of Abnormal and Social Psychology*, 51 (1955): 147–148.

Byrne, Donn. "The Influence of Propinquity and Opportunities for Interaction on Classroom Relationships," *Human Relations*, 14 (1961): 63–69.

Caplow, Theodore. "A Theory of Coalition in the Triad," *American Sociological Review*, 21 (1956): 489–493.

_____. "Further Development of a Theory of Coalition in the Triad," *The American Journal of Sociology*, 64 (1959): 488–493.

_____. *Two Against One: Coalitions in Triads*. Englewood Cliffs, New Jersey: Prentice-Hall, 1968.

Cohen, Bernard P. "Seating Position and Interaction in Five-man Groups." Unpublished paper, Harvard University, 1953.

Cook, Mark. "Experiments on Orientation and Proxemics," *Human Relations*, 23 (1970): 61–76.

Costanzo, Philip R. "Conformity Development as a Function of Self-blame," *Journal of Personality and Social Psychology*, 14 (1970): 366–374.

Deutsch, Morton; and Collins, Mary Evans. *Interracial Housing.* Minneapolis: University of Minnesota Press, 1951.

Felipe, Nancy. "Interpersonal Distance and Small Group Interaction," *Cornell Journal of Social Relations*, 1 (1966): 59–64.

Festinger, Leon; Schachter, Stanley; and Back, Kurt. *Social Pressures in Informal Groups.* New York: Harper & Row, 1950.

French, John R. P., Jr. "The Disruption and Cohesion of Groups," *Journal of Abnormal and Social Psychology*, 36 (1941): 361–377.

Gamson, William A. "A Theory of Coalition Formation," *American Sociological Review*, 26 (1961): 373–382.

Gibb, Cecil A. "The Principles and Traits of Leadership," *Journal of Abnormal and Social Psychology*, 42 (1947): 267–284.

Gibb, Cecil A. "Leadership," in Gardner Lindzey (ed.). *Handbook of Social Psychology.* Cambridge, Massachusetts: Addison-Wesley, 1954.

Gibb, Jack R. "The Effects of Group Size and of Threat Reduction upon Creativity in a Problem-solving Situation," *American Psychologist*, 6 (1951): 324–325.

Gilchrist, Jack C. "The Formation of Social Groups under Conditions of Success and Failure," *Journal of Abnormal Social Psychology*, 47 (1952): 174–187.

Gullahorn, J. "Distance and Friendship as Factors in the Gross Interaction Matrix," *Sociometry*, 15 (1952): 123–134.

Hall, Edward T. *The Hidden Dimension.* Garden City, New York: Doubleday, 1966.

Hanawalt, N. G.; Richardson, H. M.; and Morris, M. L. "Level of Aspiration in College Leaders and Nonleaders," *Journal of Abnormal and Social Psychology*, 38 (1943): 545–548.

Harding, J.; and Hogrefe, R. "Attitudes of White Department Store Employees toward Negro Coworkers," *Journal of Social Issues*, 8 (1952): 18–28.

Hare, A. Paul. "A Study of Interaction and Consensus in Different Sized Groups," *American Sociological Review*, 17 (1952): 261–267.

_____. *Handbook of Small Group Research*, 2nd ed.; New York: The Free Press, 1976.

Hare, A. Paul; and Bales, Robert F. "Seating Position and Small Group Interaction," *Sociometry*, 26 (1963): 480–486.

Heckel, Robert V. "Leadership and Voluntary Seating Choice," *Psychological Reports*, 32 (1973): 141–142.

Hemphill, John K. "Relations between the Size of the Group and the Behavior of the 'Superior' Leaders," *Journal of Social Psychology*, 32 (1950): 11–22.

Huff, Frederick W.; and Piantianida, Thomas P. "The Effect of Group Size on Group Information Transmitted," *Psychonomic Science*, 11 (1968): 365–366.

Information and Education Division of the United States War Department. "Opinions about Negro Infantry Platoons in White Companies of Seven Divisions," in Theodore M. Newcomb and E. L. Hartley (eds.). *Readings in Social Psychology*, revised ed.; New York: Holt Rinehart & Winston, 1952.

James, John. "A Preliminary Study of the Size Determinant in Small Group Interaction," *American Sociological Review*, 16 (1951): 474–477.

Kelley, Harold H.; and Arrowood, A. John. "Coalitions in the Triad: Critique and Experiment," *Sociometry*, 23 (1960): 231–244.

Kinney, Elva E. "A Study of Peer Group Social Acceptability at the Fifth-grade Level in a Public School," *Journal of Educational Research*, 47 (1953): 57–64.

Knickerbocker, I. "Leadership: A Conception and Some Implications," *Journal of Social Issues*, 4 (1948): 23–40.

Krech, David; and Crutchfield, Richard S. *Theory and Problems of Social Psychology*. New York: McGraw-Hill, 1948.

Levine, Jacob; and Butler, John. "Lecture vs. Group Decision in Changing Behavior," *Journal of Applied Psychology*, 36 (1952): 26–33.

Lippitt, Ronald; and White, Ralph K. "An Experimental Study of Leadership and Group Life," in Eleanor E. Maccoby, Theodore M. Newcomb, and Eugene L. Hartley (eds.). *Readings in Social Psychology*. 3rd ed.; New York: Henry Holt, 1958.

Lundgren, David C.; and Bogart, Dodd H. "Group Size, Member Dissatisfaction, and Group Radicalism," *Human Relations*, 27 (1974): 339–355.

Maisonneuve, Jean, in collaboration with G. Palmade and Cl. Fourment. "Selective Choices and Propinquity," *Sociometry*, 15(1952): 135–140.

Mann, John H. "The Effect of Inter-racial Contact on Sociometric Choice and Perceptions," *Journal of Social Psychology*, 50 (1959): 143–152.

Megaree, E. I. "Influence of Sex Roles on the Manifestation of Leadership," *Journal of Applied Psychology*, 53 (1969): 377–382.

Merei, Ferenc. "Group Leadership and Institutionalization," *Human Relations*, 2 (1949): 23–39.

Mills, Theodore M. "Power Relations in Three-person Groups," *American Sociological Review*, 18 (1953): 351–357.

――――――――――. "The Coalition Pattern in Three-person Groups," *American Sociological Review*, 19 (1954): 657–667.

Nacci, Peter; and Tedeschi, James T. "Liking and Power as Affecting Coalition Choices in Triads," *Social Behavior and Personality*, 4 (1976): 27–32.

Newcomb, Theodore M. "The Prediction of Interpersonal Attraction," *American Psychologist*, 11 (1956): 575–586.

Pellegrini, Robert J. "Some Effects of Seating Position on Social Perception," *Psychological Reports*, 28 (1971): 887–893.

Pelz, D. C. "Leadership within a Hierarchical Organization," *Journal of Social Issues*, 7 (1951): 49–55.

Piaget, Jean. *The Moral Judgment of the Child.* New York: Harcourt, Brace, 1932.

Roff, Merrill E. "A Study of Combat Leadership in the Air Force by Means of a Rating Scale," *Journal of Psychology*, 30 (1959): 229–239.

Rosenthal, Bernard G.; and **Delong, Alton J.** "Complimentary Leadership and Spatial Arrangements of Group Members," *Group Psychotherapy and Psychodrama*, 25 (1972): 34–52.

Shaw, Marvin E. "Changes in Sociometric Choices Following Forced Integration of an Elementary School," *Journal of Social Issues*, 29 (1973): 143–157.

_____. *Group Dynamics: The Psychology of Small Group Behavior*, 2nd ed.; New York: McGraw-Hill, 1976.

Shepherd, Clovis R. *Small Groups: Some Sociological Perspectives.* San Francisco, California: Chandler, 1964.

Smith, F. Tredwell. *An Experiment in Modifying Attitudes toward the Negro.* New York: Teachers College Bureau of Publications, Columbia University, 1943.

Smith, Robert J.; and **Cook, Patrick E.** "Leadership in Dyadic Groups as a Function of Dominance and Incentives," *Sociometry*, 36 (1973): 561–568.

Sommer, Robert. "Studies in Personal Space," *Sociometry*, 22 (1959): 247–260.

_____. "Leadership and Group Geography," *Sociometry*, 24 (1961): 99–110.

_____. "The Distance for Comfortable Conversation: A Further Study," *Sociometry*, 25 (1962): 111–116.

Stein, David D.; Hardwick, Jane Allyn; and **Smith, M. Brewster.** "Race and Belief: An Open and Shut Case," *Journal of Personality and Social Psychology*, 1 (1965): 281–289.

Stogdill, Ralph M. "Personal Factors Associated with Leadership: A Survey of the Literature," *The Journal of Psychology*, 25 (1948): 35–71.

_____. *Handbook of Leadership: A Survey of Theory and Research.* New York: The Free Press, 1974.

Stouffer, Samuel A., et al. *The American Soldier.* Princeton, New Jersey: Princeton University Press, 1949, Vol. 1.

Strodtbeck, Fred L. "The Family as a Three-person Group," *American Sociological Review*, 19 (1954): 23–29.

Stryker, Sheldon; and **Psathas, George.** "Research on Coalitions in the Triad: Findings, Problems and Strategy," *Sociometry*, 23 (1960): 217–230.

Talland, George A. "Role and Status Structure in Therapy Groups," *Journal of Clinical Psychology*, 13 (1957): 27–33.

Vinacke, W. Edgar; and **Arkoff, Abe.** "An Experimental Study of Coalitions in the

Triad," *American Sociological Review*, 22 (1957): 406–414.

White, James E. "Theory and Method for Research in Community Leadership," *American Sociological Review*, 15 (1950): 50–60.

Whyte, William Foote. *Street Corner Society*, 2nd ed.; Chicago: The University of Chicago Press, 1955.

Zander, A.; and **Havelin, A.** "Social Comparison and Interpersonal Attraction," *Human Relations*, 13 (1960): 21–32.

Chapter Eight

Small Group Structure and Process

The structural framework within which the group interaction process occurs affords each individual in the group a position within which role expectations define appropriate behavior. These three elements—position, role and interaction—are interrelated (see Figure 8-1) and are major factors in the achievement of group goals and in the development of the identity systems which bind individuals to the group (group cohesion).

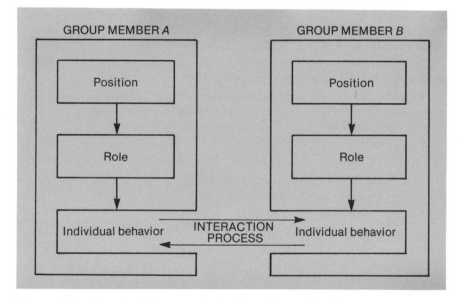

Figure 8-1.   Structural Elements in the Group Interaction Process

The two-member interaction shown in the above diagram is only one part of a group interaction system. As the size of the group increases, this simple arrangement connecting two individuals must be extended to include all group members.

Later on in the chapter we will observe the effect of the normative element in a group structure. Individuals who participate in group activity are subject not only to the demands of other group members but also to the demands of the group as a whole. In other words, maintaining positions within a social group requires that individuals are willing to internalize those group influences which originate in the normative system of the group and function as a control over individual members and their relationships. Social roles function to connect the group norms to the individual, and these roles are coordinated and complement each other. When all these elements work efficiently, groups are viewed as cohesive or integrated. The level of cohesion attained by a group is a determiner of the degree of member satisfaction within the group, the efficiency of group member performances required by the group, and the effectiveness of the group as measured by goal achievement.

These structural elements of groups and their relationships to each other will be investigated here through the eyes of the small group researcher. Research efforts into the structure of the small group are staggering in number. These efforts are also impressive in that they have provided methodologies and research designs (in the experimental laboratory and in the field) for the effective study of the small group. The findings produced from these efforts are, on the whole, consistent and have added a body of knowledge which analysts and students find indispensable in their attempts to understand the small group phenomenon.

GROUP STRUCTURE

In Chapter Two structure was identified as an essential characteristic of social groups regardless of their size. All social groups were identified, structurally, as either formal or informal, and small groups were defined as being distinguishable in the same way. The literature on group structure is clear in its distinctions between formal and informal types. The impersonal, contractual character of formal group structures is usually associated with large systems such as corporations or universities, and the personalized, affective character of informal structures with small primary-like groups such as families and friendship groups. The size differentiation suggested by this structural separation of groups is not definite nor is it realistic. The reader should be aware at this point that small subsystems of interaction within large corporate structures can develop primary-like qualities and that some small groups are characteristically formal in their structural type. Committees of all kinds, boards of directors, garden clubs, and even the weekly bridge club are to some degree formal in their organization.

The concept of structure allows us to view group interaction from a special perspective. When structure is the main consideration, human social interaction is thought of as a system of social relationships between and among individuals who occupy differentiated positions within the group. All social groups have structure, and, whether it be formal or informal, individuals behave according to expectations placed upon them by the group. The structure of the group is a clear determiner of the interaction within. Structure is a group control mechanism and, willingly or not, individuals who remain group members must conform to the expectations placed upon the positions they occupy.

Group structures are composed of differential positions which individuals occupy. When individuals who occupy these positions give value to them (ordinarily, consensus is reached on the relative worth of each position), these positions become status positions and are found to be above or below each other in hierarchy and in value. Figure 8-2 is an example of a large, formal system of positions which individuals occupy in the administration of a medium-sized university. The reader should note that the many connected blocks are positions and not individuals. One of the more interesting aspects of formal structures is that they afford us the opportunity to blueprint behavior by describing (1) the functions associated with the different positions within the structures and (2) the development of a set of criteria by which individuals are selected for occupancy. All this is indicative of the impersonal quality of formal structure. The degree of impersonality which characterizes a group is possibly the best criterion by which formal and informal structures are distinguished.

Informal structures are different in that they have positions, the functions of which are ordinarily much less explicit, as are the criteria for occupancy. For example, families obviously have only the most generalized criteria for children who enter the family by natural means. Certain expectations about the physical characteristics of the child to be adopted may be explicitly stated by the prospective parents, but to hold these rigidly would be, for many, a point of embarrassment. Similarly, friendship associations do not require explicit statements about member functions or criteria for membership. The absence of these elements does not indicate the absence of structure. There is no group which is unstructured. The absence of explicit criteria and functions indicates that friendship associations have a different kind of structure, one that is informal and affectively based.

The friendship group presents an interesting example of informal structure. A small group of college friends, unlike the college fraternity, has no rules and regulations for membership, nor is there a formal procedure for entrance. In such a group a leader may emerge although that individual may not be referred to as the leader; behavioral expectations arise from which individuals carry out certain functions which enhance the group, but these are not formalized into a code or written description of the role of each member. Common interests and mutual

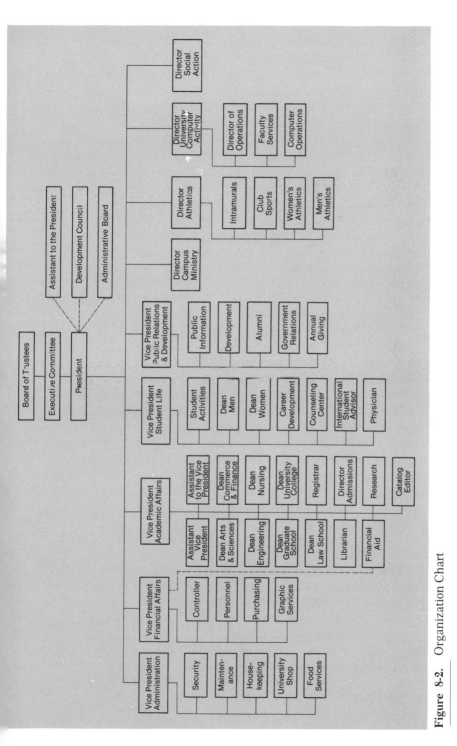

Figure 8-2. Organization Chart

Reprinted by permission of Rev. John M. Driscoll, O.S.A., President, Villanova University.

identity form the bases for the friendship association, and there are no clear regulations for entrance into the group. Each member has certain functions, and each member will evaluate[1] every other member and have a sense of status positioning within the group. All these elements form the structure of informal groups, but the informal nature of the interaction within and the affective elements which override these elements make the association qualitatively different from groups whose structures are formal.

Thus far we have distinguished structures of groups according to their formal and informal characteristics. In reality, these structures are not as separate as the analysis might suggest. One of the most interesting aspects of group structure, supported by research in industrial settings (Roethlisberger & Dickson, 1939), is referred to by Robin M. Williams, Jr. (1970:517):

> . . . if we consider a formally organized group to be one in which the members interact as occupants of explicitly defined and interrelated roles, performing prescribed functions, we can predict that continuing formal groupings will quickly develop an informal organization, simply as a by-product of action directed toward the formal objectives of the organization.

This convergence of different structural types arises, according to Williams (1970:519), from the development of subunits of large system members, which units ". . . command their own segmental loyalties." The development of subgroups within larger organizational systems also results from the proximity workers have to one another in work pools, common offices, specialized work areas, and so on, and from the communication networks which develop within the larger organization. Perhaps the most incisive explanation for the convergence of different structural types is stated by George Monane (1967:19):

> It is because of the power of past socialization, that is, the tendency for old-system norms to persist so that they may interfere with proper component action in a new system . . .

The findings from the Western Electric studies support Monane's position. The convergence of the formal structure of the company and the informal patterns of association which developed, for example, in the

---

1. In characterizing informal primary associations, Tomotsu Shibutani observed that members evaluate and are evaluated by each other. This evaluative procedure results in the development of a pattern of attraction-repulsion even in the most primary of associations. See Tomotsu Shibutani, *Society and Personality: An Interactionist Approach to Social Psychology*. Englewood Cliffs, New Jersey: Prentice-Hall, 1961, p. 407.

Bank Wiring Observation Room (see Chapter Nine) reflected the two different levels of expectations which surround the individual worker. On the one hand, the workers had internalized the company norms which controlled their work output, and they were aware of the rewards forthcoming from increasing daily and weekly production to more evenly match the company's ideal in this regard. However, the old-system norms derived from long-established family and friendship associations carried over into the work setting. The individual worker participated in the informal structure which developed within the particular work setting and derived from it a self-identity on the job which was not possible from the worker's formal association with the company.

Group structures have been studied in a variety of ways, but in large measure researchers have approached the subject in terms of role differentiation. More specifically, studies have concentrated on behavior within given organizational systems, leadership as an element in the development of structure, and the situations which prevail in various structural types of groups.

Dorwin Cartwright and Alvin Zander's (1960) criteria for the development of stable differentiations within groups should be understood in the light of the distinction just made between formal and informal groups. These criteria are applicable to both types of structures. The criteria are: (1) efficient group performance, (2) abilities and motivations of individuals, and (3) the environment of the group. Group structures, according to these authors, develop around three elements: activity, personal qualities, and physical and social enviornments (Cartwright & Zander, 1960: 643–645).

EFFICIENT GROUP PERFORMANCE

Some research in communication network analysis has indicated that efficiency in group performance is related to role differentiation within groups and to the presence or absence of reasonable or appropriate patterns of organization. Thornton Roby and John Lanzetta (1956) found that in role-differentiated networks the most efficient group performances were observed in those groups in which there were fewer communication links between the source of information and the point at which a group decision must be made. The less complex the communication channels in role-differentiated groups, the more efficient the group performance. In another study, Morrissette, Switzer, and Crannell (1965) found that appropriate organizational systems promoted increased efficiency in group performance. Research on this subject indicates that when the system within which group members function is organized in a manner which is consistent with the behavior required of them, they perform their functions in a more efficient manner. However, the pattern of organization seems to have less effect upon performance when efficiency is measured against the cohesiveness of the group. For example, the presence or absence of supervision was not a determining factor in performances in groups of high cohesion (Berkowitz, 1954). In an interesting study of B-29 bomber crews, Leonard Berkowtiz (1956) found that bomber crews which were characterized by high cohesion and who were highly motivated were more efficient in their performances than crews identified as having low cohesion and perceived as low in motivation. The study also indicated that both high- and low-cohesion crews performed with similar effectiveness if the crew members were actually motivated to perform well.

PERSONAL CHARACTERISTICS

A study by Anthony R. D'Augelli (1973) found that interpersonal skills of group members was a major factor in the development of perceived group cohesion. That is, group members identified groups which were composed of individuals with high levels of interpersonal skills as more cohesive than groups whose members scored low in interpersonal skills. D'Augelli's study implies that those individuals with particularly high interpersonal skills were viewed, at least informally, as leaders or as individuals to whom special role definitions were given. The development of role differentiation based upon interpersonal skills results in the emergence of a rudimentary group structure.

Institutionalized sex differences and occupational status were studied as factors in the structure and deliberations of a jury. Basing their results on 49 mock deliberations, Strodtbeck, James, and Hawkins (1957) found that men of higher-status occupations have higher participation, influence, satisfaction, and perceived competence for jury tasks. More particularly, those of higher occupations were most frequently selected as jury foremen. In attempting to explain these results, the authors indicate that the choice of high-status males may be a function of others' perception of these men and their comments as being of greater value. Jurors who utilized more of the time allotted for jury deliberation were perceived as jurors desired if those responding were on trial. Although the authors do not explain the causes of role differentiation among members of juries, they do suggest that status gradients emerge with great clarity, and appear to be related to the personal factors of sex and occupational status.

Qualities attributed to leaders and followers appear to have an influence upon group structure and most particularly upon how these individuals perceive group structure. For example, H. B. Gerard (1957) found that leaders tend to perform their functions more efficiently when they are free from constraint or control; followers tend to be more efficient under highly controlled conditions (rigid structure). From the point of view of the leader-follower relationship, individuals produce more when controlled by a strong formal leader than individuals who are controlled by weak informal leaders. Also, groups controlled by strong formal leaders are found to be more cohesive than those controlled by weak informal leaders (Gross, Martin & Darley, 1953).

Some individuals have a personal need for rigid structure. These individuals appear to need the security which results from participation in a highly structured group environment. L. G. Wispé and K. E. Lloyd (1955) have suggested that the barriers produced by structuring positions of superiors and subordinates alleviate, for some individuals, the fear of having negative sanctions imposed upon them for poor work performances. In this regard, low-level producers viewed their superiors as more threatening than did high producers.

Leadership-followership is the most basic form of role differentiation in groups. Since a large amount of the research in the area of group structure is devoted to or implies the leader-follower division, those physical qualities which determine leaders should be noted. Characteristics such as intelligence, specific skills and abilities, size of group members, and talkativeness have been identified as qualities which individuals bring to the leadership position. A more complete statement on leadership characteristics, leadership activity, and the relationship of these elements to group structure can be found in Chapter Seven.

GROUP ENVIRONMENTS

This writer cannot vouch for the truth of an incident which allegedly occurred in a weekend encounter group. But the truth or falsity of the matter is not as important for our purposes as the implications of what happens when changing group environments demand changes in the behavior of members of the group. The description should be read with the following proposition in mind: Changes in the group environment require changes in the behavior of all group members.

Having organized a weekend encounter, a small group of students hired a group leader and began meeting late on a Friday evening. All appeared to go well until the afternoon of the next day. At a particularly intense point in the interaction, one of the students, having made public more than she intended, was finally unable to continue. She sat rigid and would no longer speak to the group leader or to the other participants.

When the group leader realized that the situation had changed and required a proficiency which he did not possess, he rose and informed the group that he was not able to handle the situation and left. It remained for the other students to care for the disabled participant. They did so by taking her to a psychiatrist under whose care she remained for approximately six months.

The story is a sad one, but it highlights the importance of taking into account the situational environments within which group interaction occurs. The group leader was able to function very well as long as the encounter proceeded normally. He was not able to continue effectively when the demands upon him as the occupant of the position of greatest influence changed due to a situational change within the group. Carter, Haythorn, Shriver, and Lanzetta (1951) indicate that the group leader did not fulfill the requirements of the leadership role since leadership behavior is found to change as situations within groups change. The authors argue that changes in the requirements of group tasks, for example, require changes in leader behavior. In general, leadership studies (Jenkins, 1947) have shown that the traits required of a leader are directly related to the situational environments in which they are expected to function.

Physical environments have a direct effect upon the structure of groups. Festinger, Schachter, and Back (1950) found that a major determinant of the sociometric structure of groups is the physical location of residences. The authors found that the physical location of houses was directly related to the development of friendship associations and, in turn, the sociometric structure of the entire community.

The discussion on space in Chapter Seven included observations about the relationship between seating position and the development of group structure. Additionally, Robert Sommer (1961) reported that individuals who anticipate becoming group leaders tend to occupy central positions of high visibility. These individuals are most often selected as leaders because the physical location they occupy is most commonly accepted as the one from which the group members can expect authority and direction for group activity to flow. Individuals who are appointed or elected to leadership positions internalize these same expectations and do, in fact, occupy centrally located and visible positions.

The research on communication networks conducted by H. J. Leavitt (1951) supports the view that individuals who occupy central positions most often become leaders. Using four networks—circle, chain, wheel, and Y (see Chapter Five)—Leavitt found that in the wheel, where the central location is highly visible, the individual occupying that location was identified as the leader by 23 of 25 individuals. Similar results were obtained from test trials using the chain and Y patterns, both of which contain central locations. The circle network with no central position produced no clear or high-frequency leader choices. These findings and the results of other efforts (Shaw & Rothschild, 1956; Guetzkow, 1960; Mulder, 1960) indicate that individuals who occupy central positions in groups stand the best chance of emerging as group leaders.

GROUP NORMS AND SOCIAL CONTROL

Paul V. Crosbie has identified the control mechanisms used by groups to restrict individual behavior. Indicating that the ways in which groups establish control over members vary in the direction of either reward or punishment and in intensity, Crosbie (1975) lists the following group control mechanisms: rewarding conformity, punishments and sanctions, persuasion, and normative redefinition. The first three mechanisms are designed to bring the behavior of deviant group members back to within the approved limits established by the group. The last, normative redefinition, indicates that group members realize that in some instances it is more beneficial to the group to broaden the limits of acceptable behavior to include the deviant behavior of one or more members.

STUDIES IN CONFORMITY

Each of the above means used by groups to control the behavior of members is designed to increase conformity to group norms. The degree to which members conform to group norms and standards is a measure of the ability of the group to work efficiently and effectively toward established goals.

Muzafer Sherif (1936; 1937) used the autokinetic effect to illustrate informational conformity in group settings. There were no group norms established by the subjects, but informational exchange resulted in convergence of judgments about a given stimulus. Subjects were placed in a totally darkened room and asked to judge how far a pinpoint of light on the facing wall moved. The pinpoint of light is stationary in reality, but the visual effect is that it appears to move (autokinesis). Individuals placed in the room alone were asked to estimate the distance the light appeared to move. These subjects were then placed in the room in groups of two or three individuals whose earlier solitary perceptions differed substantially. Under these conditions, the subjects changed their individual estimates and developed significantly less discrepant judgments of the distance the light appeared to move. The judgments established by the group became the basis for separate judgments made by the subjects when, in a later series of tests, they experienced the autokinetic effect while alone in the room. The effect of the group experience remained and was a factor in determining the judgments made separately. In one variation of these tests, Sherif placed individuals who had no previous experience with the autokinetic effect in the room together. He found that the distance judgments among them were even closer than in the previous tests.

One of the classic experiments on conformity to group norms was conducted by Solomon Asch (1957). Groups of seven to nine individuals participated in what appeared to be a visual discrimination experiment. The subjects were asked to match the length of a standard line with one of three comparison lines (see Figure 8-3). Only one of the three comparison lines was equal in length to the standard. The lengths of the three comparison lines were sufficiently different so that there could be no ambiguity as to which one matched the standard line.

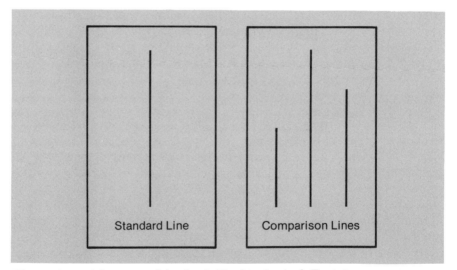

Standard Line   Comparison Lines

Figure 8-3.   Adaptation of the Cards Used in the Asch Experiment

All but one of the subjects had met previously with the experimenter and were instructed to respond with incorrect but unanimous judgments. The one subject left out was not aware of the pre-test meeting. In each test situation, all but one of the subjects who met with the experimenter responded before the uninformed subject. The uninformed subjects were, therefore, in the position of knowing the correct response (the middle comparison line) but was also in the position of having heard the incorrect but unanimous judgments of the other subjects. The uninformed subjects were in the position of either making a completely independent judgment which would contradict the judgment of the majority or go against sensory evidence and conform to the incorrect but unanimous judgments of the other subjects. Nearly 37% of the answers given by 123 college students were incorrect answers. The final results are surprising when one remembers that the comparison lines were unambiguous. There is little doubt that the incorrect answers given by the uninformed subjects were the result of pressures to conform to the unanimous responses of the other participants.

Brendan G. Rule and John Renner (1965) have demonstrated that when a group member has an opinion which differs from the majority or consensus opinion of the remaining group members, there is pressure to conform to majority opinion. The authors identified two characteristics of the distribution of values as representative of individual opinions which help to determine individual decisions about conformity to majority group opinion. These are: the dispersion of opinion and the distance between the individual group member's own opinion and the mean value of the remaining group members. Their research demonstrates that (1) individuals who differed from a group whose opinions approached consensus changed opinions more often than individuals whose opinions differed from remaining group members whose opinions were more dispersed, and (2) individual group members whose opinions were farther away from the mean of the opinions of the remaining group members changed their opinions more often than those whose opinions were closer to the mean of the remaining group members. In a more recent article, Rule and Renner (1968) measured these two characteristics against the subject's involvement/noninvolvement on issues, involvement being defined as the degree of extremity or agreement on various issues. Results indicated (1) that the observed tendency for opinion change was greater when there is less dispersion of group opinion on both involved and noninvolved issues, and (2) that when dispersion was greater, the tendency for the individual to change an opinion was less great on involved issues.

These studies suggest that conformity to the group involves a complex of forces which help determine the degree to which individuals conform to group opinion. Individual perception of the variations of opinions among other group members and the degree to which individual opinion is different from the opinion complex of the other group members are elements in the determination of individual conformity but are controlled to a significant degree by the intensity or involvement the individual has with any one issue.

The complexity of the conformity process in interaction systems is apparent in Paul V. Crosbie's (1972) report in which he tests three propositions from Homans' theory of social exchange. Crosbie adapted the three propositions to predict compliance in two-member power relationships in a laboratory setting. Compliance was identified (Crosbie, 1972:206) as " . . . the decision by Ego to comply with Other's directives, that is, the decision to engage in a power exchange." The three propositions by Homans and the compliance hypotheses developed by Crosbie combine as follows:

Proposition	The more often within a given period of time a man's activity rewards the activity of another, the more often the other will emit the activity.
Adaptation	The greater the frequency with which Other rewards Ego for compliance, the more often Ego will comply with Other's directives.
Proposition	The more valuable to a man a unit of activity another gives him, the more often he will emit activity rewarded by the activity of the other.
Adaptation	The greater the magnitude of reward which Ego receives from Other for compliance, the greater the probability that Ego will comply with Other's directives.
Proposition	The more often a man has in the recent past received a rewarding activity from another, the less valuable any further unit of that activity becomes to him and . . . the less often he will emit the activity that gets him the reward.
Adaptation	The greater the accumulation of the reward which Ego receives from Other for compliance, the less the probability that Ego will comply with Other's directives.

The experiment included a series of tests on two actors: the subject and a confederate. The test trials involved a series of exchanges between the two actors who had been told that the experiment was designed to study unilateral bargaining. The exchanges involved making and changing decisions on the part of the subject and disagreement with the initial choice of the subject by the confederate in some trials. When disagreement occurred, the confederate was expected to attempt to use rewards to induce the subject to change an initial choice. When the subject changed an initial choice, the change was viewed as representing compliance. The subject's decisions were made by selecting from 2 × 2 matrices with cells in which sums of money were represented.

The confederate held no matrices but did have a list of power directives which would be used to persuade the subject to change an initial decision in disagreement trials. As an indicator of High Frequency/High Reward, the confederate handed the subject a note which read: "I'd like you to change to row _____. If you do, I'll give you two notebooks" (nonmonetary rewards). As an indicator of Low Reward/High Frequency, the note read: " . . . I'll give you a notebook." The indicator for Low Reward/Low Frequency read: " . . . I may give you a notebook." Under this last condition, the confederate actually gave the subject a notebook one of every five times the subject changed his initial choice. The results were, for the most part, supportive of Homans' propositions. There appeared to be a significant increase in the willingness of the subject to enter a power exchange, that is, to change initial choice, with an increase in the frequency of the reward and a significant increase in the willingness of the subject to enter a power exchange when the magnitude of the reward increased. Tests of the third hypothesis (greater accumulation/less compliance) did not reach a level of statistical significance. Crosbie explains this failure as a result of being able to compare only ten test trials.

These results point to one important element in the conforming behavior of an individual. In affirming Homans' propositions in terms of compliance, the research indicates the effect of motivational elements in the process of decision making and conformity. The influences which confront individuals and which exert pressure from within group boundaries are conditioned and limited by the personal needs and reward expectations of the individual.

In summary, the Homans/Crosbie investigations suggest an economic approach to conformity. If, as Homans suggests, individuals behave toward others in a manner which will keep rewards high and reduce costs, then individuals will conform to group norms and group influences if there are expectations of rewards. Similarly, individuals will resist conformity in the face of strong group influences if the cost for conformity is greater than the anticipated rewards. The following may appear an oversimplification, but in light of the above interpretations it is reasonable to argue that individuals conform to group pressures and group influences when they are able to anticipate a net reward (rewards gained from activity as against actual costs).

The emphasis in these studies is on the individual who is doing the conforming. But there are clearly other elements which enter into consideration about the conformity process and group controls which indicate that the conformity in group settings is the result of a complex of factors. These may be combined under the following three headings: (1) conformity and the object, (2) conformity and the subject, and (3) conformity and the situation.[2]

CONFORMITY AND THE OBJECT

The early researches of Solomon Asch were conducted with unambiguous objects. These are objects which, when observed, are easily identified as what they are through the use of our senses. In the Asch experiment, the length of a line was used as the unambiguous object. There are other objects which require evaluation on the part of the subject—ambiguous objects. The Sherif experiment used the ambiguous pinpoint of light, the movement of which required a judgment on the part of each subject with no point of reference for giving a correct answer.

A. Paul Hare (1976:25) has indicated that the relationship between individual conformity to group influences and types of objects follows the proposition: " . . . the greater the ambiguity of the object, the greater will be the influence of other group members in determining the judgment of the subject." The autokinetic studies by Sherif (1952) suggested that the ambiguous object, the pinpoint of light, produced great fluctuation in individual judgment, and these fluctuations were reduced only when interaction between individuals in dyads was introduced into the investigation.

The results of research dealing with unambiguous objects are interesting and suggest a factor which appears to influence individual decisions to conform. In the Asch experiments, group pressure was coercive to a large degree; subjects responded only after numerous others responded incorrectly but unanimously. As noted earlier, the Asch report stated that nearly 37% of the subjects responded incorrectly but in conformity with the majority of responses. In a study conducted by Abraham S. Luchins and Edith H. Luchins (1956), 60 pairs of ten- to twelve-year-old children were asked to measure lines, parallelograms and other objects with linear and metric rules. Each pair included a child measuring with each rule. The child who used the linear rule was told that the answers presented were correct. These results were announced first. The announcement of

---

2. A. Paul Hare organized part of his review of the literature on conformity under these three headings. The three sections which follow in this text will use the same organizational scheme as found in A. Paul Hare, *Handbook of Small Group Research.* New York: The Free Press, 1976, pp. 24–34.

the results of the child using the metric rule followed. It was found that there was very little tendency for the second child to conform to the judgment of the first child. In these dyadic situations there was only one judgment previously announced indicating only a minor degree of influence. The contrasting results of these studies indicate that conformity is less a result of announced judgments and more a result of the number of announced results (increased coercion).

The differences might also have resulted from the age of the subjects. College students are less naïve and more sensitive to the influences which derive from others and are more impressed with the psychological and social rewards which accrue from conforming to group pressures than are children aged ten to twelve. Further research is suggested here in which the research design is held constant and the ages of the subjects are varied. Under these conditions, the nature of conformity would be suggested not only by the unambiguous or ambiguous object and by the degree to which subjects feel coerced, but also by the degree to which individuals have been socialized—a function of age—to behave in a conforming or nonconforming manner.

CONFORMITY AND THE SUBJECT

The compliance research by Crosbie discussed earlier in this chapter was concerned with the effect a subject has on conformity to group influences. Individual tendencies to conform or not to conform to certain group influences and to perceive unambiguous and ambiguous objects in a subjective way are brought into the group situation by the individual. The personality of the subject, and the subject's abilities, skills, and previous experiences are all elements which function to influence the outcome of that individual's relationship to others in the small group (Hare, 1976:26).

An individual's ability to function as a leader or at least to occupy a leadership position has been shown to produce some interesting effects in relation to conformity to group norms. Some of the research suggests that individuals whose behavior best represents the dominant norms of the small group occupy the higher ranks in the group (Bates, 1952). Similarly, in a study by R. Pellegrin (1953), individuals who function as group leaders were observed to rank highest in the assimilation of group norms. The classic research of S. A. Stouffer (1949) on the military indicated a positive relationship between high military rank and defense of the regulations and formal requirements of the organization.

This research by Stouffer on the formal military organization and the research by Pellegrin support a high correlation between leadership performance and conformity to group norms. However, O. J. Harvey (1960) found that the degree to which formal and informal group leaders conformed to group norms varied considerably. Formal leaders were observed to conform more to group norms than informal leaders. Indications of high conformity to norms by some leaders do not necessarily preclude the possibility that leaders deviate from the group norms with which they and the position they occupy are identified. Hollander (1958) suggested that the close identity of leaders with group norms during the establishment and early development of the group affords these leaders the privilege to deviate from group norms with impunity during later stages in the group's existence.

The qualities which help certain group members achieve the position of leader, then, are qualities which, in the performance of leadership functions, determine a pattern of behavior which is consistent with the normative expectations of the group. This integration of the leader with the norms of the group results in a pattern of group interaction in which the leader is identified as a model for other group members. From this perspective, the leader may be viewed as a legitimate control over group members, and the position occupied as a symbolic representation of the expectations to which group members conform.

Research on the conforming individual suggests that a number of personal characteristics are associated with conformity in group situations. High levels of anxiety (Mangan, Quartermain & Vaughan, 1960) have long been associated with dependency and, therefore, conformity to norms, as has an individual's need for approval by others (Wilson, 1960). The tendency of some individuals to look to others for support on opinions taken about some object of mutual or collective interest results in greater conformity (Bass & Dunteman, 1964). Obedience to the stated or implied expectations of groups and, specifically, of group leaders is another factor which relates directly to high conformity in groups. Referring to obedience as the uncritical acceptance of authority, Crosbie (1972:434) argues that

> . . . followers are expected to uncritically accept leadership directive, irrespective of how these directives may affect their own interests or the interests of others. This may perhaps be overstating what occurs in many groups, but at least some uncritical acceptance and suspension of judgment is involved in most leader-follower relations.

Crosbie's argument is that much of the conformity which occurs within groups is due to the definition of the leader-follower relationship as one in which followers accept the directives of their leaders in an uncritical manner. This acceptance results in conforming behavior.

CONFORMITY AND THE SITUATION

Conformity is associated with the attractiveness a group has to the individual member. A. Paul Hare (1976:30) states that members of work groups or living groups

> . . . who are highly attracted to the group either for its prestige, its productivity, or the friendship of its members will conform more to the standards of the group than will members who place low value on these criteria.

In this regard, researchers (Feather, 1964; Feather & Armstrong, 1967) have reported that one reason for the relationship between conformity and attraction to the group is that individuals like to achieve a balance in their interpersonal relationships so that conforming behavior, for example, between two individuals, is likely if the relationship is one of close friendship.

The relationship between friendship and conformity is most evident in the research conducted in the Bank Wiring Observation Room of the Western Electric Company's Hawthorne Works in Chicago (see Chapter Nine). The development of a pattern of informal association among the Bank Wiring Room workers was a major factor in controlling their daily and weekly output rates. The production standards which the workers decided upon informally were well below the maximum output hoped for by the company. These worker standards were roughly equivalent to doing a fair day's work for a fair day's pay. Having accepted the informal standards for output, the workers were willing to bear the reduced wage consequences which resulted. The pressures to conform to the standards set by the informal arrangement of workers prompted George Homans (1950:64) to remark: "About how much money did the group or an individual lose through every equipment that might have been turned out but was not?"

One explanation of the low level of output lies in the belief that conformity will increase only if the standards are set by the group itself (Hare, 1976). The workers in the Bank Wiring Observation Room, having set work standards for themselves, were willing to conform to them and suffer the consequences of reduced wages.

There is evidence that group cohesion increases member conformity and that increases in group cohesion are paralleled by increases in member conformity. Festinger, Schachter, and Back (1960:259) have observed that:

> When a cohesive group does exist, and when its realm of concern extends over the area of behavior in which we have discovered uniformity among the members of the group, then the degree of uniformity must be related to the degree of cohesiveness of the group, if a group standard is operative.

In this regard, the authors found that as group cohesiveness increases there are increased pressures to conform to group standards. Festinger, Gerard, Hymovitch, Kelley, and Raven (1952) obtained similar results. They found that greater pressures to conform were exerted in groups whose members were informed that they would be in congenial groups. In those groups in which members were not so informed, the pressures to conform were not nearly as strong.

Stephen Wilson's review of the research on the relationship between cohesion and conformity includes the observation that even highly cohesive groups do not structure a system of norms which restrict the behavior of members in situations other than those in which the group is specifically involved. He states that:

> The range of activities over which the group imposes normative expectations will vary from group to group. For instance, it may not matter much to a group of men who play poker together once a week that they have different political opinions, but it does matter that they agree on and follow the rules of the game (Wilson, 1978:106).

This view of the relationship between group cohesion and increased conformity only limits the range of influence over situations in which the group is able to function as a cohesive, controlling force over its members. Some research findings, including those by Bovard (1953) and Rotter (1967), indicate that cohesion within the group is not necessarily a significant factor in group conformity. Rotter, in an experimental situation, employed a design variation of the Asch experiment and found that member belief that other members liked them did not produce a level of conformity higher than that observed among group members who believed that other group members did not like them.

Although there is experimental evidence which supports the position that cohesion does not always produce conformity, the prevailing view, supported by a large amount of research evidence, is that cohesion is an important factor in the determination of group member willingness to succumb to group pressures and that an increase in group cohesion will result in an increase in member conformity.

GROUP COHESION

Group cohesion refers to the degree of intensity with which group members are bonded together and motivated to work as a unit toward the achievement of group goals. This adhesive quality which characterizes social groups is looked upon as a major factor in maintaining group membership, developing member satisfaction, and achieving group goals. High cohesion groups tend to have little or no membership turnover. Individuals are reticent to leave groups with which they have a strong sense of identity and through which they believe their personal needs can be met.

Individual satisfaction resulting from membership in a given group may be expressed in two ways:

(1) *In terms of the whole group.* Satisfaction with the group results from the willingness of individuals to accept the constraints placed upon them by group norms and from their development of a sense of group identity sufficiently strong so that they consider the group as a unified whole.

(2) *In terms of other group members.* Individuals not only feel a sense of satisfaction in terms of the group as a whole but also in terms of their acceptance by other individual members as worthwhile partners in the group effort. Cohesion often results from the attraction of group members toward one another. Mutual interpersonal attraction choices are expressions of a cohesive ideal. Ordinarily, a large percentage of positive choices out of a complete choice configuration becomes an expression of high cohesion within a group.

The most practical aspect of group cohesion is the high level of motivation which group members exhibit in their willingness to cooperate and coordinate activities in order to reach the goals set by the group and for the group as a whole. High levels of group cohesion, then, enhance the group's chances of achieving those ends for which the group developed and was maintained. Under conditions of less than desirable levels of cohesion, the chances of effective movement toward a group goal or set of goals are reduced. Low-cohesion groups run the risk of their membership acting independently of each other or taking divergent or colliding pathways to achieve stated or implied goals. Either condition within the low-cohesion group is nonproductive; aside from running the risk of failing to achieve desired ends, divergent or colliding efforts may produce levels of discord within the membership which might easily result in group breakdown. By any standard used to define goal achievement, high cohesion is a necessary component.

Marvin E. Shaw (1976) enumerates the three different meanings given to the term, group cohesion: (1) attraction to the group, (2) morale, and (3) coordination of efforts of group members. These would appear to be three aspects of the same bonding effect which cohesion in groups produces. Individual attraction to the group is an aspect of group cohesion measured in terms of individual perception of the group and its members. Morale identifies group cohesion in terms of *esprit de corps* or the high motivation and feeling attained from identity with the group. Coordination of efforts is the action component of cohesion which suggests the merging of such features as attraction, motivation, and the desire to work for the attainment of group goals. In the last analysis, these aspects combine to produce in the group membership a unity of thought and action which characterizes all integrated high-cohesion groups.

INTERPERSONAL CHOICE

Researchers have used the sociometric technique to establish the complex of interpersonal choices which prevail in groups. For example, in establishing task-oriented groups, the premise is that when individuals who like each other are grouped together, the group will develop higher levels of cohesion than groups of individuals who express dislike for each other or who have no opinion about other group members. In an early report by Jacob L. Moreno (1953), findings indicated that the use of interpersonal choice as a basis for regrouping delinquent girls in a cottage home institution resulted in less deviant behavior in cottage groups organized along lines of positive sociometric choices. Those delinquents housed in cottages with low percentages of choices continued behaving in a deviant manner. In the cottages which had been regrouped along lines of high-choice percentages, morale was high and there were significantly fewer expressions of deviancy (see Chapter Six).

Although studies of interpersonal choices among young children are not as meaningful or useful as those in which the subjects are adults, researchers have shown interest in the results of studies of interpersonal choice among the young (Thelen, 1966; Lott & Lott, 1966). Hare (1976:171) indicates that the interpersonal choices of children are less meaningful since they are too young to make a significant number of choices of any great strength. M. E. Shaw and L. M. Shaw (1962), in a study based upon interpersonal choices, found that high-cohesion groups composed of three second-graders were friendlier and more cooperative. The children tended to reinforce each other in the performance of their study tasks. Low-cohesion group members performed in a manner exactly opposite to members of the high-cohesion groups. They were hostile, behaved aggressively, and were unwilling to cooperate with each other.

PRODUCTIVITY

Cohesion has been found to be a major factor in increased productivity. Group members who identify strongly with group expectations tend to work harder for the achievement of group goals. There is some suggestion, however, that the intervening factor of member satisfaction is more directly associated with increased production. The argument views the development of group cohesion as a significant factor in increasing the satisfaction of each group member with the group, and this increased satisfaction as a more positive basis for motivation to work toward the achievement of the group goal, hence, increased productivity. In the study by Berkowitz cited earlier, it was noted that if members of both high- and low-cohesive bomber crews were individually motivated to perform their jobs well by giving high value to being an Air Force member, productivity did not suffer. Other studies present evidence which supports the view that cohesiveness initially results in member satisfaction. On the face of it, this relationship is an obvious one. Cohesiveness and member dissatisfaction could hardly be correlates of each other since individuals who are dissatisfied with the group to which they belong are most likely to search elsewhere for group identity. However, cohesion and member satisfaction are found to be directly related to efficient group productivity. One study (Van Zelst, 1952) found that when industrial workers were regrouped along lines of stated worker preferences for co-workers, lower turnover and increased productivity resulted.

Some studies (Lodahl & Porter, 1961) report that members of high-cohesion groups are more likely to work harder for the achievement of group goals than individuals in low-cohesion groups. If we may assume that the group members have the basic qualifications to perform the group task, we may also assume that those high-cohesion groups of harder workers are, largely, more productive than their low-cohesion counterparts. The study by D'Augelli cited earlier indicates that interpersonal behavior groups whose participants were more skilled in interpersonal behavior were seen as more cohesive. Such findings represent a view of cohesion as a group quality which results from group interaction among individuals who perceive each other as skilled in the task at hand. These results actually contradict the opinion of some that cohesion is a factor which precedes the high motivation of group members to work toward group goal achievement. The relationship between task skills of group members and cohesion is reasonable. The participants in D'Augelli's (1973:531) interpersonal behavior experiment were seen as " . . . more emphatically understanding, more honest and open, more accepting, and as discussing more personally meaningful topics." These qualities and abilities are characteristic of individuals who are skilled in interpersonal relations. Member appreciation of each other in this regard very likely results in a view of the group as one of high cohesion.

A. Paul Hare (1976) has identified an important element in the relationship of cohesion to group productivity. In his discussion, cohesion remains a significant force in group productivity, but the emphasis given cohesion is on the process of intragroup associations. Cooperation, the most obvious process in high-cohesion groups, is found to result in higher productivity than, for example, competition.

The classic statement on these two processes as bases for productivity is found in the early research of Morton Deutsch (1949), who experimented with ten five-member groups composed of fifty introductory psychology students. Each group met for three hours a week for five consecutive weeks. During the first meeting, the groups were observed as they discussed a human relations problem. The groups were rated in terms of productivity, and equivalent groups were paired off. Half the groups were designated as cooperative units and the other half as competitive units. Each cooperative group was told that performance ratings would be based upon comparisons with each of the other cooperative groups and that each member would receive the same rewards to be determined by the group's final standing in relation to the other four cooperative groups. Competitive groups were instructed that each member would be rated in terms of individual contributions to the group and that each member would receive rewards in keeping with individual productivity.

In the sessions which followed, each group was given tasks which included solving a puzzle and discussing and writing recommendations for a human relations-type problem. Deutsch found that in groups characterized by cooperation, as compared with competitive groups, there was: (1) stronger individual motivation to complete the group task and stronger feelings of mutual obligation; (2) a greater division of labor and greater coordination of effort; (3) more effective intermember communication; (4) more friendliness during discussion, and members rated themselves higher on strength of desire to win the respect of one another; and (5) more group productivity—puzzles were solved faster and recommendations produced for the human relations problems were longer and better.

Deutsch's concentration on the group process and other similar attempts (Blau, 1954; Shaw, 1958)[3] produce generally consistent findings. Cooperation among group members as a measure of group cohesion is a group process which contributes consistently to high levels of productivity. The implications which cooperation has for group cohesion are present in Deutsch's definition of the cooperative situation as one in

---

3. It is interesting to note that Shaw's study indicates that individual satisfaction ratings were higher in competitive situations.

which the entrance of one group member into a specific goal region facilitates all others' activity toward goal achievement. This view of cooperation as a cohesion-producing process is consistent with our earlier statement about cohesion, which suggested willingness of group members to cooperate and coordinate activities in the attainment of group goals.

GROUP MEMBER SATISFACTION

Let us return to the issue of group cohesion and member satisfaction. Although it is reasonable to argue that cohesive groups are composed of individual members who are satisfied with their membership, it does not follow that satisfaction with membership is automatically a quality of cohesive groups alone. In other words, it is possible that certain group situations produce expectations for individual members which members feel can be realized without cooperation with other members and without the development of a cohesive identity which cooperation ordinarily presumes. A. Paul Hare's (1976:332—333) review of the literature on this subject is excellent and forms the basis for the discussion which follows. Hare identifies three general reasons why individuals tend to join groups: (1) for the prestige of membership, (2) to help the group reach a goal, or (3) because they value the association with the group members. Individual satisfaction can be seen as a result of success in any of these three areas.

In task-oriented situations, productivity is not necessarily connected with the kind of goal achievement which results from the development of cohesion within the group. For example, although morale among clothes salesmen in a department store was reduced in competitive situations as opposed to cooperative ones, sales increased when they were in competition with each other (Babchuk & Goode, 1951). These results indicate, at the very least, that cooperation and the resultant cohesion which develops among group members does not automatically guarantee increased productivity. In some cases the rewards which are forthcoming from strong group identity and morale must be measured against rewards which accrue to individuals when motivated to compete. These individual rewards encompass those which satisfy psychological, social, and monetary needs. In some situations, the strength of these needs will function as the basis for controlling behavior in group settings, regardless of the presence of a cohesive group force.

There is evidence suggesting that in studies (Deutsch, 1949; Zander & Wolfe, 1964) which contrast individuals working for group goals with individuals working together but for individual goals, competitive groups are found to be less satisfying to group members. In these groups, individual members are found to be less efficient in the performance of goal-related activity. However, when individual group members are asked to cooperate in group activity for a group score in a task in which it is more appropriate to rate individual performances, the results are reversed. A study by Henry C. Smith (1955) reported that college students were dissatisfied with the group performance ratings given for effectiveness in group discussions. They would have preferred individual grades which they felt were more appropriate to the task performed. In this study, a group score or grade was given which some individuals strongly resented because it did not reward them for what they believed to be a better-than-average individual performance. In their view, they did not receive a grade consistent with their individual performances. One can understand the feelings of students in such a situation, especially when they may be searching for legitimate grades which would enhance their positions in the group, the classroom, or the larger academic setting.

When member satisfaction is related to groups in which status consensus is present as opposed to groups in which there is status uncertainty, individuals express greater satisfaction in those groups in which status arrangements are stabilized (Heinecke & Bales, 1953). Clear status affords each group member assurance that individual contributions to the group task will be given the credit due by virtue of the position occupied. In these studies, cohesion is not found to be the important factor otherwise assumed. It would appear that two major influences on the relationship between cohesion and productivity are the personalities and needs of individual group members.

The absence of cohesion was apparent in the findings of one study (Lewin, Lippitt & White, 1939) which measured productivity and morale in terms of types of group leaders. In groups controlled by authoritarian leaders, productivity was higher and morale lower than in democratically led groups. Higher productivity in authoritarian groups was attributed to the need of each group member to achieve, through competition rather than cooperation, a higher status position in the eyes of the leader.

Studies of group cohesion and productivity have not yielded consistent results. While considering the positive effects of cohesion on productivity, we should keep in mind the effects on productivity of those elements which individual group members bring to the interaction. Individual needs, abilities, and skills are all important factors in determining the performances of individuals. Additionally, the nature of the task assumes a certain amount of importance in judging the effects of cohesion on productivity since certain tasks are more conducive to individual performances—in some cases competitive—rather than cooperative group performance. In the last analysis, we may venture the following proposition: Group cohesion is a significant factor in determining the rate of group productivity when the value given to group goals supersedes, in the minds of the individual group members, the value given to individual needs and goals.

CONFORMITY AND GROUP COHESION

As we have seen, one aspect of group cohesion is the willingness of group members to cooperate and coordinate activities for the attainment of group goals. Cohesion within groups may also be viewed as the willingness of group members to accept the limits imposed upon them and their behavior by group norms. In this sense, group conformity and group cohesion are not distinct but complementary elements in the group process. We need only to look at the willingness of family members or members of highly integrated friendship groups to understand that the conformity exhibited by, and the cohesion which prevails in, such groups are different aspects of the same integrative mechanism working within the group as a whole. The high degree of conformity in groups which approach the primary group ideal is complemented by the cohesion of the group expressed in terms of attraction to the group, morale, and effective goal-related activity. The strength of these two elements combine to produce a system of identity which is a dominating force in the life of the individual group member.

Alan P. Bates and Nicholas Babchuk (1961) report that the intensity with which individual members identify with the norms of the primary group far outweighs their felt need to conform to the norms of secondary groups. It is important to remember that primary group norm conformity is free from coercion, and that it is the willingness on the part of members to conform which becomes an index of the level of cohesion prevalent within the group. A similar interpretation results from a report by Edward Gross (1953) in which the development of informal controls functioned as a major influence on the achievement of goals established by a formal organizational system. Again, the cohesion which develops in these informal, more primary, relationships among workers coordinates with member willingness to conform to informal group norms.

One of the most dramatic examples of the influence of cohesion and conformity to group norms is reported by David Mandelbaum (1952). The high degree of success in the integration of members of the military during World War II is accounted for by the degree to which primary-type relationships developed between and among blacks and whites. Mandelbaum stated that the development of within-group loyalties was a major factor in determining the success which resulted from integration attempts. It should be noted, of course, that wartime situations, especially those which develop during actual combat, although conducive to the development of loyalties and a sense of dependency and cooperation in the small fighting unit, do not necessarily promote maintenance of group cohesiveness beyond the limits set by the military conflict. It is possible that the primary groups referred to by Mandelbaum were short-lived and did not develop the intensity or level of integration necessary for continuation into other, more peaceful, environments.

GROUP VS. INDIVIDUAL PERFORMANCES

Ordinarily, the cohesion factor in social groups is studied in terms of the relative merits of cohesive and noncohesive groups, and the relationship of group cohesion to individual member satisfaction and productivity. However, there is a small body of research which has investigated the merits of group performance as opposed to individual performances. The question here is: Are groups more efficient in performing tasks and solving problems than individuals working alone? The reader is reminded, once again, that willingness to cooperate and coordinate activity for goal achievement is a major criterion of group cohesion. Studies (Rotter & Portugal, 1969; Husband, 1940) have shown the positive effects of group problem solving as opposed to individual attempts to solve the same types of problems. More importantly, when group members are friends, the efficiency in group problem solving increases (Husband, 1940). These reports indicate that increased cohesion (friendship as opposed to nonfriendship groups) is directly related to efficiency in problem solving. In general, these results point to the importance of group cooperation over individual performance as a significant factor in problem solving.

There are certain elements in the group process which appear to facilitate more efficient problem solving than that which results from individual performances. For example, greater efficiency is found in groups whose individual members are highly motivated, who communicate well, and who like each other (McCurdy & Lambert, 1952). The presence of one individual in the group who is extraordinarily capable as a problem solver is believed to be a factor in the ability of groups to reach solutions more efficiently than individuals performing alone (Wiest, Porter & Chiselli, 1961). When groups are composed of members who, individually, are better than other members at the task required of the group, group efficiency is increased (Graham & Dillon, 1974). Groups show a stronger tendency to report facts which are accurate than do individual performers, although fewer facts are reported by the group (Crannell, Switzer & Morrissette, 1965). In the group process, the cross-checking of facts, a procedure not available to the individual performer, allows group members to eliminate inaccuracies in their deliberations and thereby increases the efficiency of their results. This procedure may result in greater efficiency in reporting, but, at the same time, it also requires a longer period of time for the group to complete the task than is required of individual performers (Klugman, 1944). Groups also take longer to solve problems if the task at hand is not conducive to a clear division of labor. One would anticipate that specific rather than generalized types of task activities usually result in more efficient group performances requiring less time. For example, the types of tasks used in communication networks (see Chapter Five) are specific tasks in which a division of labor is possible. Research by H. J. Leavitt required participants to identify the symbols all members had in common after each had been given a list of symbols.

ROLE RELATIONSHIPS: EXPECTATIONS AND BEHAVIOR

Roles may be viewed from two different perspectives. From the group perspective, expected roles define how individuals should perform in their respective group positions. Each individual occupying a position within the group, however, may interpret the expected role in a specific way. This individual interpretation given the expected role by a group member is often referred to as the perceived role. The actual behavior of a group member is more directly associated with the role as perceived rather than with the role as expected. This being the case, individuals often behave in a manner which is, to some degree or other, at variance with the expected role. When individuals deviate from the expected roles but within acceptable limits, the variation is not thought of as hindering either to the individual or to the group. When, however, deviation is outside of that range, conflict between and among group members is likely to occur and the well-being of the group may be in jeopardy. For example, family control systems are often less rigid in regulating the behavior of children than the expected roles set for them demand. However, when the child decides to take advantage of the relaxation of clear expectations, the ensuing behavior is seen as being too much in conflict with reasonable expectations, and punishment results. Although some family groups socialize their young in open or totally permissive settings, the ordinary patterns of family control define reasonable limits for behavior and punish when those limits are violated.

The variation between expected and perceived roles is noted in the research by Sarbin and Jones (1955), who discuss the relationship between role-taking aptitude and the fulfillment of role expectations. Similarly, Rapoport and Rosow (1957) emphasize the relationship between the personality of the group member and the expected role. Role expectations are best realized by individuals whose personalities fit the role. In a study by Halpin (1955), air force commanders were found wanting in the performances of their roles as measured by ratings of members of air force crews. The two factors used in the rating procedure were "initiating group structure" and "consideration." The study reports that the actual behavior of the commanders was not only below the level of the expected role but below the level of the perceived role as well. This research suggests a downward gradation (see Figure 8-4) in the roles and actual performances of individuals from the ideal expected role to the lower-rated performances. Expected roles often differ from group members' perceptions of them, and as the study indicates, the behavior of individuals who occupy group positions is often below par when measured against both expected and perceived roles.

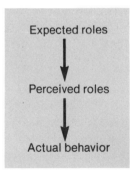

Expected roles

Perceived roles

Actual behavior

Figure 8-4.   Perceived Role and Actual Behavior Variation from Expected Role

ROLES AND GROUP STRUCTURE

Roles develop as part of the group structure which is imposed upon members or which members impose upon themselves. In initially leaderless groups, for example, the need to develop a simple group structure (leader-follower) in order to perform a task precipitates the emergence of a leader. In the performance of the task-leader role, an individual may also function as the group's socio-emotional leader. Gordon Lewis (1972) observes that these two roles are not incompatible. He observes that if an individual is capable of internalizing the expectations of the dual-leader role and if the group members perceive the performance as effective, the ensuing leader-follower structure will promote integration and will be a positive factor in the achievement of group goals. However, the results of Lewis' research should be measured against the early research of Robert F.. Bales (1966).

In studying experimental groups at the Harvard Laboratory of Social Relations, Bales noted that, over a series of four meetings in which a human relations problem was discussed, the individual chosen by the group membership as the one with the best ideas and as the one who guided the group best was the individual who was disliked most. In rankings on liking, this individual usually ranked third. The individual who received the second or third most votes on best ideas and guidance was usually selected as best-liked. Bales also found that after one meeting the highest-ranked member on best ideas and guidance was also chosen as best-liked. Although the results after the first of four meetings agreed with Lewis' findings, subsequent meetings produced a reversal of initial choices. Bales found that individuals who are able to behave according to the expectations placed upon the task leader may become the objects of member hostility. Under these conditions, another group member will likely emerge as the socio-emotional leader. Finally, although the emergence of a simple group structure may allow one individual to function as both task and socio-emotional leader, continuation of the group suggests the strong possibility that the initial choice of the two-function leader will be rejected.

THE CENTRAL PERSON

There is an interesting variation on the traditional leader-follower form of group organization which centers around the presence of a central person. The concept was developed by Fritz Redl (1942). A. Paul Hare treats Redl's typology of Central Persons as a leadership typology which breaks with the more traditional view of group leaders. Hare (1976:281) suggests that the " . . . 'leader,' in the usual sense, is only one type of central person who may have the power to control the activity of a group." Redl identifies the traditional leader as one of ten types of central persons. Other identifiable types of leaders in the typology are the patriarchal sovereign, the tyrant, and the organizer. Types of central persons who depart from the traditional interpretation of the leader include the idol, the scapegoat, the seducer, the hero, the individual who is a bad influence, and the individual who is central by virtue of setting good example. Redl places these types of central persons into categories so that the traditional leader and the patriarchal sovereign become objects of identification on the basis of love, and the tyrant an object of identification on the basis of fear. The idol and the scapegoat are central persons who are objects of drives: the idol as an object of love drives and the scapegoat as the object of aggressive drives. Redl identifies the seducer as one who acts in the service of drive satisfaction and the hero as an individual who acts in the service of drive defense. Similarly, the individual who is a bad influence is acting in the service of drive satisfaction and the individual who sets the good example is acting in the service of drive defense.

The role which determines the behavior of a central person directs the structure away from the ordinary relationships and toward emotional relationships with the central person as an object of identification or of drives and ego supports. These emotional relationships are the central foci of Redl's typology, and they identify a special level of role identity and behavior. The performance of a central-person role becomes an additional integrative group element through the establishment of identities at a level of group association other than that which derives from definitions of more traditional leadership roles.

The orientation upon which Redl based his typology is clearly Freudian. However, the utility of the typology lies not only in its assessment of the basic orientations, drives, and ego systems which individuals bring to human associations. It is also an attempt, as interpreted here, to explain the structure of social roles and the emotional bases upon which individuals build systems of patterned relationships with one another in social groups.

ROLE CONFLICT

Role conflict may be associated with the variations observed between expected and perceived roles and, more apparently, between the role and the actual behavior of the role-player. The function of roles in the development and maintenance of group structures creates, in some instances, conflict within, as for example, the individual who is both task and socio-emotional leader. In reporting on role conflicts among military chaplains, Waldo W. Burchard (1954:528) observed that:

Each person has a 'hierarchy of role obligations,' the relative positions of which are determined by the strength of the claims made upon him by the various institutions which compete for his loyalty. Therefore, his roles may not necessarily be in harmony with each other, and in some instances, where two or more institutions demand the first loyalty of a person, they may be directly antithetical.

Burchard interviewed 36 military chaplains and 35 ex-chaplains of all ranks from first lieutenant to brigadier general. The 71 respondents were from 19 denominations including 13 Catholics, 3 Jews and 55 Protestants. Questions on the interview schedule were designed to test four hypotheses which are presented here along with the study results.

Hypothesis 1	That the position of the chaplain does lead to a conflict in roles for the incumbent of that office.
Results	Strongly supported by data which indicates that the respondents were aware of the conflict between religion and war. Support for the hypothesis also came from a philosophical analysis of the social roles of military officer and clergyman.
Hypothesis 2	That the chaplain seeks to reconcile this conflict either through rationalization or through compartmentalization of role behaviors.
Results	Strongly supported by data. No member of the sample sought to escape the conflict through the abandonment of one of the roles. Of the two choices stated in the hypothesis, compartmentalization appeared to be the more successful technique for role reconciliation.
Hypothesis 3	That rationalization of conflict in roles tends to strengthen the chaplain's role of military officer at the expense of his role of minister of the gospel.
Results	Every argument given by sample members tended to assert the military claim and de-emphasize the religious claim.
Hypothesis 4	That the chaplain serves as interpreter of the values of the military organization, helps resolve value-dilemmas of individuals and helps promote smooth operation of the military organization.
Results	Less strongly supported partly because of a lack of data. Available data indicate, however, that the hypothesis is tenable.

For Burchard, the study supports the following hypotheses: (1) that the role which provides for the individual a primary identification takes first place in his hierarchy of role obligations, and (2) that for the chaplain the role of military officer provides primary identification. In attempting to explain the primacy of the military role for chaplains it might be interesting to note that assuming, as does Burchard, that the first mentioned motive for entering the military service is the primary one, 25% of the respondents entered for patriotic motives while only 10% entered for religious motives. Another 25% said they " . . . wanted to be of service." If the respondents entered the service primarily for patriotic rather than religious reasons, one might assume that for these chaplains the role of military officer provides primary identification.

Similar role conflicts were found among the members of a small group of clothing salesmen who were both friends and competitors (Wispé, 1955). In this case, the role conflict is immediately apparent due to the broad differences between the expectations placed upon individuals as friends and those of individuals in competition. The presence of role conflict under these conditions is not surprising since the differences between the two roles are differences in kind, rather than degree. Friendships are primary type relationships and are characteristically noncompetitive, although competition for the good of the relationship is not impossible. Competitors organize relationships with the understanding that the goal worked for is not a group but individual one.

Even within the family, parent roles may easily conflict on a given family issue such as child discipline. In a report on family relationships, Herbst (1952) saw the issue of role conflict in terms of who is the authority and who is the active disciplinarian. In some cases, individuals develop an awareness of role conflict from the perceptions of that role by those with whom they associate. For example, Seeman's school study (1953) indicated that some teachers perceived the role of the superintendent as strictly business, while others had no difficulty in extending the boundaries of the superintendent's role to include informal social relationships with the teaching staff. The teachers were required to give "Yes" or "No" answers to questions concerning the superintendent role: "Should an ideal superintendent invite staff members to his home for social occasions?" and "Should an ideal superintendent feel free to discuss his personal problems with the teachers?" The teacher responses to both questions were about the same (60% said yes and 40% said no). When an individual occupies the position of superintendent and becomes aware of the confusion about the superintendent role on the part of the teaching staff, that individual's perception of the role will likely incorporate the confusion expressed by those under his control. The question a superintendent might ask is: "How can I behave in a consistent manner and satisfy the expectations of all members of the teaching staff?"

Somewhat akin to the confusion which surrounds roles such as those of school superintendents is the confusion attendant upon roles which are marginal. In a report on the marginality of the professional chiropractor, Wardwell (1952:340) observes that:

A marginal role is . . . an imperfectly institutionalized one, which means that there is some ambiguity in the patterns of behavior legitimately expected of a person filling the role, and that the social sanctions attending the role tend to be inconsistently applied.

Explaining that the role of the chiropractor is marginal to the institutionalized role of the doctor, the author notes the confusion as to what a chiropractor is by the chiropractor and by others. For our purposes, the concept of marginality as used by Wardwell should be clarified. The traditional interpretation of someone caught between two cultures or two groups does not apply here. Chiropractors are to be viewed as individuals who occupy positions, the roles of which are marginal. It is this marginality in the role which determines the ambiguity with which the professional chiropractor is viewed.

summary

This chapter reviewed the research on elements of small group structure and process. Groups were distinguished according to their formal or informal structure. Viewed from the structural perspective, group interaction was identified as a system of social relationships between and among individuals who occupy different group positions. As occupants of these positions, individuals behave according to expectations placed upon them by the group. Group structures are composed of differentiated positions which individuals occupy, and individuals give value to these positions, making of them status positions.

Cartwright and Zander's criteria for the development of stable differentiations within groups were noted and observed to be applicable to both formal and informal group structures. These three criteria are: efficient group performance, abilities and motivations of individuals, and the environment of the group. Research indicates that efficient group performance is related to role differentiation within groups and also to the presence or absence of reasonable or appropriate patterns of organization. In communication network analysis it was found that the most efficient group performances occurred in groups in which there were fewer communication links between the source of information and the point at which a group decision must be made. Complex communication networks reduce the efficiency of group performances. It was also found that the organization of the group must fit the behavior required of its members for group performances to be efficient. The organizational pattern has less effect upon performance when efficiency is measured against group cohesion. Berkowitz found that high-cohesion, high-motivation bomber crews performed more efficiently than low-cohesion, low-motivation crews.

The development of a simple leader-follower structure was found to be dependent upon such factors as levels of interpersonal skill, sex differences, and occupational status. Leaders were found to perform their functions more efficiently when they were free from constraints, and followers tended to be more efficient under highly controlled conditions. Followers produce more when controlled by a strong formal leader, and groups controlled by strong formal leaders were found to be more cohesive than those controlled by weak informal leaders.

Some individuals have a personal need for rigid structure. Research by Wispé and Lloyd indicates that there is a need for the security which results from participation in a highly structured group environment. Under these conditions, low-level producers viewed their superiors as more threatening than did high producers. Other personal characteristics often associated with effective leadership are intelligence, specific skills and abilities, size of group member, and talkativeness.

Physical environments were found to have a direct effect upon the structure of groups. Festinger and others found that one major determinant of sociometric structure was propinquity. Other studies identify seating position as a factor in the development of group structure. Individuals who occupy central positions most often become leaders. Central-position networks, according to Leavitt, produce greater consistency in group member choice of a leader. In the majority of cases, the member occupying the central position in the network was chosen group leader. Therefore, individuals who occupy central positions in groups stand the best chance of emerging as group leaders.

Group norms define the limits within which behavior is deemed acceptable or appropriate. They set the standards by which individual behavior is judged. Paul Crosbie identified the control mechanisms used by groups to restrict individual behavior: rewarding conformity, punishments and sanctions, persuasion, and normative redefinition. The first three mechanisms are designed to bring the deviant behavior of some group members back to within approved limits. The last mechanism, normative redefinition, is designed to broaden the limits of acceptable behavior to include otherwise unacceptable behavior.

The early and classic experiments of Muzafer Sherif and Solomon Asch established a research standard for conformity studies. Sherif's experiment employed the autokinetic effect to illustrate conformity in group settings. Subjects, when placed in a group setting, changed earlier initial judgments as to the movement of a pinpoint of light in a darkened room to conform with judgments of the group as a whole. The judgments established by the group became the basis for separate judgments in a later series of tests. The Asch experiment used an unambiguous object which consisted of vertical lines of clearly different lengths to measure conformity to group norms. Subjects were placed in groups of seven to nine individuals. All participants except the subject were told to respond to the object unanimously and incorrectly. Under these conditions, the subject gave conforming answers about 37% of the time. The percentage is significant when one considers that the object was unambiguous and the norm established for each of the tests was unanimous but incorrect.

In order to predict compliance in two-member power relationships in a laboratory setting, Crosbie used adaptations of three social exchange propositions by George Homans. For example, Homans' proposition that the more often within a given period of time a man's activity rewards the activity of another, the more often the other will emit the activity was adapted as follows: the greater the frequency with which Other rewards Ego for compliance, the more often will Ego comply with Other's directives. Crosbie found that there was a significant increase in the willingness of the test subjects to enter a power exchange as the frequency of rewards increased. There was a significant increase in the willingness of the subjects to enter a power exchange when the mag- nitude of the reward increased. Crosbie's research suggests that if individuals behave toward others in a manner which will keep rewards high and costs low, then individuals will conform to group norms and group influences if there are expectations of rewards.

Other research findings on conformity are as follows: (1) individuals whose behavior best represents the dominant norms of the small group occupy the higher ranks in the group; (2) individuals who function as group leaders were found to rank higher in the assimilation of group norms; (3) there is considerable variation in the degrees to which formal and informal leaders conform to group norms, with formal leaders conforming more than informal leaders; and (4) leader conformity to group norms in the early period of group development gives the leader the privilege of deviating from the norms during the periods which follow. Personal characteristics associated with high conformity include high levels of anxiety (dependency resulting in conformity), an individual's need for approval, need for support from others, and a high sense of obedience to group expectations.

There appears to be a strong relationship between conformity and attraction to the group because individuals like to achieve a balance in their interpersonal relationships. Close friendships and conformity are closely related, and conformity will increase if the standards are set by the group membership and not by an outside authority. Group cohesion increases member conformity, and an increase in group cohesion is paralleled by an increase in member conformity. As group cohesiveness increases there are increased pressures to conform to group standards. In an experimental study by Festinger and others, it was found that greater pressure to conform was exerted in groups whose members were told that they would be in a congenial group. Pressures to conform in groups whose members were not so informed were significantly less strong. Highly cohesive groups do not develop norms which restrict member behavior outside the group.

Group cohesion refers to the degree of intensity with which group members are bonded together and motivated to work as a unit toward the achievement of group goals. Shaw identifies three different meanings commonly given to the term, group cohesion: attraction to the group, morale, and coordination of efforts of group members. These aspects combine to produce in the group membership a unity of thought and action characteristic of all integrated high-cohesion groups. When individuals who like each other are grouped together in task-oriented groups, the group will develop higher levels of cohesion than groups of individuals who express dislike for each other or who have no opinion about each other. Moreno's early research with delinquents supports this proposition.

Cohesion is also a major factor in productivity. Members of high-cohesion groups are prone to work harder to achieve group goals than individuals in low-cohesion groups. Groups whose members are skilled in interpersonal relations are more cohesive than groups whose members have little or no skill in interpersonal relations. Groups whose members interact cooperatively develop higher levels of cohesion than competitive groups. Extensive research by Morton Deutsch supports this proposition.

Satisfaction with group membership is not always a quality which produces cohesion. Certain group situations produce expectations for individual members who can best realize them without a cooperative effort. This is so when individual rewards are believed to be greater through, for example, a competitive effort rather than a cooperative one. This was the case in a study by Babchuk and Goode on department store salesmen whose sales increased when they were in competitive rather than in cooperative situations. When studies contrast individuals working for group goals and individuals working together but for individual goals, competitive groups are found to be more satisfying. Individuals are found to be less efficient in the performance of goal-related activity.

Individuals express greater member satisfaction in those groups in which status arrangements are stable. Clear status differentiation affords each member assurances that contributions to the group task will be given due credit.

Group cohesion may be viewed as the willingness of group members to accept the limits imposed upon them by group norms. Bates and Babchuk report that the intensity with which individuals identify with the norms of the primary group far outweighs their felt need to conform to secondary group norms. Gross observed that the development of informal controls functioned as a major influence on the achievement of group goals established within a formal organization. There appears to be a willingness on the part of members of primary groups to accept controls which, under the guise of formal systems, are seen as coercive. Integration attempts during the Second World War were enhanced by the development of primary relationships among black and white soldiers.

In research efforts concerned with the relative merits of group as opposed to individual performances, findings indicate that group efficiency is increased when members are highly motivated, when members communicate well with each other, and when members like each other. When a group includes one individual with unusually high ability in problem solving, greater efficiency results in group problem solving. When groups are composed of individuals who, individually, are better than other members at the task required of the group, task efficiency increases.

Group roles are of two types: expected and perceived. Expected roles define how individuals should perform in their respective group positions; perceived roles result from individual interpretations given to the expected roles. Roles develop out of the group structure which is imposed upon members or which members impose upon themselves. Research indicates that in initially leaderless groups, the need to develop a simple structure in order to perform a task results in the emergence of a leader. Individuals who occupy leadership positions may function as task-leaders, as socio-emotional leaders, or as both. Role conflict may result from the performance of the dual-leader role. However, if the other group members perceive the individual as effective in the dual role, the group will function efficiently. Bales reports that the individual chosen by the group membership as the one with the best ideas and as the one who guided the group best was most disliked. The individual who received the second or third most votes on best ideas and guidance was usually selected as best-liked.

One interesting variation on the traditional interpretation of the leadership role is the Central Person concept developed by Fritz Redl. Redl constructs a typology of role types which direct the structure of role relationships away from the ordinary and toward emotional relationships with the central person as an object of identification.

Role conflict may be associated with the variations observed between expected and perceived roles, and between the role and the actual behavior of the role player. Role conflict ensuing from the performance of a dual-leader role has already been noted. Additionally, Burchard's report on military chaplains and ex-chaplains indicates that the role which provides the individual with primary identification takes first place in the hierarchy of role obligations. In the case of military chaplains, Burchard concluded that, for the chaplain, the role of military officer provided the primary identification. Similar observations resulted from the study of clothes salesmen who were both friends and competitors, and within the role of the school superintendent whose role was perceived differentially by the teaching staff. The marginal role of the chiropractor also suggests role conflict due to imperfect institutionalization and ambiguity.

discussion questions

1. What is the major difference between the Sherif and Asch experiments on group conformity? Why is this difference important?
2. Why is age an important factor in studies of interpersonal choice?
3. Discuss the effects of cooperation and competition on group productivity.
4. Explain the statement: Roles control and limit the extent to which individuals will deviate from group norms.
5. Does Redl's concept of the central person offer any special insights into the concept of leadership?

references

Asch, Solomon E. "An Experimental Investigation of Group Influence," *Symposium on Preventive and Social Psychiatry*. Washington, D.C.: United States Government Printing Office, 1957.

Babchuk, Nicholas; and Goode, William F. "Work Incentives in a Self-determined Group," *American Sociological Review*, 16 (1951): 679–687.

Bales, Robert F. "The Equilibrium Problem in Small Groups," in A. Paul Hare, Edgar F. Borgatta and Robert F. Bales (eds.). *Small Groups: Studies in Social Interaction.* New York: Alfred A. Knopf, 1966.

Bass, Bernard M.; and Dunteman, George. "Defensiveness and Susceptibility to Coercion as a Function of Self-, Interaction-, and Task-orientation," *Journal of Social Psychology*, 62 (1964): 335–341.

Bates, Alan P. "Some Sociometric Aspects of Social Ranking in a Small, Face-to-face Group," *Sociometry*, 15 (1952): 330–342.

Bates, Alan P.; and Babchuk, Nicholas. "The Primary Group: A Reappraisal," *Sociological Quarterly*, 2 (1961): 181–191.

Berkowitz, Leonard. "Group Standards, Cohesiveness, and Productivity," *Human Relations*, 7 (1954): 509–519.

Berkowitz, Leonard. "Group Norms among Bomber Crews: Patterns of Perceived Crew Attitudes, 'Actual' Crew Attitudes, and Crew Liking Related to Aircrew Effectiveness in Far Eastern Combat," *Sociometry*, 19 (1956): 141–153.

Blau, Peter M. "Cooperation and Competition in a Bureaucracy," *American Journal of Sociology*, 59 (1954): 530–535.

Bovard, Everett W. "Conformity to Social Norms and Attraction to the Group," *Science*, 118 (1953): 598–599.

Burchard, Waldo W. "Role Conflicts of Military Chaplains," *American Sociological Review*, 19 (1954): 528–535.

Carter, Launor F.; Haythorn, W.; Shriver B.; and Lanzetta, J. T. "The Behavior of Leaders and Other Group Members," *Journal of Abnormal and Social Psychology*, 46 (1951): 589–595.

Cartwright, Dorwin; and Zander, Alvin (eds.). *Group Dynamics: Research and Theory*, 2nd ed.; New York: Harper & Row, 1960.

Crannell, Clarke E.; Switzer, S. A.; and Morrissette, Julian O. "Individual Performance in Cooperative and Independent Groups," *Journal of General Psychology*, 73 (1965): 231–236.

Crosbie, Paul V. "Social Exchange and Power Compliance: A Test of Homans' Propositions," *Sociometry*, 35 (1972): 203–222.

——————. *Interaction in Small Groups.* New York: Macmillan, 1975.

Deutsch, Morton. "A Theory of Cooperation and Competition," *Human Relations*, 2 (1949): 129–152.

——————. "An Experimental Study of the Effects of Cooperation and Competition upon Group Process," *Human Relations*, 2 (1949): 199–231.

D'Augelli, Anthony R. "Group Composition Using Interpersonal Skills: Analogue Study of the Effects of Members' Interpersonal Skills on Peer Ratings and Group Cohesiveness," *Journal of Counseling Psychology*, 20 (1973): 531–534.

Feather, Norman T. "A Structural Balance Model of Communication Effects," *Psychological Review*, 71 (1964): 291–313.

Feather, Norman T.; and Armstrong, D. J. "Effects of Variations in Source Attitude, Receiver Attitude, and Communication Stand on Reactions to Source and Content of Communications," *Journal of Personality*, 35

(1967): 435–455.

Festinger, Leon; Schachter, Stanley; and Back, Kurt. *Social Pressures in Informal Groups*. New York: Harper, 1950.

Festinger, Leon; Gerard, H.; Hymovitch, B.; Kelley, H. H.; and Raven, B. "The Influence Process in the Presence of Extreme Deviates," *Human Relations*, 5 (1952): 327–346.

Festinger, Leon; Schachter, Stanley; and Back, Kurt. "The Operation of Standards," in Dorwin Cartwright and Alvin Zander (eds.). *Group Dynamics: Research and Theory*, 2nd ed.; New York: Harper & Row, 1960.

Fichter, Joseph H. *Sociology*. Chicago: The University of Chicago Press, 1957.

Gerard, H. B. "Some Effects of Status, Role Clarity, and Group Goal Clarity upon the Individual's Relations to Group Progress," *Journal of Personality*, 25 (1957): 475–488.

Graham, William K.; and Dillon, Peter C. "Creative Supergroups: Group Performance as a Function of Individual Performance on Brainstorming Tasks," *Journal of Social Psychology*, 93 (1974): 101–105.

Gross, Edward. "Some Functional Consequences of Primary Controls in Informal Work Organizations," *American Sociological Review*, 18 (1953): 368–373.

Gross, Neal; Martin, William E.; and Darley, John G. "Studies of Group Behavior: Leadership Structures in Small Organized Groups," *Journal of Abnormal and Social Psychology*, 48 (1953): 429–432.

Guetzkow, Harold. "Differentiation of Roles in Task-oriented Groups," in Dorwin Cartwright and Alvin Zander (eds.). *Group Dynamics: Research and Theory*, 2nd ed.; New York: Harper & Row, 1960.

Halpin, Andrew W. "The Leadership Ideology of Aircraft Commanders," *Journal of Applied Psychology*, 39 (1955): 82–84.

Hare A. Paul. *Handbook of Small Group Research*. New York: The Free Press, 1976.

Harvey, O. J. "Reciprocal Influence of the Group and Three Types of Leaders in an Unstructured Situation," *Sociometry*, 23 (1960): 57–68.

Heinecke, Christopher M.; and Bales, Robert F. "Developmental Trends in the Structure of Small Groups," *Sociometry*, 16 (1953): 7–38.

Herbst, P. G. "The Measurement of Family Relationships," *Human Relations*, 5 (1952): 3–35.

Hollander, Edwin P. "Conformity, Status, and Idiosyncrasy Credit," *Psychological Review*, 65 (1958): 117–127.

Homans, George C. *The Human Group*. New York: Harcourt, Brace and World, 1950.

Husband, R. W. "Cooperative Versus Solitary Problem Solution," *Journal of Social Psychology*, 11 (1940): 405–409.

Jenkins, W. O. "A Review of Leadership Studies with Particular Reference to Military Problems," *Psychological Bulletin*, 44 (1947): 54–59.

Klugman, Samuel F. "Cooperative versus Individual Efficiency in Problem-solving," *Journal of Educational Psychology*, 35 (1944): 91–100.

Leavitt, Harold J. "Some Effects of Certain Communication Patterns on Group Performance," *Journal of Abnormal Social Psychology*, 46 (1951): 38–50.

Lewin, Kurt; Lippitt, Ronald; and **White, Ralph K.** "Patterns of Aggressive Behavior in Experimentally Created 'Social Climates,'" *Journal of Social Psychology*, 10 (1939): 271–299.

Lewis, Gordon H. "Role Differentiation," *American Sociological Review*, 37 (1972): 424–434.

Lodahl, Thomas M.; and **Porter, Lyman W.** "Psychometric Score Patterns, Social Characteristics, and Productivity of Small Industrial Work Groups," *Journal of Applied Psychology*, 45 (1961): 73–79.

Lott, Albert J.; and **Lott, Bernice E.** "Group Cohesiveness and Individual Learning," *Journal of Educational Psychology*, 57 (1966):61–73.

Luchins, Abraham S.; and **Luchins, Edith H.** "Discovering the Source of Contradictory Communications," *Journal of Social Psychology*, 44 (1956): 49–63.

Mandelbaum, David G. *Soldier Groups and Negro Soldiers*. Berkeley, California: University of California Press, 1952.

Mangan, G. L.; Quartermain, D.; and **Vaughn, G.** "Taylor MAS and Group Conformity Pressure," *Journal of Abnormal Psychology*, 61 (1960): 146–147.

McCurdy, Harold G.; and **Lambert, Wallace E.** "The Efficiency of Small Human Groups in the Solution of Problems Requiring Genuine Cooperation," *Journal of Personality*, 20 (1952): 478–494.

Monane, Joseph H. *A Sociology of Human Systems*. New York: Appleton-Century-Crofts, 1967.

Moreno, Jacob L. *Who Shall Survive?*, revised edition; Beacon, New York: Beacon House, 1953.

Morissette, Julian O.; Switzer, S. A.; and **Crannell, Clarke W.** "Group Performance as a Function of Size, Structure, and Task Difficulty," *Journal of Personality and Social Psychology*, 2 (1965): 452–455.

Mulder, Mauk. "Communication Structure, Decision Structure and Group Performance," *Sociometry*, 23 (1960): 1–14.

Pellegrin, Roland J. "The Achievement of High Statuses and Leadership in the Small Group," *Social Forces*, 32 (1953): 10–16.

Rapoport, Rhona; and **Rosow, I.** "An Approach to Family Relationships and Role Performance," *Human Relations*, 10 (1957): 209–221.

Redl, Fritz. "Group Emotion and Leadership," *Psychiatry*, 5 (1942): 573–596.

Roby, Thornton B.; and **Lanzetta, John T.** "Work Group Structure, Communication, and Group Performance," *Sociometry*, 19 (1956): 105–113.

Roethlisberger, F. J.; and **Dickson, William H.** *Management and the Worker*. Cambridge, Massachusetts: Harvard University Press, 1939.

Rotter, George S. "An Experimental Evaluation of Group Attractiveness as a Determinant of Conformity," *Human Relations*, 20 (1967): 273–282.

Rotter, George S.; and **Portugal, Stephen M.** "Group and Individual Effects in Problem-solving," *Journal of Applied Psychology*, 53 (1969): 338–341.

Rule, Brendan G. "Group Effects on Deviant Behavior," *Psychological Reports*, 15 (1964): 611–614.

Rule, Brendan G.; and **Renner, John.** "Distance, Group Dispersion, and Opinion

Change," *Psychological Reports*, 17 (1965): 777–778.

_____. "Involvement and Group Effects on Opinion Change," *Journal of Social Psychology*, 76 (1968): 189–198.

Sarbin, Theodore R.; and Jones, Donal S. "An Experimental Analysis of Role Behavior," *Journal of Abnormal and Social Psychology*, 51 (1955): 236–241.

Seeman, Melvin. "Role, Conflict and Ambivalence in Leadership," *American Sociological Review*, 18 (1953): 373–380.

Shaw, Marvin E. "Some Effects of Irrelevant Information upon Problem-solving by Small Groups," *Journal of Social Psychology*, 47 (1958): 33–57.

_____. *Group Dynamics: The Psychology of Small Group Behavior*, 2nd ed.; New York: McGraw-Hill, 1976.

Shaw, Marvin E.; and Rothschild, Gerald H. "Some Effects of Prolonged Experience in Communication Nets," *Journal of Applied Psychology*, 40 (1956): 281–286.

Shaw, Marvin E.; and Shaw, Lilly M. "Some Effects of Sociometric Grouping upon Learning in a Second Grade Classroom," *Journal of Social Psychology*, 57 (1962): 453–458.

Sherif, Muzafer. *The Psychology of Social Norms*. New York: Harper and Brothers, 1936.

_____. "An Experimental Approach to Social Attitudes," *Sociometry*, 1 (1937): 90–98.

Sherif, Muzafer; and Harvey, O. J. "A Study of Ego Functioning: Elimination of Stable Anchorages in Individual and Group Situations," *Sociometry*, 15 (1952): 272–305.

Shibutani, Tomotsu. *Society and Personality: An Interactionist Approach to Social Psychology*. Englewood Cliffs, New Jersey: Prentice-Hall, 1961.

Smith, Henry C. "Team Work in the College Class," *Journal of Educational Psychology*, 46 (1955): 274–286.

Sommer, Robert. "Leadership and Group Geography," *Sociometry*, 24 (1961): 99–110.

Stouffer, Samuel A., et al. *The American Soldier*. Princeton, New Jersey: Princeton University Press, 1949, Vol. 1.

Strodtbeck, Fred L.; James, R. M.; and Hawkins, C. "Social Status in Jury Deliberations," *American Sociological Review*, 22 (1957): 713–719.

Thelen, Herbert A. "Classroom Groupings," in A. Yates (ed.). *Groupings in Education*. New York: Wiley, 1966.

Van Zelst, Raymond H. "Sociometrically Selected Work Teams Increase Production," *Personnel Psychology*, 5 (1952): 175–186.

Wardwell, Walter I. "A Marginal Professional Role: The Chiropractor," *Social Forces*, 30 (1952): 339–348.

Wiest, William M.; Porter, Lyman E.; and Chiselli, Edwin E. "Relationships between Individual Proficiency and Team Performance and Efficiency," *Journal of Applied Psychology*, 45 (1961): 435–440.

Williams, Robin M., Jr. *American Society: A Sociological Interpretation*, 3rd ed.; New York: Alfred A. Knopf, 1970.

Wilson, R. S. "Personality Patterns, Source of Attractiveness, and Conformity," *Journal of Personality*, 28 (1960): 186–199.

Wilson, Stephen. *Informal Groups: An Introduction*. Englewood Cliffs, New Jersey: Prentice-Hall, 1978.

Wispé, Lauren G. "A Sociometric Analysis of Conflicting Role-expectations," *American Journal of Sociology*, 61 (1955): 134–137.

Wispé, Lauren G.; and Lloyd, K. E. "Some Situational and Psychological Determinants of the Desire for Structured Interpersonal Relations," *Journal of Abnormal and Social Psychology*, 51 (1955): 57–60.

Zander, Alvin; and Wolfe, Donald. "Administrative Rewards and Coordination among Committee Members," *Administrative Science Quarterly*, 9 (1964): 50–69.

Chapter Nine
Three Small Groups

CHAPTER PREVIEW

Long-established relations within social groups set the standards for living in the community and control the direction and content of our lives well beyond the influences they may have on any one day. The three most important small groups are the family, the friendship group, and the informal work group. In large measure, they form the center of the individual's complex of interaction and structure for the individual a collective base for all other associations within or outside social groups.

THE NUCLEAR FAMILY: A TRADITIONAL VIEW

We must begin our discussion of the nuclear family with a word of caution. The subtitle—a traditional view—should be kept in mind as the reader studies this section. The family is changing, no doubt, and we will discuss these changes later. For the present, since the nuclear family is still the major grouping for procreation and related functions, we will first concentrate upon it as a group type and try to understand the implications of its interaction framework.

When the traditional nuclear family is viewed as a closed small group, three systems emerge as important. They are: the family interaction system, the family identity system, and the family support system. We will discuss each of these as separate systems with the understanding that, in reality, the systems merge to form a complete and integrated small family group.

THE NUCLEAR FAMILY AS A SYSTEM OF INTERACTION

The *nuclear family* is a two-generation group of individuals who are bound together by ties of marriage, birth and adoption, who live in a common household, and who develop a specialized system of expectations for behaving within a closed system of reciprocal relationships. When viewed from the perspective of interaction, the nuclear family can be identified as a complex of conjugal- and consanguine-based relationships, performed in concert, and promoting the development of appropriate, common definitions and meanings which function as reinforcers of family cohesion. By definition, the nuclear family is a complex support system designed to maintain itself for life spans of time. We will return to the idea of the family as a support system shortly. First, we will identify the interaction complex within which the family support system is maintained.

The traditional nuclear family originates in the development of a marital dyad. The union of two adults of opposite sex in the relationship of marriage is the societally approved basis for producing and socializing offspring. The complexity of the nuclear family interaction system beyond the simple marital dyad is a function of the marital dyad producing children. In other words, interaction complexity, as discussed in Chapter One (see Figure 1-3), is directly related to an increase in family size.

The marital dyad is, characteristically, the family-based relationship which is least cluttered. It is the relationship in which the interacting members are able to concentrate upon each other without interruption. The addition of a child results in an interaction framework consisting of three possible dyadic relationships—those between parents, between mother and child, and between father and child—and three coalition possibilities. Traditionally, these relationships are viewed as developing high levels of integration. Practically, integration is only one possibility which accrues to the family triad. Coalition possibilities must be considered as well. Running counter to the more positive, emotionally based expectations which surround a family triad, the principles of coalition formation, discussed in Chapter Three, indicate that the addition of a third person, the child, into the dyadic relationship between spouses tends to result in the very real possibility of conflict. The reader should recall from earlier discussions that the presence of a coalition does not automatically result in the breakdown of the triad. Coalitions in families as well as in other triadic relationships will shift from one to another combination over periods of time, resulting in changing patterns of within-group associations but not necessarily in family breakdown. The point is that the presence of a third person, in this case a child, can interrupt the harmony of the marital dyad even though the marital dyad may have had high expectations about the child's coming. Along with the entrance of the child, coalition formation is a most realistic possibility.

With the addition of a second child, the complexity of nuclear family interaction increases dramatically. There are six possible relationships in the family triad. The four-person nuclear family must maintain a complex of twenty-five interaction possibilities. If we continued adding a child we would have to increase the number of interaction possibilities within the family according to the formula stated in Chapter Two. The reader, finally, upon reaching a point where a twelfth or thirteenth child is added, might begin to consider the family less as a small group and more as a small corporation! The point should be made that the traditional view of nuclear families, as characterized by closeness of members, high levels of cooperation and integration, and intense and frequent face-to-face interaction, is not nearly as clear or reasonable a possibility as the size of the family approaches the upper limits of small group size.

FAMILY IDENTITY SYSTEMS

Another view of the interaction framework within which family members maintain their in-group associations suggests that the complex of interaction is, in reality, a system of interaction within which individual members form identities. Fathers and mothers always have been identified as models for their children, siblings as models for each other, and spouses for each other.

If we consider the four-person nuclear family as the smallest-sized family possible in our present analysis, we can cover all the identity systems which can exist within a nuclear family. There are four identity systems in which family members may participate: (1) *conjugal identity systems*—identification between spouses; (2) *direct identity systems*—identification between a parent and a child of the same sex; (3) *complement identity systems*—identification between a parent and a child of opposite sex; and (4) *sibling identity systems*—identification between or among offspring (see Figure 9-1).

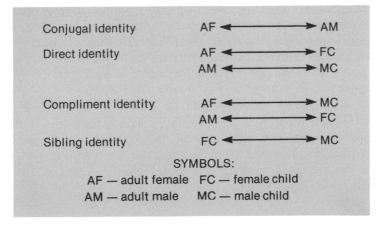

Figure 9-1. Nuclear Family Identity Systems

These identity systems which family members use are discrete systems of interaction in which they are able to understand and clarify sex roles and sexual identities. These systems are also used to clarify family positions in terms of hierarchy and to define the expectations which family membership places upon the individual. Ordinarily, these identity systems are dyadic subgroups in which family members can determine their roles and expectations in a less cluttered, less complex interaction situation. Only in the sibling identity system are the occupants interchangeable. When there are more than two, siblings may move into and out of their identity systems. In all other cases, the membership is dictated by the sex and position of each member. For example, complement identity systems must include one adult and one child of opposite sex, and direct identity systems must include one adult and one child of the same sex.

FAMILY SUPPORT SYSTEMS

The nuclear family has certain goals which the interaction support systems within it are organized to achieve. These goals are: procreation, socialization, economic maintenance, and emotional support.

Procreation. The support system present in the nuclear family begins with the extension of the marital dyad through procreation. Although there are supportive qualities present in the marital dyad, the total system of family support includes parent relations with at least one child. We will consider children who are the natural offspring of the marriage union and children who enter the family through adoption as undifferentiated participants in the support system. The full family support system begins when at least one child enters into a relationship with the marital dyad.

Nuclear-family members, as participants in a closed system of interaction, perform functions which are generally acknowledged to be mutually beneficial to all family members and to the family as a whole. Such mutuality of benefit results from the support family members receive as they cooperate with each other toward the realization of goals. These goals are usually connected to the socialization process, the security of economic maintenance, and the emotional reinforcement of all group members.

Socialization. Socialization is the process through which the individual learns how to behave according to the rules and regulations of the society. Socialization is not a one-way street; it is an interaction process in which all individuals involved influence one another.

The child is, of course, the most important object of the socialization process. It is the child who must learn how to behave appropriately and to internalize all the symbolic representations required for normal group communication. We are saying that the bulk of the content of the socialization experience is directed by the parent toward the child.

But the parent in the relationship is also a recipient of the process despite protestations from many parents that they expect nothing in return for their years of child care. Parents receive high levels of personal satisfaction from viewing the results of their labors as the child matures and enters, with increasingly appropriate performances, the world of social interaction. The support which parents receive derives from their growing awareness that the behavior of the child is, in part, a reflection, though imperfect, of the knowledge and care given. It is this reciprocity in the learning process which underscores the mutual support in the parent-child relationship.

Economic Maintenance. The implications of economic maintenance as part of the family support system are obvious. The tradition has been that the father "brings home the bacon." However, the mother has, since shortly after World War I, become, in ever increasing numbers, a participant in the economic support of the family. Children receive the benefits of such support and, depending upon the approach to work which the parents hold, learn something about the efficacy of work. Economic maintenance is not a two-way street. Parents support; children, along with their parents, receive the benefits.

Of course, the family has been, since the Industrial Revolution, a consuming unit and has retained little of the producing aspects of the pre-industrial agrarian family. The pre-industrial agrarian family was also a family of support, but it was characterized more by mutuality. It was a family in which all members cooperated in the production of goods to be consumed. We will not analyze the changeover further. It is sufficient to note that the traditional nuclear family, as a consuming unit, is characterized by a system of support which is beneficial to all, but which includes the child as a consumer.

The most interesting aspect of the nuclear family as a system of economic maintenance centers around the question of motivation. Two sources for the structure of economic maintenance characteristic of the nuclear family are apparent: (1) the expectations placed upon individuals as parents to provide at least the basic necessities of life for their children, and (2) the high level of responsibility, based upon the affective elements of family integration, felt by the parents in their positions of economic support. Joseph Monane refers to the integration within groups such as the nuclear family as systems of high integration. He (Monane, 1967:24) states that: "Systems of high organization are generally marked by a homogeneity of components and an efficiency of output toward a particular goal." If one considers economic support as efficiency of output, the need parents feel to support the family can be understood as elements of the high organization characteristic of the nuclear family.

Emotional Support. We can return now to the mutually reciprocal character of family support systems since the needs of both adults—as spouses and parents—and children include the need for emotional reinforcement. The desire to interact at intimate levels of warmth and affection is an essential part of the family support system. Along with the elements of warmth and affection, we will include understanding, love, and consideration of others as parts of the emotional support system of family groups.

The family is the ideal interaction system for meeting this human need since the character of the parent-child relationship, as suggested by its length and intensity, facilitates such emotionally based activity. Also, children enter the family group at birth and are socialized within its boundaries. If we accept the importance of emotional support, it is only logical that we place it in the group in which the early and continued socialization of the child takes place. Sound child-rearing practices for traditional nuclear families have included, for the most part, emotional support as an essential feature of the interaction system.

Because of the intensity surrounding the need of the child for parental emotional support, it has not been usual to consider the emotional support needs of parents. A failure to do so here would negate the very nature of the group as a complex of interactive relationships. Any reasonable definition of the parent role should include the expectation that the giving of emotional support within the family system will result in receiving emotional support from those to whom it is given.

The early involvement in emotionally supportive relationships which parents experienced when they were children is not lost or forgotten at any point in their lives. Children who, as adults, become parents transfer their expectations from the relationship they had with their parents to the ongoing relationship with their children. Implicit in the idea of a transfer from one object of support to another is the distinction made between families of orientation and families of procreation. The parent of today occupies an adult position in a family of procreation. That parent, as a child, held the position of child in a family of orientation.

There are other emotionally supportive systems within the nuclear family. The support which spouses receive from each other and the support which siblings receive from each other complete the family support structure and enhance the intergenerational support between the parent and child. Spouses are social, psychological, and sexual complements of each other. They form a dyadic subgroup within the family which is, in the American nuclear family system, relatively isolated from the other adult members of their respective extended-family relatives. Because of this there would appear to be a greater need for strong emotional ties between husbands and wives. Spouses receive, at best, discontinuous support from other adult extended-family members, and this produces a situation in which spouses look to each other for adult reinforcement.

The emotional support which siblings provide each other grows out of the common experiences which they have had as members of the same nuclear family. Their common socialization results in relatively common views of the larger society and, of course, of the patterns of interaction within the nuclear family. Pre-adolescent play and other family experiences, even in the face of possible sibling rivalry, result in the development of bonds which each child shares only with siblings. Such experiences create systems of reliance and cooperation between and among siblings which, as the children mature, are retained. Barring extreme disruption in the common pattern, the support developed early produces bonds which are felt, if only psychologically, for life.

Sibling support during the socialization years may take the structural form of coalition against parent or parents. The occurrence of sibling coalition is more common than is realized. They may form as a means of defiance against the expressed wishes of the controlling parents, as a means of supporting one parent against another, or as a means of defending the parent subgroup against an outside and antagonistic force. In terms of sibling emotional support, the formation of coalitions suggests the unity which can be produced between or among children who are commonly socialized and who experience similar environments. Also, it is realistic to expect that in certain situations involving behavioral differences and disagreements among siblings, a coalition of, for example, two siblings against a third will form. There are times when parents have their hands full resolving the conflicts which such coalitions produce.

Figure 9-2 depicts the various support systems which exist within nuclear families. In studying the diagram the reader should keep in mind that, although the support systems are presented as separate subsystems (spouse, parent-child, and sibling), they are all interrelated in such a way that the effect of each subsystem has serious impact upon each of the others and upon the whole.

The traditional nuclear family is a complex of interaction in which the three systems outlined above combine to produce a closed system of social behavior which many have termed primary. Charles H. Cooley's (1962:23) initial statement on primary groups included the family as one of the "most important spheres of association" for primary qualities to develop. Over the years, however, there has been some question not only about the clarity of the concept as Cooley outlined it but also about applicability of the concept to the nuclear family. Of course, the latter

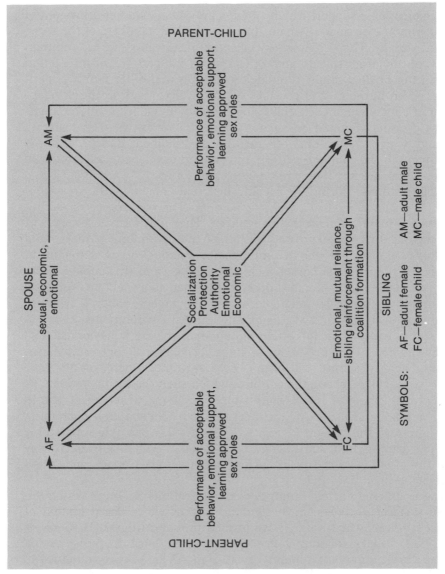

Figure 9-2. Family Support Systems

concern has surfaced along with recent changes in family life. We will discuss these changes shortly, but it might be useful at this time to discuss the family using the terminology of the primary group. Such comment is especially important because implicit in the concept of primacy is the belief that such groups are, if nothing else, highly integrated systems of mutual support.

Unfortunately, Cooley failed to extend his idea of primacy beyond the characteristic of face-to-face cooperation. Kingsley Davis (1949:290–291) noted this flaw in Cooley's reporting and extended the conditions under which primacy relations might develop:

> ... there are three essential conditions which ... tend to give rise to primary groups. The first of these is close (face-to-face) physical proximity of the group members, the second is smallness of the group; and the third, durability of the bond.

The traditional nuclear family meets these conditions which, we may argue, are conditions under which the support systems of such groups are likely to emerge.

CONTEMPORARY FAMILY GROUPINGS

Although the traditional American nuclear family, as an institution, has maintained a high degree of stability since well before the turn of the century, it has not been immune to the dynamics of change which influence the organization of all other major social groupings. Over the past twenty years family life has been characterized by diversity. The variations in family types reflect the modern tendency of some members of the society to select a lifestyle which is felt to be best suited to individual needs and expectations.

Family change is not a complete stranger to the American society, however. The pre-Industrial Revolution family involved extended relationships over three generations and was, for a great majority of individuals, the central focus of life. Activity in other institutions revolved around the family. The family was the center of agrarian work activity and was the setting for the early education of the young. Social activities were familial and inter-familial, and the community life which developed was founded upon strong ties within families functioning as support systems for the members within and for the community as a whole.

The Industrial Revolution and the attendant urbanization functioned to change the structure of the family. Small segments of the extended family began a pattern of mobility in order to establish residences in the developing urban centers. The agrarian community was fast becoming an urban community, and the family segments residing there became nuclear families. Since then, the nuclear family has functioned as the basic structure within which members interact, and has developed identity and emotional support systems.

Recently, the nuclear family system has exhibited some signs of beginning change. Contrary to the view of some, family change has presented, to date, no serious challenge to the stability of the nuclear family. There is, statistically, no serious move on the part of individuals to enter into or to maintain a type of family system other than one of nuclearity. This is another way of saying that those who have predicted the demise of the nuclear family because of observed changes are premature. There are, however, new types of family structures which have developed recently. They are: (1) the reconstructed family consisting of two partners, one of whom has been divorced, and at least one child of either spouse; (2) the single parent family in which the child is natural born or adopted; and (3) experimental families which participate as subsystems within communities called communes.

A Washington report (Engelbert, Langley & Warden, 1979:3) of the Coalition of Family Organizations states that " . . . seven out of every eight persons in the noninstitutional population of the United States in 1978 were members of nuclear families." The statistic includes one-parent households which comprised 10% of the total number of individuals who were nuclear family members. Of the total number of individuals in the population, 76% were in married-couple households. Our definition of the nuclear family would parallel this last figure. Of the remaining noninstitutional population, 8% were living alone as one-person households, 1% were in households of unmarried couples, and 5% were in various other living arrangements.

Although the patterns of family life are changing, the degree of change is not sufficient at this point to warrant an interpretation of family life based upon themes of group disorganization. As we shall see later, if the effects of change in the nuclear family are having an impact on organizational systems, the system most affected is the nuclear family itself. This is particularly true of the changing patterns of socialization of children during the pre-school years.

The reasons for changes in nuclear family life are many. There are, however, factors which emerged during World War II and immediately afterward which give direction to the changes in family life noted above. A key factor throughout the ensuing years has been the changing role of the female and the effects of this dramatic role shift on the system of interaction within the nuclear family.

In order to free the male for active military service during World War II, it became necessary for the female to function as a replacement for her male counterpart in industry and other traditionally male-dominated job settings. Upon war's end, it was difficult to release the female from her new-found occupation and demand that she return to the traditional role of housewife and mother. Three reasons, economically based, required that the female continue working in industrial and other settings: (1) the female was willing to work for less wages, (2) the female was willing to work for longer hours, and, (3) most importantly, the efficiency with which the female performed required work functions was as high as that of males in most cases. The combination of these three factors produced a profit situation for employers which demanded that they rethink their position on the dominance of the male and the traditional view of the female as child-bearer, child-carer and homemaker.

These factors, which resulted in dramatic changes in the female's role, are mentioned as preface to the concerns we have about the family as a small group. They are important because, with a shift in the role of the adult female family member, shifts in the entire system of family interaction and support result, and one of the most significant of these is the changing pattern of early child socialization. The pattern of part-time and full-time employment of the adult female parent militates against that parent's spending the amount of time in the home socializing the young, as the traditional view of the adult female parent role requires. One early view of the time element centered around observations about the changing role of the adult male parent. Arguments were forwarded which accounted for the loss of adult female parent time spent with children by asserting that, as the remunerative function of the female increased, the child socialization functions of the male parent would increase. Although there has been some shifting of roles on the part of each parent, the shifting has not been sufficient to allow for the continuation of full socialization of the child within the confines of the home.

With the advent of a clear pattern of dual-parent remunerative employment outside the home, the question of who will care for the children has been raised and answered in a manner which has led to the suspicion that the primary, integrative qualities of early age socialization in the home have been lost, or, at least, severely reduced. The answer, at least for the present, appears to be institutional care with strong educational overtones.

Today, children can be placed in learning centers while still in the cradle. The educational orientation in these institutional settings is based upon the view that children who are with surrogate parents are best served by organized attempts to educate them rather than babysitting them in an aimless nondevelopmental fashion. Whatever the reasoning behind the institutionalization of the child, the fact remains that children from their cradle years to the time of mandatory education are exposed to patterns of interaction which will significantly affect their development. In other words, children are being placed in settings in which there develops a new caring system, educationally oriented, which forms a structure of associations paralleling but not necessarily coordinating with the caring system within the family itself.

The impact of early institutional care on the child is considerable. It is particularly important to recognize that the child during the first few years of life is not sufficiently alert to the roles specific others are expected to use as a basis for effective socialization of the young. Children are not discriminating of individuals who meet their physical, emotional, and social needs. Parents who develop expectations that a child will be able to respond differently to them than they will to the nonparent carers will likely be dismayed when the child develops, for example, affective bonds for the surrogate parent which are the same as those expressed toward parents. Additionally, as the child matures and is able to differentiate the roles of others, the need to cope with feelings which run counter to the role expectations of others may result in a sense of conflict and guilt.

This analysis requires a word of caution. The assumption that a child will have difficulties in coping with others who perform the same or similar functions as parents is based upon the belief that the root socializers of the child should be the child's parents, and that no others are expected to fill these positions, especially in terms of the love bond between parent and child. Under conditions in which the societal expectations for roles change, the responses of those involved will be interpreted differently. In this regard, Gilbert D. Nass has remarked on the persistence of societal expectations that early socialization should take place in the home and under the supervision of the mother except in cases of financial need. Nass (1978:78) observed that " . . . mothers are still expected to stay home with their children, even if this leads to personal frustration and underutilization of the woman's talents and abilities." Nass's statement suggests that the primary qualities attributed to family life have been retained, at least at the level of expectations.

Realistically, the family as a small group is in a period of transition. Whereas the expectations about the functions of within-family interaction and support systems remain intact, the pattern of relationships, particularly in reference to parent-child relations, which has emerged appears to be moving in the direction of increased institutionalization of the child at earlier and earlier ages.

THE FRIENDSHIP GROUP

It is difficult to separate the many variables which are associated with groups identified as friendship groups. We accept the fact that such groups have the same common bases as are described for all social groups. The question is: What characteristic makes friendship groups distinct from all other social groupings?

To say that a friendship group is a relationship among friends or that it is a friendly association is not sufficient. Neither is it appropriate to identify the friendship group as one having primary group characteristics. Not all primary groups are friendship groups.

The following is an attempt to isolate one characteristic, affectivity, which is, or should be, commonly identified with friendship associations. Affectivity suggests a high level of liking, warmth, personal interest, sociability, support, and highly valued association. We will use this idea as the basic and unique characteristic of friendship groups. In definition form, then, a *friendship group* is a collection of individuals whose associations with each other are based upon high affectivity[1] and who value the relationship sufficiently to make the continuation of the affective relationship the dominant group goal.[2] Affectivity is the single most important common element in the friendship. There are, of course, other factors which determine the origins and development of friendship groups. These factors are: (1) propinquity (physical proximity), (2) physical characteristics (age, sex, ethnic or racial origins, strength, and

---

1. Two other words, liking and love, were considered to describe the quality of the friendship relation. *Liking* was rejected since its use is too generalized in our language, referring to a host of relationships which are not true friendships. Unfortunately, the word *love* was rejected since the reference is strongly toward sexual associations and, therefore, too limiting. *High affectivity* was chosen because it has a strong psychological as well as sociological referent. This combination of referents carries the desired connotation for true friendship associations.

2. The most recent investigations into friendship associations have been conducted in the field of Social Networks. The definition used by social network analysts carries the same "affectivity" theme as used in our definition. Accordingly, Edward O. Laumann offers the following definition: "Friendship *denotes* a voluntarily formed and maintained relationship between two persons who more or less mutually regard each other as having a special, affectively toned relationship of mutual trust and esteem." See Edward O. Laumann, *Bonds of Pluralism: The Form and Substance of Urban Social Networks*. New York: Wiley, 1973, p. 83.

so on), (3) common interests and values, and (4) self-presentation (personality). These are the common bases for many associations, but there must be an overlay of affectivity which pervades them if they are to develop as friendships.

THE INTERACTION SYSTEM OF FRIENDSHIP GROUPS

The relationships which develop within a friendship group are characteristically informal in type. Along with such characteristics as cooperation, group identity, emotional involvement, and personal knowledge of membership is, of course, the qualifying characteristic of affectivity. Figure 9-3 is a diagram of the interactive relationships as they develop out of the factors of friendship group origin and as they direct individual and group energies to the common goal of the friendship. The reader should remember that the development of a hierarchy of positions along leader-follower lines is as much a part of the structure of the friendship group as it is a part of all other social groups. This element of structure is not represented in the diagram because it is not an explicit force in the maintenance of the group. In the friendship group one can assume that there is a willingness on the part of áll members to change the structure of any informally developed hierarchy for the good of the group and to aid the group in maintaining itself as a complex relationship of affectivity.

HOMOGENEITY IN FRIENDSHIP GROUPS

Friends tend to be more like each other than not. We all assume that individuals who associate with each other as friends have something in common. The common element may be age or sex, common ethnic or racial background, common interests, or common values. A. Paul Hare (1976:207) remarks: "Since friendship is based upon common characteristics, persons who choose each other may well be of the same age, sex, social class, and ethnic group." Early research on the subject of homogeneity among friends suggests other common factors, such as intelligence and temperament (Richardson, 1939). These common elements, although strongly suggestive of the homogeneous nature of the friendship association, are not so definitive as to reject the suspicion that in some instances opposites attract. Although some research reports point to personality traits (Byrne, Griffit & Stefaniak, 1967) as a common basis for associations, other research indicates that similarity in personality traits is not a significant basis for friendship association (Zimmer, 1956).

There appear to be two possible views on the subject of homogeneity and friendship associations. They are: (1) friendship associations are

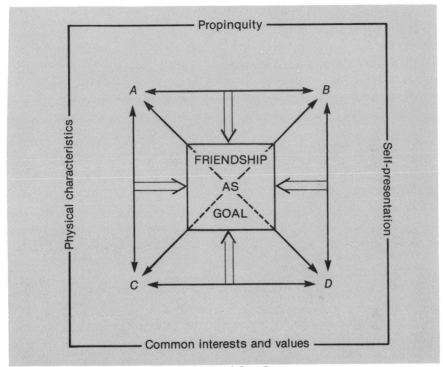

Figure 9-3.   Interaction System of Friendship Groups

homogeneously based, and (2) friendships may be homogeneously and heterogeneously based. Some friendships may include significant differences among the members. Although a friendship may include significant differences, the basic references for the friendship are not the differences but the perceived similarities between and among the group members.

Friendship associations are, by definition, based upon high affectivity, and if the affective character pervades the entire system of interaction among friends the resultant mutuality of affectivity will provide a common system of motivation and experience for all group members. Mutuality of affectivity is a common bond strong enough to reinforce elements of common identity and strong enough to overcome differences which, in less intense affective relationships, might be factors in group breakdown.

There is an assumption concerning homogeneity and heterogeneity in friendship groups which should be discussed. The assumption is that maintaining the group process toward goal achievement requires a variety of skills and information. The assumption suggests that heterogeneous groups are more likely to succeed. The argument is a commanding one for groups interested in task performance or decision making. For friendship groups, a variety of skills and information within the membership is no more important than are similarities among members since the dominant concern of the group is simply to maintain the friendship regardless of similarities or differences.

Since the tendency in group association appears to be strongly in the direction of homogeneity, let us describe the relationship between member similarity and the possible emergence of a high level of affectivity. Stein, Hardwyck, and Smith (1965) studied a population of white ninth-grade students. The researchers found that these students, when asked about their feelings toward other individuals of similar age who were black and white and who were either similar to or different from the ninth-graders in beliefs and interests, perceived similarities in beliefs and interests as more important in determining interpersonal attractiveness than the factor of racial differences. The researchers are suggesting that racial difference is not as important a factor in interpersonal attraction as beliefs and interests. In terms associated with high affectivity, the implication of the research is that, although individuals may be aware of racial differences at least at the visibility level, common beliefs and interests are perceived as a more important basis for the emergence of interracial associations of high affectivity. Since the study was directed toward discovering information about feelings and attraction, one is prompted to ask if the results of the study fit real-life situations. For present purposes, however, the research of Stein and his colleagues suggests two conclusions: (1) that there is a relationship between perceived similarities and possible high affectivity, and (2) that similarities (common beliefs and interests) and differences (racial) should be viewed on a scale of priorities. The implication of such a scale is that when more than one similarity or difference is involved in the determination of a friendship, the chances of developing high levels of interpersonal attraction (affectivity) depend upon the value individuals place upon a particular similarity as compared to a particular difference.

FRIENDSHIP GROUPS AS CLOSED SYSTEMS

The specialization of relationships and the intensity which develops around the element of high affectivity in friendship groups is not conducive to frequent replacement of members. In this sense, the group is a closed system into which and out of which members seldom move.

In a more general sense, all groups are closed systems of interaction, but in most of them there are procedures built into the group structure which facilitate the entrance and exit of members. For example, work groups are controlled by larger-system regulations concerning hiring and firing. Also, work groups which are small and which develop on-the-job, informal associations develop informal techniques for ostracizing individuals and, in extreme cases, for causing their firing. Small committees may organize and maintain membership through election or by appointment for limited periods of time. In these groups there is a system for controlling the flow of individuals into and out of the group.

The friendship group, once established at the level of high affectivity, is not prone to eliminate or to add members for four reasons:

1. Qualifications for membership are generalized and it is difficult to find individuals who have the mix of characteristics desired by groups of friends.
2. There is a reticence to change the structure of interaction which the given members find comfortable. It is difficult for new members to adapt to the familiarity and ease characteristic of long-standing friendships. In instances in which there is an absence of verbal or other external forms of communication, friends are capable of feeling comfortable with each other; new members are not.
3. Friendships are associations among individuals who are open with each other (see the discussion of the Johari window in Chapter Five) and who share private experiences and feelings. Most individuals are unwilling to accept into their circles of secret sharing others who are not part of the established relationship.
4. Friends develop a highly specialized system of communication. This system includes symbols and meanings which derive, in large measure, from past situations which friends experience as a whole. Learning the symbols and understanding their meanings is a difficult task for new members. When friends use the phrase "private joke" or suggest to nonmembers that they wouldn't understand, they are, in effect, stating the limits of the closed system of friendship. At the same time, they are telling the outsider that it is a closed system and that it is difficult to gain entrance.

These observations identify friendship groups as primary systems of interactions, and the "we" feelings attached to these systems are restrictive. Implicit in the use of the word "we" is the opposite word "they."

"We" identifies the closed system; "they" identifies those outside the system or those who would enter the system but do not. Rudyard Kipling understood the "we-they" theme of group relations in his poem:

> All good people agree
>   And all good people say
> All nice people like Us are We
>   And everyone else is They:
> But if you cross over the sea,
>   Instead of over the way
> You may end by (think of it!) looking on We
>   As only a sort of They.

"We and They" copyright 1926 by Rudyard Kipling from *Rudyard Kipling's Verse: Definitive*. Reprinted by permission of the Executors of the Estate of Mrs. George Bambridge and Doubleday & Company, Inc.

The Kipling "sea" may be identified symbolically as the boundary line of the closed group system. It is this boundary which clearly delineates in-groups and out-groups. The limitations which such rigid boundaries produce often result in tensions between members of different social groupings or anxiety for individuals who might otherwise wish to enter into certain group associations. The final reality is that the boundaries surrounding groups such as friendship groups also result in high levels of within-group integration and is one of the most important elements in the development and maintenance of high levels of affectivity.

COALITION FORMATION IN FRIENDSHIP GROUPS

Friendship groups may possess high levels of integration which support the strong emotional ties that bind members to each other. However, high integration among friends does not exempt them from the principles of subgroup development to which all social groups are subject. The following propositions are basic to all friendship groups:

Proposition 1. As groups of friends increase in size, they experience increased difficulty in maintaining their integrative quality.

Proposition 2. Friendship groups of three or more are subject to the principles of group coalition formation.

Proposition 3. Coalition formation does not necessarily threaten friendship group unity.

Proposition 4. Coalitions within friendship groups produce coalitions characterized either by conflict or by enhancement.

Proposition 1. Understanding the relationship between group size and the number of possible within-group relationships discussed in Chapter Two, we will proceed to describe the impact of group size on friendship groups. Friendship groups have as their goal the maintenace of the friendship associations developed among *n* individuals. Considering ten or more as the upper range, if the size of the friendship group is in this range of small group size there is a greater chance that difficulties will arise in maintaining the group's informal/affective character than in smaller groups. Although laboratory research on this subject has not included investigations of friendship groups as such, the results suggest that in small groups of relatively larger size, individual resources are not sufficient to cope with the increase in the complexity of the possible relationships in which the individual is involved (Zimet & Schneider, 1969; Williams & Mattson, 1942).

Proposition 2. The fact that friendship groups possess a special quality which we have termed high affectivity does not rule out the possibility that coalitions will form within them. Charles H. Cooley pointed out that primary groups in general, and for our purposes, friendship groups in particular, are characterized not only by face-to-face cooperation but also by status and positional differentiation, competition, and "various appropriate passions" (see Chapter Two). These latter qualities underscore the possiblity of restructuring friendship groups along lines of coalition formation. Reasonably, specific situations will produce circumstances which require or suggest group restructuring. Friends will disagree, for example, on a specific issue. Some members will combine to take one position on the issue and other members will combine to take an opposing position. Lines of argument will be drawn and the subject discussed. The issue may or may not be resolved to the satisfaction of all members. Whatever the result, when the situation changes the coalition will disappear and restructuring along other lines will occur. The process is a familiar one and the continuation of the friendship associations will follow a line of coalition shifting as suggested in Chapter Three, Figure 3-4.

Proposition 3. Implicit in the shifting character of friendship group coalitions is the fact that coalitions, although indicators of intra-group conflict, are not necessarily destructive of the whole. In other words, that conflict within the group will result in group breakdown is not a foregone conclusion. Two group tendencies are worthy of note here: (1) that coalitions will form, and (2) that coalition shifting will occur over time. In discussing coalitions in triads, George Monane (1967:28) observed:

In social systems involving three people, two of them are found to combine against the other. These systems form a twosome, corner the flow of energy/information within the system, and isolate the one left out. . . . Threesomes maintain themselves well although their internal coalitions may shift from time to time.

One early research effort by Theodore M. Mills (1953) supports the first tendency. Mills (1953:356) states that " . . . findings confirm Simmel's basic point that the threesome tends to break up into a pair and another party."

In their researches on gang behavior, Muzafer and Carolyn Sherif (1964) suggest the formation and shifting of coalitions with gangs in their report on social control mechanisms and gang sanctions. The authors report instances in which individual members became the object of insult and hazing from coalitions. The failure of one member to conform to gang expectations regarding hair style resulted in the remaining members of the gang insulting him and subjecting him to intense hazing. When, finally, the member conformed to getting his hair cut in the prevailing gang style, the other members warmly greeted him for conforming to their expectations. Isolation of one member from the gang occurred when one member, after attempting to get needed money from other gang members through gambling with them, was given the cold shoulder. The individual is subject to group pressures which result from coalitions formed by remaining gang members. The effectiveness of group controls, in these instances, results from the force of the coalition and not any individual gang member. The one variation is to be found in the authority of the leader who may use gang approved means for sanctioning any one member. If the leader is sufficiently established in his position he may be exempt from the pressures of gang coalitions. All other members, however, are usually subject to such pressures if they choose to deviate from the normative expectations of the gang.

Proposition 4. At various points in the text, including the material covered just above, we have discussed the group tendency to form coalitions in the traditional sense of subgroups uniting against third elements. Since the early writings of Georg Simmel, this usage has been the acceptable mode of interpretation for group coalition formation. However, in attempting to apply these traditional interpretations to the coalition possibilities in groups of friends, we observe that the shifting realignments within these groups do not fit the normal analytical model nearly as well as other types of small groups.

From a research point of view two developments are relevant here: (1) the body of coalition research, most of which is carried out in laboratories, has concentrated upon coalitions of two members against a third and upon within-group conflict which results from coalition formation; and (2) small group research on friendship groupings is sparse; research on coalition formation in friendship groups is nonexistent. There are studies such as the one discussed above by the Sherifs from which we have been able to "tease out" some understanding of friendship group coalitions. The effect of all this is that our use and interpretations of the coalition theme in small groups, and particularly in small friendship groups, has followed the party line. The following analysis of friendship groups is an attempt to broaden the sociological basis of group coalition formation and to suggest a typology which may increase our understanding of this unique and interesting group process.

Friendship associations are centered around the high affectivity of the interactive bonds and are characterized by continuing levels of high integration. Although friendship groups are subject, as are all small groups, to the development of conflict between and among members, the range of possibilities for coalition formation would appear to be broader than the range suggested by conflict possibilities alone. If, in fact, friendship groups are composed of high affect relationships there appear to be realistic possibilities that some of the coalitions which form are designed not to resolve differences within a situation of group conflict but to enhance the integrative forces already existing within the group.

Coalitions in friendship groups are not necessarily indicators of a loss of the high affectivity shared by all group members. Ordinarily, the assumptions made earlier about the primary qualities of friendship groups and the high levels of integration which characterize them remain intact. When coalitions develop, the relationship of those who participate in them are characterized by an increase in the intensity of the group affect and reinforced by group members outside the coalition.

Coalitions produced in friendship groups are of two types:

(1) *Conflict coalitions* —these are coalitions formed *against* the remaining group members, isolating them or penalizing them, as in the phrasing "two against one." Conflict coalitions are viewed as negative and are potentially disruptive of group integration.

(2) *Enhancing coalitions* —these are coalitions from which the remaining group members are *excluded* without fault or penalty. Enhancing coalitions are viewed as positive, helpful to all group members, and supportive of group integration.

Conflict coalitions are usually the result of efforts to control and sanction individuals so that the friendship group may resolve some internal conflict and continue to function smoothly. Such coalitions form at the risk of disrupting group interaction and can result in the breakdown of the group. Enhancing coalitions, on the other hand, are alignments within the group which develop as aids to the larger group in maintaining its high level of integration. For example, groups of friends may find themselves in situations requiring decision making or the performance of certain tasks. Group members who have the required knowledge or skill will not only form the effective enhancing coalition, but will be expected to do so by noncoalition members.

The identification of an enhancing coalition type suggests a moving away from the traditional conflict view of coalitions and points toward a more positive and broader interpretation of coalition formation in friendship groups as well as in other group types. In families, sibling coalitions may form in an attempt to persuade parents in favor of a third noncoalition sibling. In informal work groups, a coalition of high-output workers may form to protect a less productive member. In each case, the coalition formed was not based upon conflict within but upon the desire to enhance the position of a noncoalition member.

In structuring the coalition typology above we are not suggesting that the importance of the conflict coalition in small groups is less significant than it has been since Simmel's early interpretations. The enhancing coalition theme suggests only that in some types of small group associations coalition development has nothing to do with elements of disorganization but with activities in groups which serve as reinforcers of the integration developed and maintained by the group as a whole.

THE INFORMAL WORK GROUP

Informal work groups develop as a result of individual workers performing their expected formal functions in a setting conducive to the development of a system of personalized interaction among them. The frequency with which such a development has been observed and reported has made the informal work group a basic concept in the small groups field.

The *informal work group* may be defined as a collection of individuals whose common work experiences result in the development of a system of interpersonal relations beyond those expected of them by virtue of their employment. Such groups are characterized by friendliness, common interests and, in some cases, group goals which are not required for the efficient performance of their expected work activity. Some informal work groups continue functioning in settings outside the work environment. In some instances, members of informal work groups may develop relationships of a primary nature, relationships lasting longer than their common work experiences.

Although these informal work groups cannot be divorced totally from the formal systems of production in which they are rooted, the relationships which develop promote a sense of loyalty and common identity, which elements are not part of the workers' contractual relations with the larger formal organization. From a functional point of view, the informal work group is a second, but not necessarily secondary, point of reference from which the worker may view the elements of his work environment. The worker, then, has a dual system of references which are used to determine performance while on the job.

MOTIVATIONAL FACTORS

The first question one must ask when considering the impact of informal groups on formal organization systems is, "How do they develop?" In other words, why do workers exhibit a strong tendency to behave informally with other workers in settings already regulated by explicit rules and regulations? There is little doubt that the motivation behind the formation of informal work groups stems from common work experiences and worker agreement about those experiences. The following is a list of factors which motivate workers to develop informal patterns of relationships:

(1) *Large system failure.* Large formal organizations often fail to satisfy the social interaction needs of its members. When relationships of companionship are denied (as in line assembly work) there is a tendency for individuals to search for means outside the system.

(2) *Worker consensus.* Workers may view the formal system as a common antagonist or "enemy." The conflict which results when the economic and production expectations of workers differ from those of the formal system may force worker consensus which, in turn, may result in the formation of an informal pattern of worker relationships.

(3) *Common interests.* Workers may become aware of common interests associated with or apart from their common work experience. As discussed in Chapter One, common interests are a frequent basis for group formation.

(4) *Propinquity.* Physical proximity in the work situation is conducive to the development of interpersonal relations. If workers remain in a common work setting over a significant period of time, there is a strong tendency to develop a pattern of interpersonal associations.

(5) *Common work experience.* Workers whose job requirements are the same, similar, or, at least, connected in some way may use the common experience as a basis for developing an informal relationship.

The most basic motivating factor is the common work experience. Such experiences form the connecting link between the two systems for the workers. Common work experiences include elements of the formal system such as formal rules and regulations which define productivity expectations about work efficiency and the level of remuneration which each worker may expect. Common work experiences also include the physical environment of the workers, their relationships with immediate superiors, and worker interaction. All these elements combined form the common ground for work activity. Figure 9-4 indicates the nature of the workers' two interaction systems and the involvement of each worker with the elements common to both systems.

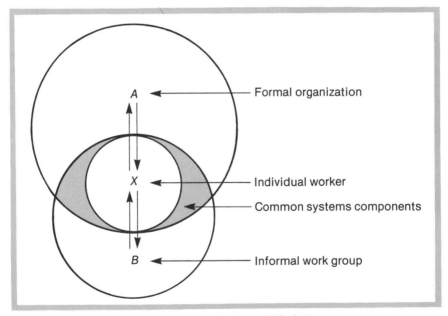

Figure 9-4. Overlapping Formal and Informal Work Systems

If we view the two work systems of the individual as one complex system of behavior, we can identify four system elements which combine to influence behavior in the work environment:

(1) *The individual.* The worker is influenced by each system in the complex and, in turn, influences each system. This complex system functions in terms of the individual's interaction with each system, as well as in terms of each system as an influencer of the individual worker.

(2) *The formal structure.* A system of rules and regulations which define expected behavior for each individual within it.

(3) *The informal structure.* A system of interpersonal relations which interprets and attempts to control the worker's view of elements in the work environment.

(4) *Common systems components.* These are work-related factors (output, efficiency, and so on) which are important concerns of both systems.

Changes in any of these four elements or in any combination of them will have an effect upon each other element and upon the entire system complex.

THE HAWTHORNE EXPERIMENTS

Our concern is mainly with the development of informal work relationships and their impact upon the formal system. The classic research which produced findings on this subject was carried out in the Hawthorne Works, a Chicago subdivision of the Western Electric Company, during the years 1927–1932 (Turner, 1933; Mayo, 1933).

We will concern ourselves only briefly with the results of the controlled experiments in the Relay Assembly Test Room for reasons we will discuss shortly. We will deal more extensively with the results of experiments conducted in the Bank Wiring Observation Room.

Experiments in the Relay Assembly Test Room (Roethlisberger & Dickson, 1939) were conducted on six cooperative females who were experienced in telephone relay assembly. They were under no formal supervision and were free to talk and move about without negative sanctions for their informal behavior. Initial interpretations of the impact of such informal relationships suggest that the operators were able to control levels of production without the imposition of rigid rules and regulations from outside the group. The only control was a friendly observer from the test team. As informal work relationships increased among the operators, production increased dramatically. Although the researchers were not looking in the direction of informal factors as having significant effects upon production, that is exactly what they found.

Initial findings suggested that the elimination of isolation and the incorporation of a "working together" scheme increased group morale and productivity as well.

These results are not as impressive as they might have been because of the presence of uncontrolled circumstances such as the workers' awareness of their superiors' favorable reactions to the experiment. Since the operators knew of the support given the experiment by their superiors, their production might have reflected their desire to impress the boss. Other factors such as changes in the incentive program and replacing less productive operators with operators of greater skill were also likely influences on the increasingly high rate of productivity.

Recently, a statistical interpretation critical of the Hawthorne studies by Richard Franke and James Kaul (1978; Carey, 1967) indicates that factors such as those listed immediately above and others such as the benefits resulting from fatigue reduction and the exercise of managerial discipline were significant determiners of the increased productivity of the operators. Franke and Kaul also suggest that the economic depression which began in October, 1929, might have had a positive effect upon production due to the increased fear of losing one's job. They conclude their findings with the following observation:

> This first statistical interpretation of the major Hawthorne experiment leads to conclusions different from those heretofore drawn. Most of the variance in production rates during the first relay experiment could be explained by measured variables. To assume that output changes result from unmeasured changes in the human relations of workers therefore seems injurious, even though it was the assumption of the Hawthorne researchers and has been accepted and built upon by many social scientists over the past several decades (Franke & Kaul, 1978:638).

The development of a set of informal group norms for controlling elements in the work environments is chronicled most impressively in the reporting on experiments conducted in the Bank Wiring Observation Room. Because we are particularly interested in the impact of informal groups on the formal work system, we will use the interpretation of George Homans (1950) as the basis for our discussion. Homans' report centers around the output situation and the effect of informal worker relations upon it.

There were fourteen operators in the Bank Wiring Observation Room, of whom nine were wiremen. Of the five operators remaining, three were soldermen, and two were inspectors. The operators worked with two types of equipment: connectors and selectors (types of central office telephone switches). The operators were paid by group piecework, being paid for the number of equipments turned out by the department as a whole. As Homans (1950:61) suggested: "A man's earnings depended on the output of the whole group, not just on his own. . . . " Although the efficiency of each worker and the speed with which he worked contributed to the financial well-being of the entire group, the payment of a wage depended largely on the cooperation of all the workers as reflected in the products at the end of each day and week.

The importance of informal group controls upon each of the workers can be identified in the responses of fellow workers to individuals who produced more than they, as a group, believed to be acceptable. Operators who worked too fast were called such names as "rate-buster" or "speed king"; they were ridiculed in the presence of other operators and they were "binged." Operators who produced less than was expected of them were called "chiselers." They were also "binged." Binging, although a childish game,[3] was used as a form of control or penalty over the individual worker who deviated above or below the accepted group definition of reasonable output.

The use of daywork allowances by the operators is another example of the informal controls the workers used in determining the rate of production; in this case, production restriction by handing in unjustifiable allowances for work stoppages. Operators were allowed to claim daywork allowances for all time lost because of material shortages, defective material, waiting for another operator to complete his work, repairs, and power shortages. Daywork allowances were manipulated by the operators, with some claiming very little and others claiming a great deal of time lost. Many of these claims could not be justified, and some men claimed much more time out than was fact. The group chief allowed the great majority of claims to go through. As with stated output by the operators, the group chief allowed claims on the word of the operator reporting them.

Helping others is, by definition, a support factor among individuals who have a sense of togetherness or who have developed personalized relationships. Such a condition of support existed among the operators in the Observation Room. Homans (1950:66) observed that one of the most common activities practiced by the operators " . . . was helping another man out by doing some of his wiring for him when he has fallen behind."

Among the 14 workers, the development of a pattern of informal association produced numerous subgroups (cliques), as one might expect

3. The reader might recall the word "binging" from childhood. Binging is a game in which individuals hit each other on the upper arm to see who is the hardest hitter.

with a small group of this size. However, there developed an overriding set of behavioral expectations which all men were constrained to follow. Although all operators did not conform equally (clique formation developed along lines of conformity to these expectations), each group member knew what was expected of him and defined his behavior in those terms. Roethlisberger and Dickson (1939:522) refer to these behavioral expectations as group sentiments and offer the following list:

1. You should not turn out too much work. If you do, you are a "rate buster."
2. You should not turn out too little work. If you do, you are a "chiseler."
3. You should not tell a supervisor anything that will react to the detriment of an associate. If you do, you are a "squealer."
4. You should not attempt to maintain social distance or act officious. If you are an inspector, for example, you should not act like one.

The Hawthorne experiments directed early interest toward the importance of informal group relationships in the on-the-job experiences of workers. There are other factors, certainly, which, as Franke and Kaul suggest, influence worker productivity. As a last word of caution, we agree with the observation of Stephen Wilson (1978:203):

It is inaccurate to assume that all workers in all work organizations form highly solidary informal groups. Informal relationships are neither formally required nor restricted, thus allowing the nature of the formal structure to influence the extent to which solidarity develops among members of the same subsystem.

Nevertheless, it seems clear that the development and maintenance of informal relationships among workers is one significant factor in the determination of worker behavior in formal organizational systems.

ASSEMBLY LINES, BOREDOM, AND AUTONOMY

Earlier, we discussed the failure of the formal system to provide for the social interaction needs of its workers and the development of patterns of informal relations which result. Donald F. Roy's (1959) reporting on "banana time" points directly to this issue. The author, as participant observer, studied a group of machine operators who worked with punching machines called "clickers." The work area was referred to as the clicking room. It soon became clear to Roy that the two major characteristics of the work day were monotony and intense boredom. The following description of the work area and manual activity of the workers highlights the problem:

This was standing all day in one spot beside three old codgers in a dingy room looking out through barred windows at the bare walls of a brick warehouse, leg movements largely restricted to the shifting of body weight from one foot to the other, hand and arm movements confined, for the most part, to a simple repetitive sequence of place the die, ____ punch the clicker, ____ place the die, ____ punch the clicker, and intellectual activity reduced to computing the hours to quitting time (Roy, 1959:160).

Workers interrupted the tedium of their work with very short breaks during which time the workers participated in playing jokes on each other, deactivating another worker's machine, and stealing fruit from the lunch of another worker, hence "banana" time. The short breaks occurred continuously throughout the work day. Other childish games were played: "window" time occurred shortly after "banana" time. The worker whose banana was taken would retaliate by opening the thief's window so that he would be hit with a blast of cold air. Such pranks would include a great deal of verbal teasing and insulting.

As Roy became more involved with the activities of the other workers, he began to recognize a pattern in the horseplay and verbal insults:

> . . . the disconnected became connected, the nonsense made sense, the obscure became clear, and the silly actually funny. And, as the content of the interaction took on more and more meaning, the interaction began to reveal structure. There were "times" and "themes," and roles to serve their enaction (Roy, 1959:161).

Roy's research in the industrial setting serves to reinforce the generally accepted belief that informal systems of interaction develop under work conditions in which the formal system fails to account for the social needs of its workers.

Although formal system failure is often conducive to the development of informal worker relationships, certain structural developments in, for example, industrial plants work against the formation of informal relationships. William A. Faunce (1958) describes the restrictions placed upon worker relationships and the difficulty in developing friendly associations among workers when assembly line production systems are introduced into a factory. The research was conducted in an automobile engine plant which had introduced automatic transfer machines. His findings (Faunce, 1958:404) suggest that ". . . many workers are virtually isolated socially on automated production lines. Under such conditions, it might be expected that fewer close relationships or friendships would develop on the job."

Fred E. Katz (1968:47), in assessing the effect of formal systems upon the development of informal work groups states that " . . . the culture of informal work groups is a manifestation of autonomy within the confines of the organization. . . . " Worker autonomy, which may be defined as freedom from external controls over the work environment, produces an unrestricted work environment in which the workers are free to interact and form friendly informal relationships. Katz suggests that such informal relationships alleviate boredom and, in some cases, help get work done. He cautions that, in other cases, informal patterns can work contrary to the goals of the formal system. Whatever the effects of informal systems upon behavior in the work situation, Katz's thesis is clear: undefined autonomy is conducive to the development of informal patterns of interaction among workers.

A SMALL GROUPS LIST

There are numerous other types of small groups, to be sure. Included in any small groups list would be therapy groups, committees, decision-making groups, adolescent and child peer groups, and informal groups which develop in military systems, prisons, and political bureaucracies. There are semi-formal groups whose character is informal, such as garden and bridge clubs. There are high-achievement groups such as Scouts of America troops and competition groups such as baseball, football, and hockey teams. There are boards of directors, liaison groups, and academic groups of students and faculty. We should include, also, laboratory experimental groups of all types.

All these and the three small groups which we have subjected to our scrutiny have one thing in common: they are small. The groups selected for our analysis and interpretation are, in this writer's view, the most significant and all-encompassing in the life situations of a large majority of individuals. The patterns of behavior which emerge in them are root patterns of interaction. If these patterns do not fit all other groups in the list, they at least function as reference systems for social interaction and afford the reader a framework for understanding the basic structure of interaction found in all other small groups.

summary

There are relationships which occur in our daily lives which are of very short duration and which never achieve the status of a full-fledged social group relationship. This chapter identified these types of relationships as temporary social relations, which are in many ways very much like group relationships. Temporary social relations are characterized by rudimentary social structures, and explicit or implied goals; they also satisfy individual needs.

This chapter was devoted to interpretations of three small groups which are more important in the determination of our life directions than temporary social relations. These three groups—the nuclear family, the friendship group, and the informal work group—involve long-established relationships, set the standards for living in the community, and control the direction and content of our lives. It was noted that they form the center of an individual's complex of interaction and structure a collective base for all other associations.

In presenting a traditional interpretation of the modern American nuclear family, three within-family systems were identified. They are: the interaction system, the identity system, and the support system.

The nuclear family was defined as a two-generation group of individuals who are bound together by ties of marriage, birth, and adoption, who live in common households, and who develop a specialized system of expectations for behaving within a closed system of reciprocal relationships. In an interaction system, the family was found to be a complex of conjugal- and consanguine-based relationships, performed in concert, and promoting the development of appropriate, common meanings which function as reinforcers of family cohesion.

The complexities of family interaction systems were defined in terms of the size of the family unit. For example, the marital dyad is a simple, two-person relationship maintained in terms of the give-and-take between two interdependent individuals. The addition of one offspring increases the family numerically by one but increases the interaction complex from one to six possible relationships. In a family system of four individuals, the number of possible relationships increases to twenty-five. It was observed that the traditional view of nuclear families as characterized by closeness of members, high levels of cooperation and integration, and intense, frequent face-to-face interaction is not nearly as clear or reasonable a possibility as the family approaches the upper limits of small group size.

The nuclear family includes four separate subsystems of identity: *conjugal* (between spouses), *direct* (between parent and child of the same sex), *complement* (between parent and child of opposite sex), and *sibling* identities (between or among offspring). These systems afford family members discrete subsystems of interaction in which sex roles and sexual identities can be determined and clarified. These systems also function to define family positions in terms of hierarchy and continuing and changing expectations which family members place upon each other.

The family as a support system is organized to achieve the essential goals of procreation, socialization, economic maintenance, and emotional support. The last-stated goal is less clear than the first three and includes the structuring of within-family relationships which are conducive to fulfilling the need for interaction at the intimate level. Traditionally, the family has been identified as the interaction system within which warmth and affection are necessary requisites for the development of a mutual support system. It was noted that discussions of family support usually centered around the emotional needs of the child while developing to maturity. However, any reasonable definition of emotional support in a family structure must also include an understanding of the needs of adult members, both as parents and as spouses. The sibling mutual support system was also discussed and observed to be the result of long-term, common experiences which offspring have as members of the same nuclear family. The integration achieved between and among siblings creates a climate of reliance and cooperation which may, at times, result in the formation of sibling coalitions against one or both parents.

The friendship group was discussed in terms of the unique characteristic which separates friendship groups from other social groupings. Rejecting the qualities of friendly associations and primacy, we observed that the characteristic of affectivity is the one factor most commonly associated with friendship relationships. In consideration of this, we defined the *friendship group* as a collection of individuals whose associations with each other are based upon high affectivity and who value the relationship sufficiently to make the continuation of the affective relationship the dominant group goal.

Friendship associations develop out of the same bases as other social groups: propinquity, physical characteristics, common interests and values, and self-presentation (personality). Characterizations of friendship associations as homogeneous (based upon common factors such as age, sex, social class, and ethnicity) were only partially supported by researchers of the subject. Friendship groups were also characterized as closed support systems into which and out of which there is little or no movement. Four reasons were given for the tendency of friendship groups to remain closed. (1) Qualifications for membership are generalized and it is difficult to find individuals who have the correct mix of requirements. (2) There is a reticence to change the structure of interaction which members find comfortable. Membership changes would require a change in group structure. (3) Such associations include the sharing of private meanings, experiences, and feelings. These are elements which preclude the easy acceptance of new members. (4)

Friends develop a highly specialized system of communication, the meanings within which are frequently based upon past associations commonly experienced. Changing membership would disrupt the unity and integration which develops from sharing past experiences.

When the principles of coalition formation in groups were applied to friendship associations, it was noted that although there is the real possibility in all friendship associations for coalitions to form against one or more members, there was also the possibility that coalitions may also form which are not conflict-oriented; such coalitions form in order to enhance the friendship group as a whole. Four propositions were discussed in this regard:

1. An increase in the size of friendship groups results in increased difficulty in maintaining the informal structure.
2. Friendship groups of three or more are subject to the principles of group coalition formation.
3. Coalition formation does not necessarily threaten group unity.
4. Coalitions within friendship groups may be conflict-oriented or enhancing.

The view of some friendship group coalitions as enhancing grew out of the difficulties associated with holding to the position that all subgroup development within friendship groups was necessarily conflict-based or conflict-producing. The following typology developed:

1. *Conflict coalitions* —coalitions formed against the remaining group members, isolating them or penalizing them, as in the phrase, "two against one."
2. *Enhancing coalitions* —coalitions from which the remaining group members are excluded without fault or penalty, which coalitions develop as supportive of larger group integration.

Informal work groups were observed to develop as a result of individual workers performing their expected work functions in a setting conducive to the development of more primary systems of interaction. The *informal work group* was defined as a collection of individuals whose common work experiences result in the development of a system of interpersonal relations beyond those expected of them by virtue of their employment. Characteristically, individuals who formed such groups were friendly, and developed common interests and collective goals not required for the efficient performance of their expected work activity.

The factors which motivate workers to develop informal group relationships were listed as follows: large system failure, worker consensus, common interests, propinquity while on the job, and common work experiences. The famous Hawthorne experiments were cited to support the presence of informal work group development. Included in the discussion were criticisms which do not support the Hawthorne experiment or the generalizations about the development of informal work groups. It was also noted that large-system failure results in some kind of informal association of workers even under the most difficult working conditions, but that assembly line work is not as all conducive to such development.

discussion questions

THE NUCLEAR FAMILY

1. Is the socialization of an infant possible outside the family support system?
2. Discuss the effects of changing female roles on the traditional structure of the nuclear family.
3. Do you agree that there is a decline in the quality of primary relationships in nuclear family groups as the size of the family group increases?

THE FRIENDSHIP GROUP

1. Why do sociologists consider friendship groups homogeneous?
2. Is affectivity absolutely necessary for a continuing friendship?
3. Have you ever experienced coalition formation in your friendship associations?

THE INFORMAL WORK GROUP

1. Does the presence of informal work group relationships always result in increased productivity?
2. Are the criticisms made of the Hawthorne experiments reasonable?
3. Why is work on assembly lines not conducive to the development of informal work groups?

references

Byrne, Donn; Griffit, William; and **Stefaniak, Daniel.** "Attraction and Similarity of Personality Characteristics," *Journal of Personality and Social Psychology,* 5 (1967): 82–90.

Carey, Alex. "The Hawthorne Studies: A Radical Criticism," *American Sociological Review,* 32 (1967): 403–416.

Cooley, Charles H. *Social Organization: A Study of the Larger Mind.* New York: Shocken, 1962.

Davis, Kingsley. *Human Society.* New York: Macmillan, 1949.

Engelbert, Steven; Langley, Patricia; and **Warden, Barbara** (eds.). *The Washington Cofo Memo.* A publication of the Coalition of Family Organization, Vol. 2, 1979.

Faunce, William A. "Automation in the Automobile Industry: Some Consequences for In-plant Social Structure," *American Sociological Review,* 23 (1958): 401–407.

Franke, Richard Herbert; and **Kaul, James D.** "The Hawthorne Experiments: First Statistical Interpretation," *American Sociological Review,* 43 (1978): 623–643.

Hare, A. Paul. *Handbook of Small Group Research,* 2nd ed. New York: The Free Press, 1976.

Homans, George C. *The Human Group.* New York: Harcourt, Brace and World, 1950.

Katz, Fred E. *Autonomy and Organizations: The Limits of Social Control.* New York: Random House, 1968.

Kipling, Rudyard. *Rudyard Kipling's Verse: Definitive.* Garden City, New York: Doubleday, 1940.

Laumann, Edward O. *Bonds of Pluralism: The Form and Substance of Urban Social Networks.* New York: Wiley, 1973.

Mayo, Elton. *The Human Problems of an Industrial Civilization.* New York: Macmillan, 1933.

Mills, Theodore M. "Power Relations in Three-person Groups," *American Sociological Review,* 18 (1953): 351–357.

Monane, Joseph H. *A Sociology of Human Systems.* New York: Appleton-Century-Crofts, 1967.

Nass, Gilbert D. *Marriage and the Family.* Reading, Massachusetts: Addison-Welsey, 1978.

Richardson, Helen M. "Studies of Mental Resemblance between Husbands and Wives and between Friends," *Psychological Bulletin,* 36 (1939): 104–120.

Roethlisberger, F. J.; and **Dickson, William J.** *Management and the Worker.* Cambridge, Massachusetts: Harvard University Press, 1939.

Roy, Donald F. "'Banana Time': Job Satisfaction and Informal Interaction," *Human Organization,* 18 (1959): 158–168.

Sherif, Muzafer; and Sherif, Carolyn W. *Reference Groups*. New York: Harper & Row, 1964.

Stein, David D.; Hardwyck, Jane Allyn; and Smith, M. Brewster. "Race and Belief: An Open and Shut Case," *Journal of Personality and Social Psychology*, 1 (1965): 281–289.

Turner, C. E. "Test Room Studies in Employee Effectiveness," *American Journal of Public Health*, 23 (1933): 577–584.

Williams, Ruth M.; and Mattson, Marion L. "The Effect of Social Groupings upon the Language of Pre-school Children," *Child Development*, 13 (1942): 233–245.

Wilson, Stephen. *Informal Groups: An Introduction*. Englewood Cliffs, New Jersey: Prentice-Hall, 1978.

Zimet, Carl N.; and Schneider, Carol. "Effects of Group Size on Interaction in Small Groups," *Journal of Social Psychology*, 77 (1969): 177–187.

Zimmer, Herbert. "Motivational Factors in Dyadic Interaction," *Journal of Personality*, 24 (1956): 251–261.

Glossary

Activity   The observable acts that group participants perform.

Altruistic Behavior   The performance of costly behavior for the benefit of others with little or no expectation of rewards in the exchange.

Beliefs   Mental concepts by which we judge elements of culture to be true or false and that exert control over individuals in certain situations.

Coalition Formation   The breakdown of the three-party relationship into a relationship of two against the third.

Communal Conflict   Conflict over how to behave or "the best action for behaving" once principle agreement has been reached.

Communication Network   The arrangement of lines of communication that are open between and among members of groups.

Communicative Act   A transmission of information that includes discriminative stimuli from one individual (point of origin) to another (a recipient).

Culture   A system of standards of conduct that orients individuals in their organized, meaningful relationships with one another.

Duration   Amount of time sufficient to allow for the attainment of the desired group goal or goals.

Dyad   A two-party group relationship.

Exchange Balance   The results of a relationship in which the interacting parties are able to maintain the interaction, having received (and with the expectation of continuing to receive) at least minimally acceptable rewards in relation to the costs involved in the relationship.

Expected Role   A statement of how individuals should perform in their respective group positions.

Formal Structure   Clearly defined positions in fixed relationships to other positions which are governed by explicit rules and regulations for individual and interpersonal behavior.

Friendship Group   A collection of individuals whose associations with each other are based upon high affectivity and who value the relationship sufficiently to make the continuation of the affective relationship the dominant group goal.

Group Cohesion   The degree of intensity with which group members are bonded together and motivated to work as a unit toward the achievement of group goals.

Group Goals   The ends to which social groups are organized and maintained.

Group Identity   A sense of group belonging that group participants experience.

Group Needs   Forces that develop out of group affiliation, and that promote concerted activity directed toward the achievement of a goal acceptable to the group as a whole.

Group Norms   Systems of expectations or standards of conduct which define appropriate behavior in specific situations.

Group Structure   A set of positions that individuals occupy in relation to each other and that carry with them levels of expectations for behavior. Each group member can more or less rely upon these positions as a basis for ordering present as well as future behavior.

Helping Relationship   One in which a help agent intervenes between a person and that person's problem.

Individual   A symbol-using animal who is capable, by nature and through social care, of participating in patterned interaction within human social groups.

Individual Needs   Forces within the individual, the existence of which is inferred through behavior directed toward the achievement of a goal.

Induced Goals   Goals given the group member by the leader to replace a goal previously accepted by the group member.

Informal Structure   An arrangement of positions in relationships within groups governed by an informal code of behavior that develops out of previous experiences between and among group members.

Informal Work Group   A collection of individuals whose common work experiences result in the development of a system of interpersonal relations beyond those expected of them by virtue of their employment.

Interaction The exchange of meaningful activity between two or more individuals.

Interaction Distance The measurable distance between and among group members while they are interacting with each other.

Interpretation A process going on inside an individual by which that individual attempts to understand the meanings intended by others as they interact with each other.

Intimate Distance From point of contact to eighteen inches.

Leadership A group process by which an individual in a given situation is able to direct and control group interaction more influentially than any other group member.

Life-Space Situational regions within which behavior (group or individual) is free, prohibited, or intermediate between freedom and prohibition.

Meaning The significance given to a symbol by an individual.

Model Construction A device for putting information together in a manner that helps us to understand the relationships between and among the elements under investigation.

Negative Valences Restrictive, prohibitive forces that work against group goal achievement.

Nuclear Family A two-generation group of individuals who are bound together by ties of marriage, birth, and adoption, who live in a common household, and who develop a specialized system of expectations for behaving within a closed system of reciprocal relationships.

Patterned Interaction Behavior in groups that has become a habit.

Perceived Role Individual interpretation given the expected role by a group member.

Personal Distance From eighteen inches to four feet.

Personal Space "Owned" space surrounding an individual while he is interacting with others.

Physical Environment The sum total of concrete objects and spatial elements that surround activity within a group.

Positive Valences Forces that are attractive to the group's goal orientation.

Primary Group Face-to-face relationships based upon intimacy and cooperation.

Principled Conflict Conflict over a basic truth, law, or ethical code.

Proxemics The interrelated observations and theories of man's use of space as a specialized elaboration of culture.

Proximity (Propinquity) The physical distance between and among individuals who are interacting with each other.

Psychodrama The science which explores personal truth through the use of drama in therapeutic settings.

Public Distance Twelve feet and more.

Reciprocity The constant interchange of meanings and intentions through the use of verbal and other symbols.

Roles Sets of expectations that members in groups share concerning the behavior of every individual who occupies a position within the group structure.

Secondary Group Impersonal relationships based upon contract and ability.

Self-Control An individual's ability to make appropriate decisions about, to organize, and to execute a plan of action within the group that will satisfy individual needs and the needs of the group as a whole.

Sentiments The feelings, emotions, needs, and attitudes of group members toward each other.

Separation The breakdown of the three-party relationship resulting in loss of group identity.

Situational Environment The sum of all the social elements at a given point in time that individuals perceive as determiners of how they will perform their group roles.

Small Group A group whose size ranges from a minimum of two to a maximum of twenty.

Social Distance From four feet to twelve feet.

Social Forms Clusters of elements abstracted from human interaction that describe the structure (or process) characteristic of a given relationship regardless of its content.

Social Frame of Reference The accumulation of all past experiences from birth to the present.

Socialization The process in which the individual, through interaction with others, learns how to behave according to the rules and regulations of the society of which he is a member.

Sociation A sense of unity between and among interacting parties.

Society The complex of patterns of interaction (communication) between and among a large number of individuals.

Sociogram A graphic representation of preferred associations based upon feelings and interpersonal attractions among group members, or upon some specific criterion such as preference of a partner for the performance of a task or some other goal requiring cooperation.

Symbol   Something which represents something else, the meaning of which is given by the user.

Symbolic Interaction   A framework for understanding human social behavior that combines the concepts of human interaction and the symbolic nature of the individual's relationship to the external world.

Total Communication   The process of transmitting meanings and intentions through the use of verbal, gestural, facial, and other external communication modes.

Triad   A system of interaction among three members who maintain their identity as a group over a significant period of time.

Unification   Integration of all three members of a triad into a balanced relationship.

Valences (positive and negative)   Equivalents of group forces that influence goal-related activity.

Values   Ideas that are shared and that define behavior as appropriate or inappropriate, good or bad.

Vector   The direction taken by a group in relation to positive or negative valences.

Verbal Behavior   A means whereby two or more individuals communicate their intentions and meanings to each other.

Bibliography

Albert, Robert S.; and Brigante, Thomas R. "The Psychology of Friendship Relations: Social Factors," *Journal of Social Psychology*, 56 (1962): 33–47.

Aldous, Joan; and Straus, Murray A. "Social Networks and Conjugal Roles: A Test of Bott's Hypothesis," *Social Forces*, 44 (1966): 576–580.

Angell, Robert C., "Introduction," in Albert J. Reiss, Jr. (ed.). *Cooley and Sociological Analysis.* Ann Arbor, Michigan: The University of Michigan Press, 1968.

Asch, Solomon E. "Opinion and Social Pressure," *Scientific American*, 193 (1955): 32.

_____ . "An Experimental Investigation of Group Influence," *Symposium on Preventive and Social Psychiatry*, Washington, DC: United States Government Printing Office, 1957.

Babchuk, Nicholas; and Goode, William F. "Work Incentives in a Self-determined Group," *American Sociological Review*, 16 (1951): 679–687.

Bales, Robert F. *Interaction Process Analysis: A Method for the Study of Small Groups.* Cambridge, Massachusetts: Addison-Wesley, 1950.

_____ . "Adaptive and Integrative Changes as Sources of Strain in Social Systems," in A. Paul Hare, Edgar F. Borgatta and Robert F. Bales (eds.). *Small Groups: Studies in Social Interaction.* New York: Alfred A. Knopf, 1966.

_____ . "The Equilibrium Problem in Small Groups," in A. Paul Hare, Edgar F. Borgatta and Robert F. Bales. *Small Groups: Studies in Social Interaction.* New York: Alfred A. Knopf, 1966.

Bales, Robert F. *Personality and Interpersonal Behavior.* New York: Holt, Rinehart and Winston, 1970.

Bales, Robert F.; and Borgatta, Edgar F. "Size of Group as a Factor in the Interaction Profile," in A. Paul Hare, Edgar F. Borgatta and Robert F. Bales (eds.). *Small Groups: Studies in Social Interaction.* New York: Alfred A. Knopf, 1966.

326   Bibliography

Bales, Robert F.; and Cohen, Stephen P. *SYMLOG: A System for the Multiple Level Observation of Groups*. New York: The Free Press, 1979.

Bales, Robert F.; Strodtbeck, F. L.; Mills, T. M.; and Roseborough, M. E. "Channels of Communication in Small Groups," *American Sociological Review*, 16 (1951): 461–468.

Bass, Bernard M. "The Leaderless Group Discussion," *Psychological Bulletin*, 51 (1954): 465–492.

Bass, Bernard M.; and Dunteman, George. "Defensiveness and Susceptibility to Coercion as a Function of Self-, Interaction-, and Task-orientation," *Journal of Social Psychology*, 62 (1964): 335–341.

Bass, Bernard M.; and Norton, Fay-Tyler. "Group Size and Leaderless Discussions," *Journal of Applied Psychology*, 35 (1951): 397–400.

Bass, Bernard M.; and Wurster, C. R. "Effects of the Nature of the Problem on LGD Performance," *Journal of Applied Psychology*, 37 (1953): 96–99.

Batchelor, James P.; and Goethals, George R. "Spatial Arrangements in Freely Formed Groups," *Sociometry*, 35 (1972): 270–279.

Bates, Alan P. "Some Sociometric Aspects of Social Ranking in a Small, Face-to-Face Group," *Sociometry*, 15 (1952): 330–341.

Bates, Alan P.; and Babchuk, Nicholas. "The Primary Group: A Reappraisal," *Sociological Quarterly*, 2 (1961): 181–191.

Bates, Frederick L. "A Conceptual Analysis of Group Structure," *Social Forces*, 36 (1957): 103–111.

Bavelas, Alex. "A Mathematical Model for Group Structures," *Applied Anthropology*, 7 (1948): 16–30.

––––––– . "Communication Patterns in Task-oriented Groups," *Journal of the Acoustical Society of America*, 22 (1950): 725–730.

Bennis, Warren G. "Leadership Theory and Administrative Behavior: The Problems of Authority," *Administrative Science Quarterly*, 4 (1959): 259–301.

Berkowitz, Leonard. "Group Standards, Cohesiveness, and Productivity," *Human Relations*, 7 (1954): 509–519.

––––––– . "Group Norms Among Bomber Crews: Patterns of Perceived Crew Attitudes, 'Actual' Crew Attitudes, and Crew Liking Related to Aircrew Effectiveness in Far Eastern Combat," *Sociometry*, 19 (1956): 141–153.

Bertrand, Alvin L. *Basic Sociology: An Introduction to Theory and Method*. New York: Appleton-Century-Crofts, 1967.

Blake, R. R.; and Morton, J. S. "The Fifth Achievement," *The Journal of Applied Behavioral Science*, 6 (1970): 413–426.

Blau, Peter M. "Cooperation and Competition in a Bureaucracy," *American Journal of Sociology*, 59 (1954): 530–535.

Blumer, Herbert. "Society as Symbolic Interaction," in Arnold M. Rose (ed.). *Human Behavior and Social Process*. Boston: Houghton Mifflin, 1962.

––––––– . *Symbolic Interactionism: Perspective and Method*. Englewood Cliffs, New Jersey: Prentice-Hall, 1969.

Borgatta, Edgar F.; and Bales, Robert F. "Task and Accumulation of Experience as Factors in the Interaction of Small Groups," *Sociometry*, 16 (1953): 239–252.

Borgatta, Edgar F.; Couch, Arthur S.; and Bales, Robert F. "Some Findings Relevant to the Great Man Theory of Leadership," *American Sociological Review*, 19 (1954): 755–759.

Bossard, James H. S. "The Law of Family Interaction," *American Journal of Sociology*, 50 (1945): 292–294.

Bossard, James H. S.; and Boll, Eleanor Stoker. *The Sociology of Child Development*, 4th ed.; New York: Harper & Row, 1966.

Bovard, Everett W. "Conformity to Social Norms and Attraction to the Group," *Science*, 118 (1953): 598–599.

Burchard, Waldo W. "Role Conflicts of Military Chaplains," *American Sociological Review*, 19 (1954): 528–535.

Burns, Tom. "The Reference of Conduct in Small Groups: Cliques and Cabals in Occupational Milieux," *Human Relations*, 8 (1955): 467–486.

Byrne, Donn. "The Influence of Propinquity and Opportunities for Interaction on Classroom Relationships," *Human Relations*, 14 (1961): 63–69.

Byrne, Donn; and Buehler, J. A. "A Note on the Influence of Propinquity upon Acquaintanceships," *Journal of Abnormal and Social Psychology*, 51 (1955): 147–148.

Byrne, Donn; Griffit, William; and Stefaniak, Daniel. "Attraction and Similarity of Personality Characteristics," *Journal of Personality and Social Psychology*, 5 (1967): 82–90.

Caplow, Theodore. "A Theory of Coalition in the Triad," *American Sociological Review*, 21 (1956): 489–493.

_____ . "Further Development of a Theory of Coalition in the Triad," *The American Journal of Sociology*, 64 (1959): 488–493.

_____ . *Two Against One: Coalitions in Triads*. Englewood Cliffs, New Jersey: Prentice-Hall, 1968.

Carey, Alex. "The Hawthorne Studies: A Radical Criticism," *American Sociological Review*, 32 (1967): 403–416.

Carter, Launor F.; Haythorn, W.; Shriver, E.; and Lanzetta, J. T. "The Behavior of Leaders and Other Group Members," *Journal of Abnormal and Social Psychology*, 46 (1951): 589–595.

Cartwright, Dorwin; and Zander, Alvin. *Group Dynamics: Research and Theory*, 2nd ed.; New York: Harper & Row, 1960.

Cattell, Raymond B. "New Concepts for Measuring Leadership in Terms of Group Syntality," *Human Relations*, 4 (1951): 161–184.

Cohen, Bernard P. "Seating Position in Five-man Groups." Unpublished Paper, Harvard University Press, 1953.

Cook, Mark. "Experiments on Orientation and Proxemics," *Human Relations*, 23 (1970): 61–76.

Cooley, Charles Horton. *Social Organization: A Study of the Larger Mind*. New York: Schocken, 1962.

_____ . *Human Nature and the Social Order*. New York: Schocken, 1964.

Coser, Lewis A. (ed.). *Georg Simmel*. Englewood Cliffs, New Jersey: Prentice-Hall, 1965.

_____ . *Masters of Sociological Thought*. N.Y.: Harcourt Brace Jovanovich, 1971.

Costanzo, Philip R. "Conformity Development as a Function of Self-blame," *Journal of Personality and Social Psychology*, 14 (1970): 366–374.

Crannell, Clarke W.; Switzer, S. A.; and Morrissette, Julian O. "Individual Performance in Cooperative and Independent Groups," *Journal of General Psychology*, 73 (1965): 231–236.

Crosbie, Paul V. "Social Exchange and Power Compliance: A Test of Homans' Propositions," *Sociometry*, 35 (1972): 203–222.

———. *Interaction in Small Groups*. New York: Macmillan, 1975.

D'Augelli, Anthony R. "Group Composition Using Interpersonal Skills: An Analogue Study of the Effect of Members' Interpersonal Skills on Peer Ratings and Group Cohesiveness," *Journal of Counseling Psychology*, 20 (1973): 531–534.

Davis, Kingsley. "Final Note on a Case of Extreme Isolation," *American Journal of Sociology*, 50 (1947): 432–437.

———. *Human Society*. New York: Macmillan, 1949.

Deutsch, Morton. "A Theory of Cooperation and Competition," *Human Relations*, 2 (1949): 129–152.

———. "An Experimental Study of the Effects of Cooperation and Competition upon Group Process," *Human Relations*, 2 (1949): 199–231.

Deutsch, Morton; and Collins, Mary Evans. *Interracial Housing*. Minneapolis: University of Minnesota Press, 1951.

Dunphy, Dexter. *The Primary Group: A Handbook for Analysis and Field Research*. New York: Appleton-Century-Crofts, 1972.

Engelbert, Steven; Langley, Patricia; and Warden, Barbara (eds.). *The Washington Cofo Memo*. A publication of the Coalition of Family Organization, 2, 1979.

Faunce, William A. "Automation in the Automobile Industry: Some Consequences for In-plant Social Structure," *American Sociological Review*, 23 (1958): 401–407.

Feather, Norman T. "A Structural Balance Model of Communication Effects," *Psychological Review*, 71 (1964): 291–313.

Feather, Norman T.; and Armstrong, D. J. "Effects of Variations in Source Attitude, Receiver Attitude, and Communication Stand on Reactions to Source and Content of Communications," *Journal of Personality*, 35 (1967): 435–455.

Felipe, Nancy. "Interpersonal Distance and Small Group Interaction," *Cornell Journal of Social Relations*, 1 (1966): 59–64.

Festinger, Leon; Gerard, H.; Hymovitch, B.; Kelley, H. H.; and Raven, B. "The Influence Process in the Presence of Extreme Deviates," *Human Relations*, 5 (1952): 327–346.

Festinger, Leon; Schachter, Stanley; and Back, Kurt. *Social Pressures in Informal Groups*. New York: Harper, 1950.

———. "The Operation of Group Standards," in Dorwin Cartwright and Alvin Zander (eds.). *Group Dynamics: Research and Theory*, 2nd ed.; New York: Harper & Row, 1960.

Fichter, Joseph H. *Sociology*. Chicago: University of Chicago Press, 1957.

Franke, Richard Herbert; and Kaul, James D. "The Hawthorne Experiments: First Statistical Interpretation," *American Sociological Review*, 43 (1978): 623–643.

French, John R. P., Jr. "The Disruption and Cohesion of Groups," *Journal of Abnormal and Social Psychology*, 36 (1941): 361–377.

Gamson, William A. "A Theory of Coalition Formation," *American Sociological Review*, 26 (1961): 373–382.

Gerard, Harold B. "Some Effects of Status, Role Clarity, and Group Goal Clarity upon the Individual's Relations to Group Progress," *Journal of Personality*, 25 (1957): 475–488.

Gibb, Cecil A. "The Principles and Traits of Leadership," *Journal of Abnormal and Social Psychology*, 42 (1947): 267–284.

———. "Leadership," in Gardner Lindzey (ed.). *Handbook on Social Psychology*. Cambridge, Massachusetts: Addison-Wesley, 1968. Vol. II.

Gibb, Jack R. "The Effects of Group Size and of Threat Reduction upon Creativity in a Problem-solving Situation," *American Psychologist*, 6 (1951): 324–325.

Gilchrist, Jack C. "The Formation of Social Groups under Conditions of Success and Failure," *Journal of Abnormal Social Psychology*, 47 (1952): 174–187.

Goffman, Irving. *The Presentation of Self in Everyday Life*. Garden City, New York: Doubleday, 1959.

Graham, William K.; and Dillon, Peter C. "Creative Supergroups: Group Performance as a Function of Individual Performance on Brainstorming Tasks," *Journal of Social Psychology*, 93 (1974): 101–105.

Gross, Edward. "Some Functional Consequences of Primary Controls in Informal Work Organizations," *American Sociological Review*, 18 (1953): 368–373.

Gross, Neal; Martin, William E.; and Darley, John G. "Studies of Group Behavior: Leadership Structures in Small Organized Groups," *Journal of Abnormal and Social Psychology*, 48 (1953): 429–432.

Guetzkow, Harold, "Differentiation of Roles in Task-oriented Groups," in Dorwin Cartwright and Alvin Zander (eds.). *Group Dynamics: Research and Theory*. 2nd ed.; New York: Harper & Row, 1960.

Guetzkow, Harold; and Dill, William R. "Factors in the Organizational Development of Task-oriented Groups," *Sociometry*, 20 (1957): 175–204.

Gullahorn, J. "Distance and Friendship as Factors in the Gross Interaction Matrix," *Sociometry*, 15 (1952): 123–134.

Hall, Edward T. *The Hidden Dimension*. Garden City, New York: Doubleday, 1966.

Halpin, Andrew W. "The Leadership Ideology of Aircraft Commanders," *Journal of Applied Psychology*, 39 (1955): 82–84.

Hanawalt, N. G.; Richardson, H. M.; and Morris, M. L. "Level of Aspiration in College Leaders and Nonleaders," *Journal of Abnormal and Social Psychology*, 38 (1943): 545–548.

Harding, J.; and Hogrefe, R. "Attitudes of White Department Store Employees toward Negro Coworkers," *Journal of Social Issues*, 8 (1952): 18–28.

Hare, A. Paul. "A Study of Interaction and Consensus in Different Sized Groups," *American Sociological Review*, 17 (1952): 261–267.

———. *Handbook of Small Group Research*, 2nd ed.; New York: The Free Press, 1976.

Hare, A. Paul; and Bales, Robert F. "Seating Position and Small Group Interaction," *Sociometry*, 26 (1963): 480–486.

Hare, A. Paul; Borgatta, Edward F.; and Bales, Robert F. *Small Groups: Studies in Social Interaction*. New York: Alfred A. Knopf, 1966.

Harvey, O. J. "Reciprocal Influence of the Group and Three Types of Leaders in an Unstructured Situation," *Sociometry*, 23 (1960): 57–68.

Heckel, Robert V. "Leadership and Voluntary Seating Choice," *Psychological Reports*, 32 (1973): 141–142.

Heinicke, Christopher M.; and Bales, Robert F. "Developmental Trends in the Structure of Small Groups," *Sociometry*, 16 (1953): 7–38.

Hemphill, John K. "Relations between the Size of the Group and the Behavior of 'Superior' Leaders," *Journal of Social Psychology*, 32 (1950): 11–22.

Herbst, P. G. "The Measurement of Family Relationships," *Human Relations*, 5 (1952): 3–35.

Hollander, Edwin P. "Conformity, Status, and Idiosyncrasy Credit," *Psychological Review*, 65 (1958): 117–127.

Homans, George. *The Human Group*. New York: Harcourt, Brace and World, 1950.

———. "Social Behavior as Exchange," *The American Journal of Sociology*, 63 (1958): 597–606.

Huff, Frederick W.; and Paintianida, Thomas P. "The Effect of Group Size on Group Information Transmitted," *Psychonomic Science*, 11 (1968): 365–366.

Husband, R. W. "Cooperative Versus Solitary Problem Solution," *Journal of Social Psychology*, 11 (1940): 405–409.

Information and Education Division of the United States War Department, "Opinions about Negro Infantry Platoons in White Companies of Seven Divisions," in Theodore M. Newcomb and E. L. Hartley (eds.). *Readings in Social Psychology*, revised ed.; New York: Holt, Rinehart and Winston, 1952.

James, John. "A Preliminary Study of the Size Determinant in Small Group Interaction," *American Sociological Review*, 16 (1951): 474–477.

Jenkins, John G. "The Nominating Technique as a Method of Evaluating Air Force Group Morale," *Journal of Aviation Medicine*, 19 (1948): 12–19.

Jenkins, W. O. "A Review of Leadership Studies with Particular Reference to Military Problems," *Psychological Bulletin*, 44 (1947): 54–59.

Katz, Fred E. *Autonomy and Organizations: The Limits of Social Control*. New York: Random House, 1968.

Kelley, Harold H.; and Arrowwood, A. John. "Coalitions in the Triad: Critique and Experiment," *Sociometry*, 23 (1960): 231–244.

Kephart, William M. "A Quantitative Analysis of Intragroup Relationships," *American Journal of Sociology*, 55 (1950): 544–549.

Kinney, Elva E. "A Study of Peer Group Social Acceptability at the Fifth-Grade Level in a Public School," *Journal of Educational Research*, 47 (1953): 57–64.

Kipling, Rudyard. *Rudyard Kipling's Verse*, definitive ed.; Garden City, New York: Doubleday, 1940.

Klugman, Samuel F. "Cooperative Versus Individual Efficiency in Problem-solving," *Journal of Educational Psychology*, 35 (1944): 91–100.

Knickerbocker, I. "Leadership: A Conception and Some Implications," *Journal of Social Issues*, 4 (1948): 23–40.

Krech, D.; and Crutchfield, R. S. *Theory and Problems of Social Psychology*. New York: McGraw-Hill, 1948.

Kuhn, Manford H. "Major Trends in Symbolic Interactionist Theory in the Past Twenty-five Years," *The Sociological Quarterly*, 5 (1964): 61–84.

Laumann, Edward O. *Bonds of Pluralism: The Forms and Substance of Urban Social Networks*. New York: Wiley, 1973.

Laurence, Alfred E. "Georg Simmel: Triumph and Tragedy," *International Journal of Contemporary Sociology*, 12 (1976): 33–47.

Leavitt, Harold J. "Some Effects of Certain Communication Patterns on Group Performance," *Journal of Abnormal Social Psychology*, 46 (1951): 38–50.

Levine, Donald N., "Some Key Problems in Simmel's Works," in Lewis A. Coser (ed.). *Georg Simmel*. Englewood Cliffs, New Jersey. Prentice-Hall, 1965.

_____ . "The Structure of Simmel's Social Thought," in Georg Simmel, et al. Trans. and ed. by Kurt H. Wolff. *Essays on Sociology, Philosophy and Aesthetics*. New York: Harper & Row, 1965.

Levine, Jacob; and Butler, John. "Lecture Vs. Group Discussion in Changing Behavior," *Journal of Applied Psychology*, 36 (1952): 29–33.

Lewin, Kurt. "Psycho-sociological Problems of a Minority Group," *Character and Personality*, 3 (1935): 175–187.

_____ . "Experiments in Social Space," *Harvard Educational Review*, 9 (1939): 21–32.

_____ . "Field Theory and Experiment in Social Psychology: Concepts and Methods," *American Journal of Sociology*, 44 (1939): 868–896.

_____ . "The Background of Conflict in Marriage," in Moses Jung (ed.). *Modern Marriage*. New York: F. S. Crofts, 1940.

_____ . *Resolving Social Conflicts*. Edited by Gertrud W. Lewin. New York: Harper and Brothers, 1948.

Lewin, Kurt; Lippitt, Ronald; and White, Ralph K. "Patterns of Aggressive Behavior in Experimentally Created 'Social Climates,' " *Journal of Social Psychology*, 10 (1939): 271–299.

Lewis, Gordon H. "Role Differentiation," *American Sociological Review*, 37 (1972): 424–434.

Lewis, Helen B. "An Experimental Study of the Role of the Ego in Work: I. The Role of the Ego in Cooperative Work," *Journal of Experimental Psychology*, 34 (1944): 113–126.

Lippitt, Ronald. "Field Theory and Experiment in Social Psychology: Autocratic and Democratic Group Atmospheres," *American Journal of Sociology*, 45 (1939): 26–49.

Lippitt, Ronald; and White, Ralph K., "An Experimental Study of Leadership and Group Life," in Eleanor E. Maccoby, Theodore M. Newcomb and Eugene L. Hartley (eds.). *Readings in Social Psychology*, 3rd ed.; New York: Henry Holt, 1958.

Lodahl, Thomas M.; and Porter, Lyman W. "Psychometric Score Patterns, Social Characteristics, and Productivity of Small Industrial Work Groups," *Journal of Applied Psychology*, 45 (1961): 73–79.

Lott, Albert J.; and Lott, Bernice E. "Group Cohesiveness and Individual Learning," *Journal of Educational Psychology*, 57 (1966): 61–73.

Luchins, Abraham S.; and Luchins, Edith H. "Discovering the Source of Contradictory Communications," *Journal of Social Psychology*, 44 (1956): 49–63.

Luft, Joseph. *Of Human Interaction*. Palo Alto, California: National, 1969.

Lundgren, David C.; and Bogart, Dodd H. "Group Size, Member Dissatisfaction, and Group Radicalism," *Human Relations*, 27 (1974): 339–355.

MacIver, R. M.; and Page, Charles H. *Society: An Introductory Analysis*. New York: Holt, Rinehart and Winston, 1949.

Maisonneuve, Jean, in collaboration with G. Palmade and Cl. Fourment. "Selective Choices and Propinquity," *Sociometry*, 15 (1952): 135–140.

Mandelbaum, David G. *Soldier Groups and Negro Soldiers*. Berkeley, California: University of California Press, 1952.

Mangan, G. L.; Quartermain, D.; and Vaughan, G. "Taylor MAS and Group Conformity Pressure," *Journal of Abnormal Psychology*, 61 (1960): 146–147.

Mann, John H. "The Effect of Interracial Contact on Sociometric Choice and Perceptions," *Journal of Social Psychology*, 50 (1959): 143–152.

Mayo, Elton. *The Human Problems of an Industrial Civilization*. New York: Macmillan, 1933.

McCurdy, Harold G.; and Lambert, Wallace E. "The Efficiency of Small Human Groups in the Solution of Problems Requiring Genuine Cooperation," *Journal of Personality*, 20 (1952): 475–494.

Mead, George Herbert. *Mind, Self, and Society*. Edited by Charles W. Morris. Chicago: The University of Chicago Press, 1934.

Mead, Margaret; and Byers, Paul. *The Small Conference*. Paris: Mouton, 1968.

Megaree, E. I. "Influence of Sex Roles on the Manifestation of Leadership," *Journal of Applied Psychology*, 53 (1969): 377–382.

Mendelson, Edward (ed.). *W. H. Auden Collected Poems*. New York: Random House, 1976.

Merei, Ferenc. "Group Leadership and Institutionalization," *Human Relations*, 2 (1949): 23–39.

Mills, Theodore M. "Power Relations in Three-person Groups," *American Sociological Review*, 18 (1953): 351–357.

_____. "The Coalition Pattern in Three-person Groups," *American Sociological Review*, 19 (1954): 657–667.

_____ . "Some Hypotheses on Small Groups from Simmel," _The American Journal of Sociology_, 63 (1958): 642–650.

_____ . _The Sociology of Small Groups_. Englewood Cliffs, New Jersey: Prentice-Hall, 1967.

Mitchell, J. Clyde (ed.). _Social Networks in Urban Situations_. Manchester, England: Manchester University Press, 1969.

Monane, Joseph H. _A Sociology of Human Systems_. New York: Appleton-Century-Crofts, 1967.

Moore, Merritt H. (ed.). _Movements of Thought in the 19th Century_. Chicago: The University of Chicago Press, 1936.

Moreno, Jacob L. _Who Shall Survive?_ Revised edition; Beacon, New York: Beacon House, 1953.

Morrissette, Julian O.; Switzer, S. A.; and Crandell, Clarke W. "Group Performance as a Function of Size, Structure, and Task Difficulty," _Journal of Personality and Social Psychology_, 2 (1965): 451–455.

Mulder, Mauk. "Communication Structure, Decision Structure, and Group Performance," _Sociometry_, 23 (1960): 1–14.

Nacci, Peter; and Tedeschi, James T. "Liking and Power as Affecting Coalition Choices in Triads," _Social Behavior and Personality_, 4 (1976): 27–32.

Nass, Gilbert D. _Marriage and the Family_. Reading, Massachusetts: Addison-Wesley, 1978.

Newcomb, Theodore. "An Approach to the Study of Communicative Acts," _The Psychological Review_, 60 (1953): 393–404.

_____ . "The Prediction of Interpersonal Attraction," _American Psychologist_, 11 (1956): 575–586.

Nisbet, Robert. _The Social Bond_. New York: Alfred A. Knopf, 1950.

Olmstead, Michael S.; and Hare, A. Paul. _The Small Group_, 2nd ed.; New York: Random House, 1978.

Parsons, Talcott; and Shils, Edward A. (eds.). _Toward a General Theory of Action_, Torchbook edition; New York: Harper & Row, 1951.

Pellegrin, Roland J. "The Achievement of High Status and Leadership in the Small Group," _Social Forces_, 32 (1953): 10–16.

Pellegrini, Robert J. "Some Effects of Seating Position on Social Perception," _Psychological Reports_, 28 (1971): 887–893.

Pelz, D. C. "Leadership within a Hierarchical Organization," _Journal of Social Issues_, 7 (1951): 49–55.

Piaget, Jean. _The Moral Judgment of the Child_. New York: Harcourt, Brace, 1932.

Rapoport, Rhona; and Rosow, I. "An Approach to Family Relationships and Role Performance," _Human Relations_, 10 (1957): 209–221.

Redl, Fritz. "Group Emotion and Leadership," _Psychiatry_, 5 (1942): 573–596.

Richardson, Helen M. "Studies of Mental Resemblance between Husbands and Wives and between Friends," _Psychological Bulletin_, 36 (1939): 104–120.

Roby, Thornton B.; and Lanzetta, John T. "Work Group Structure, Communication and Group Performance," _Sociometry_, 19 (1956): 105–113.

Roethlisberger, F. J.; and Dickson, William J. _Management and the Worker_. Cambridge, Massachusetts: Harvard University Press, 1939.

Roff, Merrill E. "A Study of Combat Leadership in the Air Force by Means of a Rating Scale," *Journal of Psychology*, 30 (1959): 229–239.

Rosenthal, Bernard G.; and Delong, Alton J. "Complimentary Leadership and Spatial Arrangement of Group Members," *Group Psychotherapy and Psychodrama*, 25 (1972): 34–52.

Rotter, George S. "An Experimental Evaluation of Group Attractiveness as a Determinant of Conformity," *Human Relations*, 20 (1967): 273–282.

Rotter, George S.; and Portugal, Stephen M. "Group and Individual Effects in Problem Solving," *Journal of Applied Psychology*, 53 (1969): 338–341.

Roy, Donald F. "Banana Time: Job Satisfaction and Informal Interaction," *Human Organization*, 18 (1959): 158–168.

Rule, Brendan G. "Group Effects on Deviant Behavior," *Psychological Reports*, 15 (1964): 611–614.

Rule, Brendan G.; and Renner, John. "Distance, Group Dispersion, and Opinion Change," *Psychological Reports*, 17 (1965): 777–778.

———. "Involvement and Group Effects on Opinion Change," *Journal of Social Psychology*, 76 (1968): 189–198.

Sarbin, Theodore R.; and Jones, Donal S. "An Experimental Analysis of Role Behavior," *Journal of Abnormal and Social Psychology*, 51 (1955): 236–241.

Schellenberg, James A. *An Introduction to Social Psychology*. New York: Random House, 1970.

Seeman, Melvin. "Role Conflict and Ambivalence in Leadership," *American Sociological Review*, 18 (1953): 373–380.

Shaw, Marvin E. "Some Effects of Problem Complexity upon Problems Solution Efficiency in Different Communication Nets," *Journal of Experimental Psychology*, 48 (1954): 211–217.

———. "Some Effects of Irrelevant Information upon Problem-solving by Small Groups," *Journal of Social Psychology*, 47 (1958): 33–37.

———. "Communication Networks," in Leonard Berkowitz. *Advances in Experimental Social Psychology*. New York: Academic Press, 1964, Vol. 1.

———. "Changes in Sociometric Choices Following Forced Integration of an Elementary School," *Journal of Social Issues*, 29 (1973): 143–157.

———. *Group Dynamics: The Psychology of Small Group Behavior*, 2nd ed.; New York: McGraw-Hill, 1976.

Shaw, Marvin E.; and Rothschild, Gerard H. "Some Effects of Prolonged Experience in Communication Nets," *Journal of Applied Psychology*, 40 (1956): 281–286.

Shaw, Marvin E.; and Shaw, Lilly M. "Some Effects of Sociometric Grouping upon Learning in a Second Grade Classroom," *Journal of Social Psychology*, 57 (1962): 453–458.

Shepherd, Clovis R. *Small Groups: Some Sociological Perspectives*. San Francisco: Chandler, 1964.

Sherif, Muzafer. *The Psychology of Social Norms*. New York: Harper and Brothers, 1936.

———. "An Experimental Approach to Social Attitudes," *Sociometry*, 1 (1937): 90–98.

Sherif, Muzafer; and Harvey, O. J. "A Study of Ego Functioning: Elimination of Stable Anchorages in Individual and Group Situations," *Sociometry*, 15 (1952): 272–305.

Sherif, Muzafer; and Sherif, Carolyn W. *Reference Groups*. New York: Harper & Row, 1964.

Shibutani, Tomotsu. *Society and Personality: An Interactionist Approach to Social Psychology*. Englewood Cliffs, New Jersey: Prentice-Hall, 1961.

Smith, F. Tredwell. *An Experiment in Modifying Attitudes toward the Negro*. New York: Teachers College Bureau of Publication, Columbia University, 1943.

Smith, Henry C. "Team Work in the College Class," *Journal of Educational Psychology*, 46 (1955): 274–286.

Smith, Robert J.; and Cook, Patrick E. "Leadership in Dyadic Groups as a Function of Dominance and Incentives," *Sociometry*, 36 (1973): 561–568.

Sommer, Robert. "Studies in Personal Space," *Sociometry*, 22 (1959): 247–260.

_____ . "Leadership and Group Geography," *Sociometry*, 24 (1961): 99–110.

_____ . "The Distance for Comfortable Conversation: A Further Study. *Sociometry*, 25 (1962): 111–116.

Sorokin, Pitirim. *Social and Cultural Dynamics*. Boston: Porter Sargent, 1970.

Sprott, W. J. H. *Human Groups*. Baltimore, Maryland: Penguin Books, 1969.

Spykman, Nicholas J. *The Social Theory of Georg Simmel*. Chicago: The University of Chicago Press, 1925.

Stein, David D.; Hardwyck, Jane Allyn; and Smith, M. Brewster. "Race and Belief: An Open and Shut Case," *Journal of Personality and Social Psychology*, 1 (1965): 281–289.

Stogdill, Ralph M. "Personal Factors Associated with Leadership: A Survey of the Literature," *The Journal of Psychology*, 25 (1948): 35–71.

_____ . *Handbook on Leadership: A Survey of Theory and Research*. New York: The Free Press, 1974.

Stouffer, Samuel A., et al. *The American Soldier*. Princeton, New Jersey: Princeton University Press, 1949. Vol. 1.

Strauss, Anselm (ed.). *George Herbert Mead on Social Psychology*. Chicago: The University of Chicago Press, 1956.

Strodtbeck, Fred L. "The Family as a Three-person Group," *American Sociological Review*, 19 (1954): 23–29.

Strodtbeck, Fred L.; James, Rita M.; and Hawkins, C. "Social Status in Jury Deliberations," *American Sociological Review*, 22 (1957): 713–719.

Stryker, Sheldon; and Psathas, George. "Research on Coalitions in the Triad: Findings, Problems and Strategy," *Sociometry*, 23 (1960): 217–230.

Talland, George A. "Role and Status Structure in Therapy Groups," *Journal of Clinical Psychology*, 13 (1957): 27–33.

Tenbruck, F. H., "Formal Sociology," in Georg Simmel, et al. Trans. and ed. by Kurt H. Wolff. *Essays on Sociology, Philosophy and Aesthetics*. New York: Harper & Row, 1965.

Thelen, Herbert A. "Classroom Groupings," in A. Yates (ed.). *Groupings in Education*. New York: Wiley, 1966.

Turner, C. E. "Test Room Studies in Employee Effectiveness," *American Journal of Public Health*, 23 (1933): 577–584.

Van Zelst, Raymond H. "Sociometrically Selected Work Teams Increase Production," *Personnel Psychology*, 5 (1952): 175–186.

Vernon, Glenn. *Human Interaction: An Introduction to Sociology*. New York: Ronald, 1965.

Vinacke, W. Edgar; and Arkoff, Abe. "An Experimental Study of Coalitions in the Triad," *American Sociological Review*, 22 (1957): 406–414.

Wallace, David. "Reflections on the Education of George Herbert Mead," *American Journal of Sociology*, 72 (1967): 396–408.

Wardwell, Walter I. "A Marginal Professional Role: The Chiropractor," *Social Forces*, 30 (1952): 339–348.

Wheaton, Blair. "Interpersonal Conflict and Cohesiveness in Dyadic Relationships," *Sociometry*, 37 (1974): 328–348.

White, James E. "Theory and Method for Research in Community Leadership," *American Sociological Review*, 15 (1950): 50–60.

White, Leslie A. *The Science of Culture*. New York: Farrar, Straus and Giroux, 1969.

Whyte, William Foote. *Street Corner Society*, 2nd ed.; Chicago: The University of Chicago Press, 1955.

Wiest, William M.; Porter, Lyman W.; and Chiselli, Edwin E. "Relationship between Individual Proficiency and Team Performance and Efficiency," *Journal of Applied Psychology*, 45 (1961): 435–440.

Williams, Robin M., Jr. *American Society: A Sociological Interpretation*, 3rd ed.; New York: Alfred A. Knopf, 1970.

Williams, Ruth M.; and Mattson, Marion L. "The Effect of Social Groupings upon the Language of Pre-school Children," *Child Development*, 13 (1942): 233–245.

Wilson, R. S. "Personality Patterns, Source of Attractiveness, and Conformity," *Journal of Personality*, 28 (1960): 186–199.

Wilson, Stephen. *Informal Groups: An Introduction*. Englewood Cliffs, New Jersey: Prentice-Hall, 1978.

Wispé, Lauren G. "A Sociometric Analysis of Conflicting Role-expectations," *American Journal of Sociology*, 61 (1955): 134–137.

Wispé, Lauren G.; and Lloyd, K. E. "Some Situational and Psychological Determinants of the Desire for Structured Interpersonal Relations," *Journal of Abnormal and Social Psychology*, 51 (1955): 57–60.

Wolff, Kurt H. (Trans. and ed.). *The Sociology of Georg Simmel*. New York: The Free Press, 1950.

Zander, A.; and Havelin, A. "Social Comparison and Interpersonal Attraction," *Human Relations*, 13 (1960): 21–32.

Zander, Alvin; and Wolfe, Donald. "Administrative Rewards and Coordination among Committee Members," *Administrative Science Quarterly*, 9 (1964): 50–69.

Zimet, Carl N.; and Schneider, Carol. "Effects of Group Size on Interaction in Small Groups," *Journal of Social Psychology*, 77 (1969): 177–187.

Zimmer, Herbert. "Motivational Factors in Dyadic Interaction," *Journal of Personality*, 24 (1956): 251–261.

Name Index

Subject Index